Jamaica's

FIRST

President

1992-2010

His Rise - His Reign - His Demise

A Chronology of Lawlessness

Researched, Investigated and Compiled

By

K.C. Samuels

Published by PageTurnER Publishing House
Email: pageturnerja@gmail.com

Copyright © 2011 by PageTurnER Publishing House

ISBN #: 978-1-4276-4940-9

REGISTERED TRADEMARK

Cover Design: Klyf Antonio
Edited By: I. Abrahams
Photo Editing: KLJ Photography

Jamaica's FIRST President
First Printing 2011

*Dedicated To The Memory
Of
All the lives lost during The Tivoli Gardens Incursion
May 24, 2010
Rest In Peace...*

Contents

Preface

History has recorded the names and legacies of many men, some great, some famous, and some, infamous. The famous and great are many and interesting in their own right, but the infamous seem to possess a different sort of power; they are colourful, dangerously intriguing, and more interesting than we are at times willing to admit, and when it comes to the Caribbean, specifically Jamaica, none has elevated to such a status in recent times than the infamous, and now world renowned, Michael Christopher *Dudus* Coke.

But who is this man, who not many Jamaicans have ever seen, prior to him becoming front page news, even though they may've all heard his name before the now tragic storming of his stronghold (located in one of Jamaica's West Kingston residential communities, known as Tivoli Gardens, on May 24, 2010), by Jamaican Security Forces?

Who is this man; whom the US Justice Department described as one of the most dangerous drug lords in the world? The same man, the US Government apparently wanted so badly that it's said to have caused diplomatic strain between Jamaica and Washington. Who is he, the same man who is said to have been shielded by the Jamaican Government during his bid to avoid extradition to face drugs and weapons charges in New York City?

According to official reports, seventy-four civilians died for, and or because of this same man, during the incursion of the security forces dragnet. Seventy-four (74) - a number that many [including former

Jamaica Labour Party – [JLP] - leader, Edward Seaga] are saying was much more; quite possibly numbering into the hundreds.

Who is this man, the *President* as he is affectionately called?...Who elected him *President*, and how can a *President* operate with what many say was immunity, when the country's constitution labels the leader of the country as a Prime Minister, a position a *President* tops any day, in any regime...Who is this man?

The questions are many and the answers have been few, and it is with that focus that this volume was penned. Not for sensationalism, but more so for understanding...Understanding who this man really was, and at the same time, this volume also makes a bold attempt at separating the speculations and myths, from the truth.

To understand the present, we must first investigate the past, and to understand any human being, the same is true, we must first investigate their past; where they have been, what and who influenced them, what they have been through, etcetera, in order to fully understand what they eventually became: *THE PAST* is very important in order for us to understand the present and prepare for the future. *THE PAST* - the key ingredient to what we see in the present, which is merely the end results - the manifestation if you may, of what could be considered the writing on the wall.

The media paints one picture of this man, and the masses far and wide paint a variety of other portraits - some breathtaking in more ways than one, some admirable, almost noble in nature and magnitude, and those who knew him best (residents of his community) have nothing but the best to say about him – so much that many have even made the ultimate sacrifice of laying down their lives for him.

So who was this man?

How did he, (not a public figure, entertainer, politician or the holder of any other job description that warrants such magnetism) become so influential – and not only over situations, but more so over people - so many people that his influence was said to have even encompassed the very leadership of Jamaica?

The suggestions, assumptions and even the accusations are at times either too grotesque or too remarkable, so much so that it has left many to still question (even after his extradition) if any, some or all of what has been said about this man, is indeed true.

A lot has been said, written, and even televised about *Dudus* and his exploits, and by no means will this volume even begin to tout itself as the *gospel* according to the situation, but what this volume will claim - is that it is an investigative effort aimed at presenting the facts – the facts as they have been discovered. That is the aim of this volume, to present facts, not to decide on guilt or innocence – that's for a jury and a court of law to decide – but with so much already said, it is crystal clear that the court of public opinion is in session, and with that I have taken the liberty to add depth to the conversation by presenting this volume as evidence for your analysis - as our investigation uncovered.

Is *Dudus* the monster the media has made him out to be – murderer, drug trafficker, gun runner, and according to some, judge, jury and executioner - or is he merely a scapegoat for something or someone way more sinister and powerful than we are even allowing ourselves to imagine; an entity, person or situation that now has no more need for him?

The theories are many, speculations insurmountable, opinions endless, but what are the facts?

How did *Dudus* become the *President*?

9

Did he actually run the city of Kingston, or like some say – the entire Island of Jamaica?

Did parliamentarians really answer to him – The *President*?

Was he as powerful as people say he was, or was all that just a figment of the masses' imaginations?

Was he set up, and if so, by whom?

How political, (if at all) was all this – the *Dudus* saga?

What happens now that the smoke has cleared – where do those left behind in the aftermath go, what do they do?

What happens to *Dudus* now?

What happens to Tivoli Gardens?

This is what this volume is all about, not just questions, but ANSWERS – the main one being, who is Michael Christopher *Dudus* Coke, and how did he become - *Jamaica's FIRST President*?

Who is Dudus?

On Monday, May 24, 2010 - a media release was published in the local Jamaican press that got the attention of literally everyone across the island of Jamaica. The headline came in the form of a question, and one which was already being asked all across the island, and even across the globe at the time it was printed - WHO IS DUDUS? Below those words were printed the following: *The Police yesterday released their profile of Christopher 'Dudus' Coke, who is wanted in the United States to answer to drug and gun charges.*

Michael Christopher 'Dudus' Coke

- And just like that everyone went berserk; newspapers flew off the stands and out of the hands of vendors – everyone was curious to read the details beyond the headlines.

The profile came as the security forces issued yet another appeal for Coke to surrender after their initial effort to apprehend him, (which started on May 23, 2010), came up short. So naturally, this was one of those headlines that came with enough drama to warrant the attention it received upon being released.

This was what was released to the public:

Name: Michael Christopher Coke, otherwise called 'Dudus'

Alias: Dudus, Paul Christopher Scott, Presi, President, General, Shortman, Omar Clark

Date of birth: 13/03/1969

Address: 33 Asquith Drive, Plantation Heights, Red Hills, St Andrew – (Originally from Albert Street)

Telephone: (876) 847-4573

School: Ardenne High

Mother: Patricia Halliburton

Address: Building 25, Seaga Boulevard

Girlfriend: Stephanie Gayle

Address: 33 Asquith Drive, Plantation Heights, Red Hills, St Andrew - (Born, grew up in Tivoli Gardens)

Vehicles: 1994 Blue Nissan Bluebird

2000 Silver Honda CR-V

Brothers: Omar Coke, Everton Jones, otherwise called 'Corn Pipe', Andrew [Leighton] Coke, otherwise called 'Livity'

Businesses: Incomparable Enterprise Limited

Address: 59 Spanish Town Road, Kingston

Type: Construction

Directors: Michael Christopher Coke, otherwise called 'Dudus', Justin Ogilvie, Everton Russell

Trading company: Presidential Click - Entertainment Promotions

Passport expired: Passport will be obtained by the National Intelligence Bureau.

Driver's licence: He has no driver's licence. He said he had one in the name Omar Clark, but it was confiscated (he could not remember the date). His explanation for not having a driver's licence is that if he is stopped on the road by police and they see the name, he may be harassed.

This was what was released to the public, but is that all there is to the man, the myth and the legend? - What about the rest?

TO UNDERSTAND THE PRESENT, FIRST WE MUST REVISIT THE PAST:

Michael Christopher *'Dudus'* Coke was born into what could easily be considered as gangster royalty; the son of Pauline 'Patsy' Halliburton and the now infamous, Lester Lloyd Coke, aka Jim Brown. Not many knew that Dudus would one day ascend to the throne of what has been labeled, the mother of all garrisons; Tivoli Gardens, but as fate would have it...he did.

Lester Llyod 'Jim Brown' Coke

By the time Dudus was born, one thing had led to the next and by then his father, Lester Lloyd 'Jim Brown' Coke, had already forged a path that was to be both his and his sons to follow, (unknown to them at the time), all the way to their demise.

Contrary to popular belief, Lester Lloyd Coke - one of the key architects of the infamous Shower Posse dynasty - was not always the combative gunslinger and dope dealer that he was reputed to be in the years leading up to his death.

In the early stages of his life their was none of that, Jim Brown was just another youth from the inner city of Kingston's Denham Town community, going about the business of making something of his life, like most of his peers at the time.

Those who knew Jim Brown before he started to make headlines, remember a totally different person in comparison to the one who made headlines years later. Back then there wasn't even a *Jim Brown*; the name was Ba-Bye. A well-built Denham Town resident, who despite proving that he could defend himself in a fight on more than one occasion, was still not known to be an aggressor. Instead, Ba-Bye was known as a good soccer player, active and handy.

At one stage in his early teenage years, Ba-Bye (later called Jim Brown) was an apprentice to a locksmith by the name of Miller in a shop between Regent Street and Chestnut Lane, in the downtown section of Jamaica's capital; a far cry from what he would eventually become, which all started to take shape in classic dramatic irony in 1966.

Back then Tivoli Gardens had not yet taken shape, and the center of Western Kingston was Denham Town. This was the same year (1966) when the boiling point of political warfare in Western Kingston had ushered in a state of emergency. Although not a known player on either side at the time, Jim Brown, then in his late teens, was shot multiple times in what was later determined to be political mischief.

14

To some this may sound a bit crazy, but keep in mind, though callous as it may sound, behaviour of this nature was commonplace practice at the time.

It was a Sunday afternoon, and according to actual accounts of those who were present, political activity was in full swing throughout the entire community. According to them, the lines in the sand had been drawn, and many had aligned themselves on the whim of a promise, gravitating to either the PNP (People's National Party) or the JLP (Jamaica Labour Party).

No one knows for sure if Jim Brown had taken a particular side back then, but what is known is that during a political melee, he was shot by some gunmen a reported five times and left for dead in a gutter.

Those who recall the incident all gave accounts of everyone being so scared, it was as if they were hesitant in assisting him - not that they thought he was guilty or got what he deserved, but this was 1966, and all this was new to Jamaica. However, as scared as everyone was, one good and brave Samaritan eventually came to his rescue, riding up on a motorbike, and in unadulterated paramedic fashion, grabbed him, got him on the motorbike, and in seconds was whisking off to the newly constructed, Tivoli Gardens, where he was saved and treated back to health by the medical professionals at the health facility.

When Jim Brown re-emerged, it is said that all bets were off; everything had changed. His attitude towards life, his attitude towards people, all that had changed - he was a different man, a man who had now been to the doors of death and back, and with this attitude change, Ba-Bye was now not just a bad man, but according to one of his childhood friends, he was now a bad, bad man.

A brush with death has been known to rearrange quite a few things in ones life, but Jim Brown's brush with death was only one element to the change. The other element was the then seventeen year old, and already infamous, Claudius Massop.

Massop was born in nineteen forty nine (1949) in the West Kingston area of Denham Town. He spent his early life in petty criminal activities as a street hustler, and at one time was said to have even been a pimp. However, by the time he was eighteen, (1967) he was already the acknowledged leader of what would later become known as the infamous Shower Posse.

ALSO: By 1967, although only eighteen, Massop had somehow managed to become a big influence in Tivoli Gardens, which at the time was nothing more than a new emerging housing development for the urban poor.

Upon being shot and taken to a Tivoli Gardens health facility, the meeting of Jim Brown and Claudie Massop became a reality. Both men were no strangers to each other, they were from the same community, and more than likely even knew some of the same people, they were just from different sides of the fence, but that was until then.

Regardless if you had taken a side or not, being shot by one set of party supporters, literally predetermines where ones support would be after recovery - and Jim Brown was no different from any other man. He knew who had shot him, and according to him, it wasn't the Labourites, (Jamaica Labour Party – [JLP] Supporters), it was the other side, the Socialists (Supporters of the PNP - Peoples National Party), and that was enough to seal his allegiance.

Massop, who was by then a well recognized figure in the community, and one who had always been a supporter and activist for the JLP (Jamaica Labour Party), was quick to act upon hearing that the baller, (soccer player) Ba-Bye was shot by Socialists; and just like that,

Massop and his team of cronies decided to make Jim Brown's problem their own.

What happened next is a mystery that has gone to the grave with those who knew the facts as they actually unfolded, but according to speculation, supposition and hearsay, the retaliation was swift and bloody; and bought with it the loyalty of yet another respected force in the community; Ba-Bye, who would later become known as Jim Brown. .

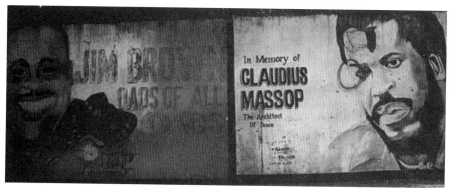

Mural of Jim Brown and Claudie Massop – Tivoli Gardens – West Kingston Ja.

With this new alliance formed, it took very little time for Jim Brown to mark his territory. Massop may've been the pimp, but Jim was just good with the ladies. Surviving five shots now with modern technology is a literal miracle, and back then in 1966, it was considered more so than now, and that alone added to Jim Brown's characteristic of power and magnetism.

By the time Dudus was born in 1969, three years after Jim Brown was shot and left for dead, later re-emerging as a totally different man; he, now in his early twenties was already a proven ladies man, or like one of his former lovers puts it, *"he fought hard, but loved harder."* He was young, well-built, well-known, and was now linked with the big man himself, Claudie Massop, and he had survived being shot multiply times; a key element that separated him from most, because most who got shot even once back then, died!

Pauline 'Patsy' Halliburton then twenty-two years old, gave birth to Michael Christopher Coke in 1969, to a father that was already notorious in his own right; [some have disputed that Jim Brown was actually Dudus' biological father, but was rather adopted, but that has remained one of those issues yet to be resolved, and has since been left to speculation and suspicion].

By the time of Dudus' birth, Jim Brown's reputation had taken a dramatic turn. No longer was he known only as the avid soccer player and humble youth, but by then his name was being called in the same conversations as some of the most notorious men of his day, from the likes of Claudius Massop to William 'Burrey Boy' Blake, Aston 'Bucky' Marshall, Dennis 'Copper' Barth, Glenford 'Early Bird' Phipps, [older brother to Donald 'Zekes' Phipps] and Vivian Blake (all deceased), except for Zekes who's now incarcerated: - These were some of, and the likes of some of the men who Dudus' father was known to associate with, or was being compared to – hence these were the same men, or the calibre of men who were Dudus' *god fathers, uncles, protectors and role models*. This was his foundation - a cast of Jamaica's most infamous and notorious characters!

NOTE: *Statistics show that murders in Jamaica soared by approximately 69 percent from 1965 to 1966 – acts which were mostly committed in the garrisons of Jamaica's capital, and in particular, West Kingston. In addition to that fact, what also needs to be understood here, is that at this particular moment in time, (mid to late 60s) Tivoli Gardens was not the political powerhouse it eventually became, [Tivoli Gardens was developed between 1963 and 1965 when the bulldozing of a slum known as Back O' Wall was ordered and redeveloped into what we know today] back then Denham Town was the heart of West Kingston, and Tivoli was just a new housing development for the under privileged. ALSO, another key point to be* *aware of is that of the above names mentioned, not all were of the same political persuasion; at one point they all held the same views, as poverty made them equals, but with politics, lines were drawn, and with gifts and promises aplenty, persuasion and manipulation were both achieved that much easier: Such was the case in West Kingston back then, so much that until this very day, the very area remains divided along political lines.*

UNDERSTANDING THE PLAYERS:

Claudius Massop (Born 1949 - Died February 4, 1979) - infamous gang leader and strongman of the Jamaica Labour Party (JLP), who was a huge influence in what would later become the Tivoli Gardens that the world now knows and some even fear. By 1972, Massop - then only 23, had solidified himself as the top man, or an area leader in the areas now known as Arnett Gardens (Jungle), Tivoli Gardens and Rema. In his early years he had a string of arrests under his belt, which included several charges of murder, armed robbery (according to police reports the firearm recovered from the scene of Massop's shooting was involved in a recent robbery a month prior), perjury and shooting with intent, but none of these charges ever led to a conviction; a somewhat early version of the Teflon Don of sorts. His chief claim to fame was the so called *'political truce'* between himself and Aston 'Buckie Marshall' Thomson in January 1978 – on behalf of the two opposing political forces which they supported – The JLP and The PNP: - Up until then a brutal on going bloody battle had ensued between the two political factions, infamously producing more than eight hundred (800) deaths in the 1980 general elections; a staggering record, even to date.

Massop met his waterloo on February 4, 1979 when he was shot dead by police, (shot at least 40 times according to newspaper reports) along with two other men, Lloyd Frazer and Alphonso Trevor Tinson. All three were shot in what the police described as a car chase that developed after being signalled to stop upon leaving a football match in Spanish Town involving the Tivoli Gardens team.

Controversy surrounding his death: In an interview with **The Gleaner** (Jamaica's premier daily newspaper) at the time of the incident, Samuel Evans, the driver of the ill-fated taxi, gave a story that out rightly contradicted the official police report, a report which claimed that Massop and his accomplices were armed and had opened fire on them (the police). He (Mr. Samuel Evans, driver of an Austin Cambridge yellow cab) said the men were unarmed and that the policemen had blocked his vehicle, took the men out and searched them, before killing them all in cold blood.

Massop was reportedly shot 40 times – a bloody end to a life that had been moulded and tainted by violence.

Following the controversial outcry surrounding the killings, the policemen involved were eventually all charged with three counts of murder, but were all later cleared after a three-week trial in Jamaica's Circuit Court system, in December of 1982.

Over 15,000 mourners came out to bid Massop farewell.

- **William** *'Burrey Boy'* **Blake,** another infamous West Kingston area leader and political activist, who was also instrumental in paving the path that was to be followed by many a copycat. A supporter of the PNP (Peoples National Party), Burrey Boy was considered by some to be a murderous maniac, who was responsible for a number of heinous criminal acts, which included murder, rape, arson and petty theft. It is said that one of the main reasons he sided with the PNP was because he refused to be an underboss to Massop, who was one of the key advocates for the JLP's cause.

Even before Tivoli Gardens welcomed its first residents, it was clear where Massop's support was, and with the emergence of said housing project, not only did this become more distinct, but it also empowered Massop to heights never before seen, and like they say in Jamaica, *'two bulls cannot reign in one pen,'* and that alongside whatever other personal reasons there may've been, and then add the divider of promises and gifts, and it didn't take much more for William 'Burrey Boy' Blake, to became one of the earliest forces of PNP dominance to be reckoned with, right up until his demise in 1975. He was such a force that his funeral procession saw the then Prime Minister and leader of the PNP, Michael Manley and several other Cabinet members leading a procession of over 20,000 mourners; a clear sign of the side he had taken, and just how much they [the PNP] regarded his support.

Retraction: The late Prime Minister Michael Manley, at a news conference at the Jamaica Conference Centre on March 15, 1992 where he announced his intention to resign as Prime Minister and president of the PNP, had this to say when asked if there was anything he had done during his administration that he regretted: He said the biggest mistake of judgement he ever made as the head of the party was to have attended the (gun salute) funeral of (PNP badman) Winston "Burrey Boy" Blake, because it had sent the wrong signal to the people, who he (Mr. Manley) was a role model to. **NOTE**: This was 17 years after the fact.

- **Aston** *'Bucky Marshall'* **Dennis** was another of the early infamous bloodletting circle. Bucky Marshall was a PNP supporter and enforcer from his late teens – starting in the late 1960s. His power increased when Michael Manley, the then leader of the PNP was elected Prime Minister of Jamaica in 1972. Almost immediately Manley embarked on a socialist agenda intended to redistribute wealth by privatizing the country's major export industries. His agenda proved to be financially unsustainable, as his policies deterred foreign investment in Jamaica, which led to unemployment and shortages of basic products. Opposition to his policies were widespread, but beginning in 1974, the opposition went into high gear when the opposition came in the form of the more conservative Edward Seaga of the Jamaica Labour Party (JLP). Things escalated for the worst and the *'chuckies,' as* they were called back then, (the equivalent of today's Shottas) were said to have quickly found favour with the political leadership of both parties (the JLP and the PNP). These were the men or youths who were both respected and feared by those that knew or even heard of them, and with this level of notoriety in and outside of their communities, they became ideal in keeping things in check for their new political puppet masters, who kept them motivated with all that they were unable to provide for themselves.

What came next may eventually be considered as one of the worst political moves in Jamaica's history, as both politicians were said to have, and in some cases known to have hired local gangsters to help them increase their hold on power in their respective constituencies. Bucky Marshall wasn't very different from the typical thug of his era; carrying out and being accused of all manner of evils known to man. However, his real claim to fame ironically is that he was instrumental in the formulation of the idea that led to *Jamaica's first One Love Peace Concert*; a plan, which was orchestrated by two gangsters from rival political factions, who by sheer happenstance were locked up in the same jail cell together and who it seemed both wanted to bring the violence to an end.

Claudius 'Claudie' Massop (JLP) and Aston 'Bucky' Marshall (PNP) - together both decided that enough was enough and that the best way to bring the country together was to use music as a uniting factor and organize a major concert. Quickly realizing that Bob Marley was a critical element upon which their success depended, Massop flew to London after being released from jail to convince Marley to perform at the event. Marley accepted the invitation, and the concert was Marley's first performance in Jamaica since he was almost assassinated at his home (now the Bob Marley Museum) in 1976.

Bob Marley and Claudius Massop

Unfortunately, as successful and revered as the event was, with even the legendary on-stage hand shake (seen in photo – next page) of the political rivals, Edward Seaga and Michael Manley, in reality it did very little in terms of quelling the political tension and violence that had been plaguing the nation, and to make matters worse, the event's two organizers and key architects, Massop and Marshall were both killed within two years of the inaugural staging.

Massop was killed by police in Jamaica, and Bucky Marshall was gunned down by unknown assailants on March 8, of the same year - 1979 - in a New York City nightclub after fleeing Jamaica.

**Michael Manley (then Prime Minister of Jamaica),
Bob Marley (Reggae Superstar)
and Edward Seaga (then leader of the opposition)**

- **Dennis** *'Copper'* **Barth:** - PUBLIC ENEMY NUMBER ONE - 'Copper' may not have been on what many Jamaicans remember as the infamous wanted flyer of 1980 – he was already dead by then, but although he did not make it to the eighties, the seventies was his. Before Copper, Jamaica's criminals kept it basic, brute force and violence, but Copper was different; he did all that, but he also did more. He was the most infamous Public Enemy Number One in the 1970s. A member of the Hot Steppers gang out of East Kingston. Before he was eighteen years old he was given two life sentences for murder and shooting two policemen. **Sentenced:** Copper however escaped from the General Penitentiary, not once, but twice.

Besides his reputation as a cold-blooded murderer, Copper was also a prolific bank robber. He was the most wanted man (by the police) at the time of his death on April 30, 1978. He was

24

killed by police while attempting to pull off his biggest caper yet; robbing the Caymanas Park racetrack, located in Portmore, St. Catherine.

Unlike most gangsters of his day, Copper never assumed the rude boy persona. Instead, he was always well-shaved, dapper and smooth with the ladies. He was never known to have hurt a woman. And even back then, gangsters drove well, Copper's car of choice being BMWs or like he and his cronies renamed them, *Bad-Man-Wagons.*

Incidentally, crime fighters of the day all viewed him as one of the best drivers they had ever seen in a high pressure situation. His wanton disregard for the police was common knowledge, almost legendary, and with superior firepower at his disposal - (it was well-known at the time that Copper was armed with a sub-machine gun) - he made the challenge of the police a sport.

INTERESTING FACT: *Unlike most chuckies / gangsters / thugs of that era who forged alliances with either of the two major political parties, PNP or JLP, Copper wasn't affiliated with neither - he was actually a political enforcer aligned to the Workers Party of Jamaica (WPJ) –* [One of Jamaica's then minor political players]. *ALSO, unlike most of the notorious of his day, who committed wanton acts of violence in the name of political affiliations; Copper was different, most of his wanton acts of violence and criminality were done in the name of the almighty dollar. Copper was about money and material acquisition, not merely violence; confirmed above by his attire and his mode of transportation – and keep in mind, this was Jamaica in the 1970s.* **CASE IN POINT:** *On what would be Copper's final dance with fate; the robbery that claimed his life, he had orchestrated an elaborate scheme to rob the racetrack, which involved the forging of alliances with leading criminal figures from various garrison communities. The robbery was supposed to bring about somewhat of a stimulus package to the various dons in different communities, with the undertone, or excuse if you wish, to* *ease the economic depression those communities were facing – an ambitious and almost revolutionary thought even in today's society.*

- The robbery attempt was carried out on a Saturday evening, May 1978, at the end of a lucrative race day. It is said that Copper, in his fearless style, led the alliance of gangsters to a room where large sums of cash was being stored, but he never managed to leave the racetrack alive. He did however manage to shoot two police officers in the melee, killing one in the process. He was said to have then grabbed a bag with cash, but was then shot once in the stomach by one of the injured police officers, which Copper had shot, and who he apparently thought was dead.

As heroic as the efforts of the police officer were, his efforts amounted to *too little, too late*; surrendering to his injury in a tragic ironic twist, which found his body, along with Copper's, at the morgue that very evening.

There was a $5,000 bounty on the head of 'Jamaica's Most Wanted' at the time of his death – a pretty decent reward in 1978.

ADDITIONAL FACTS ON COPPER: Born and raised in the Bond Street area of Western Kingston - described by the Police as a career criminal and a cold-blooded killer. Known also as a master in the art of disguise; he would oftentimes even wear women's clothing during the commission of certain criminal acts. Records show that his first murder was carried out in his early teens, which according to the police, eventually earned him the reputation of being the most dangerous criminal to ever walk the streets of Kingston at the time - so much that it is said that the mere mention of his name would leave police officers serving (at the time), on edge.

Copper: *Arguably the most cunning and dangerous man to have ever made the Jamaica's most wanted list.*

[Agreed upon by most senior law enforcement officers; retired and presently in service].

- **Vivian Blake** (May 11, 1956 – March 21, 2010) reputed leader of the notorious *Shower Posse*, was born to a poor family in West Kingston, but was the recipient of a Marcus Garvey Scholarship while attending St. Anne's Primary, which granted him access to the then prestigious private high school, St. George's College, located on North Street in Jamaica's capitol, where he excelled both academically and in sports. He first traveled to New York as part of a cricket team in 1973, but instead of returning to Jamaica, Blake remained, and eventually established the American arm of the *Shower Posse*; the entity of death and mayhem that the world ultimately came to know and fear.

In the United States, Mr. Blake developed a marijuana and cocaine distribution network that spanned throughout major cities from Miami to New York to Los Angeles, reaching even as far as Anchorage, Alaska.

Vivian Blake

NOTE: *In 1981 a Time Magazine article reported that an estimated US$ 1 Billion was earned annually from illegal drugs (mainly marijuana) shipped or flown into the US from Jamaica. News Week Magazine at the same time put the figure at an estimated US$1.1 Billion.*

A warrant for his arrest was first issued in 1988 after he and other members of the gang were accused in the November 1984 killing of five people in a Miami crack house. According to a 2008 profile of the Shower Posse on the BET series "American Gangster," Blake escaped arrest and prosecution by hopping on a cruise ship in Miami bound for Jamaica.

According to New York Daily News columnist Patrice O'Shaughnessy, in an article printed on March 30, 2010, Blake is credited with the dubious distinction of being "one of the creators of crack."

During the 1980s, also according to O'Shaughnessy, Blake was responsible for flooding Bronx neighbourhoods such as Soundview, Crotona Park and Bronx River with tons of cocaine and crack cocaine.

After escaping apprehension for the multiple homicides in Miami, and the whole posse fiasco hit the fan, additional charges were eventually added, and subsequent to being featured on America's Most Wanted, he was extradited to the United States in 1999 after fighting extradition from 1994.

On what can be described as the dawn of the new millennium, Y2K, Vivian Blake pleaded guilty to charges including racketeering and conspiracy, and admitted to his role in the Shower Posse gang. He was sentenced to 28 years, but was released on parole after eight.

Upon his release from prison, Blake returned to Jamaica and was said to be working on a screenplay about his life.

Vivian Blake died on March 21, 2010 at the age of 53, after being admitted to the University Hospital of the West Indies for a heart attack. At the time of his death, he was suffering from kidney disease and undergoing dialysis.

WITH VIVIAN BLAKE THE STORY IS SOMEWHAT DIFFERENT, he may've been accused of some major atrocities, and even did time behind them, but even with all that, Blake was never known as a *chuckie,* a *thug or* a *badman.* Instead Vivian was just Vivian, another youth from the inner city who was going to school, enjoyed playing cricket and played the game well; he was an athlete. However, what must not be overlooked here for the purpose of complete understanding is that although not one of the rudies, [rude boys] one of his best friends, Jim Brown, by now was.

Role models were hard to come by in those days, and there is little doubt that Vivian was fascinated by all that Jim was into by the time he was making his exit of Jamaica. From all accounts, the avenues of communication remained opened, and soon business was birth out of friendship - with Jim orchestrating from a distance [Jamaica], and Vivian handling business on the ground [New York] – and within a short period, Jim Brown's status was on the rise, because unlike most who came before him, he now had plans that went way beyond the shores of Jamaica and politics.

ADDITIONAL NOTE: Vivian Blake can also be viewed as a godfather to Dudus in literal terms. This was one of his best friend's son, and there is little doubt that Dudus was an early patron of Blake's generosity.

Excerpt from an interview before Vivian Blake's demise:

Exhibit A

"I did 15 years in prison. I've never had a crime in Jamaica. Never had a crime in Jamaica. Had nothing to do with Jamaica and their politics. But they keep mixing me up in politics. I'm a family man. Me commit my crimes dem in America, and finish my time. All I want right now is

just finish out me life peacefully. I ain't got no time fi go in gun ting and all type of thing deh. I'm 54 years old. Y'understand me? I have to more try to be checking about my health, more than trying to be gangster."

_____End of Excerpt

Vivian Blake: Dead at 54, March 21, 2010 - after returning to Jamaica just over a year before, in January 2009 – following an eight year stint in a US federal prison. In life he was said to be larger than life, celebrated by many, but in death the mourners were few, as just over 20 showed up to pay their last respects– and in

Vivian Blake upon his return to Jamaica

a cinematic twist of irony, the contingent of police officers deployed to the funeral was even greater than the number of mourners in attendance. It must also be noted that there were no notable figures of any sort among the mourners in attendance – neither from the political arena or the underworld.

OTHER KEY NOTABLES OF THE ERA: **Push Wood**, a JLP enforcer who ruled the community known as Rema, also a Jamaica Labour Party affiliated community. He was the mentor and forerunner to the highly revered (in Jamaican gangster circles) Howard Hewitt, popularly known as **'Curly Locks'** - also a JLP enforcer from the community of Rema, which it is said he ruled with an iron first for almost a decade – (his reign was simultaneous with that of Massop, Mitchell and Jim Brown) – he was known to be involved in daring bank and payroll robberies at various locations across the city of Kingston. Curly Locks was known primarily as the head of the Rema 13 gang, which included (among its ranks), some of the most notorious of the day - 'Bigness', 'Pearl Harbour', 'Little Jack',

'Stealer', 'Mutt', 'Peazy', '39', 'Riley', 'Bobo Charles,' and a young and dangerous youth known only as Crackers.

According to police reports of the day, the gang was known to have staged multiple robberies, with each gang member at times brandishing two guns or more. Many persons inside Rema and outside the garrison community met their deaths at the hands of the Rema 13 gang. Locks was said to be so evil that he was respected, and maybe even a little feared by both his counterparts - Claudius Massop and his successor, 'Jim Brown'. The stories surrounding his cruelty are numerous, with probably the most evil and deranged being (so it is said) – that in a jealous rage, Curly Locks was reported to have shot and injured one of his many women over what was said to be his steady advances on her sister, who he impregnated six months later, only to end her life in her eight month of pregnancy.

His demise came at the hands of a young Tivoli Gardens enforcer with whom he had a dispute, inside the garrison community. The enforcer in question was known as 'Paper Man.' It's reported that he was handling security and had refused Curly Locks entry to a yard where Jim Brown was said to be distributing the weekly cheques for community work done in Tivoli Gardens, Rose Town and Rema.

What transpired next was one of those tragic misunderstandings, as it has since been ascertained that Paper Man, did not know that he was dealing with the Rema don, and had even gone as far as disrespecting him with derogatory *'coolie boy'* terms, even reportedly threatening to punch him in his mouth, before chasing him away from the entrance to the premises at gun point.

Reports are that *Locks* left the scene and returned with a .357 magnum, and after a brief scuffle, in which he reportedly pistol-whipped Paper Man to the stage of near unconsciousness, dislodging his right eye in the process – Jim Brown and other top Tivoli Gardens enforcers rushed in; diffusing the situation, all the time explaining to Paper Man that the 'coolie boy', was in fact the notorious Curly Locks. Only then and because of their intervention - Paper Man's life was spared – but a move that would quickly proved to be tragic – with Curly Locks being ambushed and shot just a few weeks later as he rode his Honda Motorbike through West Kingston. The triggerman was a one-eyed *Paper Man.*

Anthony Tingle, aka 'General Starkey': People's National Party (PNP) political thug - General Starkey and his crony, 'Hutch' came to prominence in the Arnett Gardens and Jones Town communities after the death of PNPs top man, Burry Boy and Feathermop in 1975.

Ironically, Starkey and Hutch took their name from a popular American television crime series of the day which featured two police officers named - Starksy and Hutch.

In 1977, Starkey, still only a teenager, topped the police most wanted list with a bounty of $3,000 for his capture. At the time the posting of General Starkey as a most wanted criminal by police was frowned upon by then PNP's youth organisation, who issued a statement saying the PNPYO was "extremely disturbed by such a practice." (*Starkey was 17 years old*).

INTERESTING TWIST: A little over six months after going public with that statement, the PNP's disciplinary committee suspended the then PNPYO President, Mr. Paul Burke; a suspension which was said to be based solely on the issuing of such a statement. According to many, including published reports, Burke's suspension was a signal that the inventors of the political monsters and their offspring, had simply had enough of their little creations, and were now literally authorizing their *extermination.*

NOTE: One year later, 1978, police killed more than 30 persons who were on their top 40 most wanted list – most of who had some political affiliation of one sort or another.

Starkey's running gun battles with legendary crime fighter of the day, Keith Gardner, known in the streets as 'Trinity,' are the type of stuff blockbuster movie scripts are made of.

In January of 1978, General Starkey...still wanted, turned himself over to the police and was charged with two counts of rape and shooting with intent – but this was Jamaica, witnesses seldom ever turn up for court, and with that being the deciding factor, General Starkey was soon back on the streets as no evidence was ever offered up against him.

A year later, 1979, General Starkey's name was again on the lips of law enforcement, again wanted for his suspected role and involvement in a series of disparaging and wanton shootings.

With the heat in the kitchen becoming just a little too hot for his liking, Starkey, again a fugitive, fled the island, only to turn up in Canada, with the same old tricks. It is said that only two days subsequent to his arrival, The Royal Canadian Mounted Police arrested and charged him with three counts of attempted murder and other related charges. He was sentenced by a Toronto court to four years imprisonment at hard labour.

By July 1980, General Starkey was deported to Jamaica, where he was again faced with the charges he had absconded from - shooting with intent and illegal possession of a firearm.

However, on September 19, of that same year, General Starkey was back on the streets after no one turned up at the Gun Court to again give evidence against him.

With Starkey's return to the island, and the climate being what it was, politically, it is rumoured that he and his gang made some moves out of desperation that caused them to fall out of favour with the main elements inside the community, a development that led to them being literally forced to relocate to nearby Jones Town.

The dispute that led to General Starkey's expulsion from Arnett Gardens or Concrete Jungle, as the area is called, is said to have came about due to the murder of a betting shop clerk on Lincoln Crescent in Arnett Gardens in May 1981. The killing of the woman was said to have not gone down well with some of key 'Junglists,' who all in one way or the other, blamed Starkey's gang for the senseless act of violence.

According to residents who recall the period – the body of the betting shop clerk might've still been warm when a man accused of being involved or known to be apart of Starkey's gang, was held and dragged to the scene of the crime and shot dead, *execution style*. The perpetrators of this act then tagged his body *'This killer of the betting shop woman'*. Shortly after, same day, another man was taken to the scene and also murdered.

WHAT GOES AROUND, COMES AROUND: Just over a month after the betting shop incident, on June 1, 1981, Anthony 'General Starkey' Tingle would meet his waterloo.

HOW HE DIED: The gangster and his cronies are said to have just left a dance in Jones Town on the *fateful* morning of his death. The word is that most of the gang members were either drunk or high upon retiring to bed, when heavily armed policemen alongside members of the military (who were in the area in search of Starkey and his gang, and who had already gotten credible information on their whereabouts), swooped down on their Jones Town location - 32 Love Street.

The law men swooped down on the premises, but reported that they were met with gun fire, and after a lengthy gun battle; the clearing the smoke revealed: General Starkey and seven of his cronies, including his brother Michael McLeod, all laid dead.

The other dead men were identified as Barrington Fitzroy, Paul Johnson - both of Septimus Street, Jones Town - Errol Shorter, Conrad Bryan and Leroy Reid of Orange Street, and a man known as Michael Jackson.

The Police report at the time stated that they recovered a M16 assault rifle, 80 rounds of ammunition, gas masks and military uniforms. Two law men were reportedly injured during the gun battle.

General Starkey was 26 years old at the time of his death.

IN CONCLUSION: The list of notable notorious figures and their exploits are too numerous to mention, but regardless what other name(s) may or may not have been brought into the conversation – one thing is clear – this was the reality that Dudus was born into - this was the era, the environment, the situations, the people and types of people who were instrumental in one way or the other when it came to his moulding and preparation for his future role. Sure other children were born in the same year and even in the same area as he was, and sure not all of them turned out like he did, but to those children's benefit, and in Dudus' defence, let's not forget that they didn't have a father by the name of Lloyd Lester 'Jim Brown' Coke.

Proverbs 22:6 *"Train up a child in the way he should grow, and when he is old, he will not depart from it."*

HAUNTED BY VIOLENCE AND DEATH:

On TUESDAY, May 3, 2005, Christopher 'Chris Royal' Coke [1987-2005] was shot and killed by the police. His death made him the fourth family member in the Coke dynasty to have met a violent end. The other members include; the head of the dynasty himself, Lester Lloyd "Jim Brown" Coke – who was burnt to death under what some have labelled mysterious circumstances in his jail cell in Jamaica [1992], while awaiting extradition to the United States to face multiple murder and drug and gun charges. Then there was Mark "Jah T" Coke, [1967-1992] - who was shot along Maxfield Avenue in Kingston, while riding his motorcycle [he was in preparation for an anniversary dance for a fallen area leader, and his father's predecessor, Claudius Massop] - *police say at least twelve (12) persons were killed in retaliation within a two-week period after his murder.* The violent *end* was not limited to the male members of the dynasty, as there was also the killing of a female sibling known only as "Mumpi" – who was also killed by the gun in downtown, Kingston [shortly before Jah T's demise]. Information surrounding her death is sketchy, but it's alleged that she was sleeping with the enemy, and her demise came about because of who she was, and where she should *not* have been.

NOTE: Three police officers were killed shortly after Chris Royal's death, and were all thought to be acts of reprisal for his slaying.

Fig. 1. The final resting place Christopher St. Aubin Coke aka Chris Royal

Fig. 2. The final resting place of Mark Anthony Coke aka Jah - Tl

• *Dudus — The Boy*

To understand Dudus the boy, first we must understand Jim Brown the Man, because without understanding, or at least having some level of understanding of Jim Brown the man, then understanding Dudus the boy will be a desire nestled in the bosom of impossibility.

Someone once said that *when laws get involved, the lines that separate the heroes from the villains get blurred, sometimes even erased or replaced all together.* Some have argued that Jim Brown was such a man; a man who got caught up in the bureaucratic rigmarole of society's blatant twisting of what was once okay, but suddenly becomes outlawed for whatever reason it is that those in

A young Dudus

charge decide - (at that particular time) - should be the reason for such a change.

A lot has been said about him [Jim Brown], but according to his wife, Bev Brown, [not Dudus' mother] in an interview after his death, she was quick to point out that Jim Brown was not the monster the media had made him out to be – **QUOTE:** *"people love him for real,"* she said, continuing with *"they love him for real, because of the person he is, always trying to help someone, always giving words of encouragement, especially to the kids, always encouraging them to stay in school and achieve a better tomorrow,"* – in said interview, his widow went on to say that, *"he was a principle person,"* - a claim that many agree with, but a claim also disputed by an equal number, if not more, because with a reputation like the one he left behind, what principles did he really stand on, or for?...Mayhem and confusion?

Some would be quick to agree to that, while some would beg to differ, but let's analyze the FACTS as we have uncovered them.

A lot has been said about the man, but from what we have uncovered, it seems that most of it was sensationalized for a variety of reasons. The truth however lacks no vibrancy, and with that said, these are some of the FACTS we uncovered:

Although Tivoli Gardens and Jim Brown have been almost synonymous in mention for as long as most of us can remember, what needs to be made clear is that at the time Jim Brown allegedly took up arms, he was not the front-line or top-man in Tivoli Gardens, and wasn't so for *many* years to come. One of the greatest facts missed by many is that Jim Brown's reign as the Tivoli boss was even shorter than that of his mentor, Claudius Massop, but unlike Massop, his reign had so much impact that it has overwhelmed and eventually dwarfed the memory of Massop all together.

RECAP: To further clarify this point, what needs to be remembered is that at the time when Jim Brown was first shot in 1966, and rushed to the Tivoli Gardens Health Centre for medical assistance, all he was, was a mere soccer player, doing odd jobs and apprentice work; another youth from the inner city trying to see a brighter day. In the bigger scheme of things, Jim Brown was still a literal nobody; his involvement was from a spectator's prospective; like most members of the community.

Mural of Jim Brown inside Tivoli Gardens

In the early years of Tivoli Gardens, the prominent players were the likes of (Claudius) Claudie Massop and (Carl) Byer Mitchell, but eventually it was Jim Brown who emerged as the leader of what has become a Tivoli Gardens dynasty of tyranny.

BUT HOW DID ALL THAT COME TO BE?

AFTER the demise of Tivoli Gardens enforcer, Claudius Massop; who died in a hail of police bullets on February 4th 1979, the Tivoli Gardens reign of control fell into the hands of his chief honcho, Carl 'Byah' Mitchell. Mitchell's reign was however short lived, lasting just over a year, when he succumbed to a drug overdose, [he was a reputed cocaine abuser], which resulted in an opening for the then popular and only logical leader...Lester Lloyd 'Jim Brown' Coke.

Jim Brown stepped in to fill the breach left by the two men just before the Jamaica Labour Party's

Claudie Massop greeted by Tivoli Garden residents

landslide victory at the polls in 1980 and with him at the helm of the Jamaica Labour Party's political stronghold, his power increased sevenfold, even before victory was declared.

Another important fact that must also be noted is that although Jim Brown was not the top-man in Tivoli Gardens before 1980, he still maintained a high level of prominence and respect in the community from the moment he was introduced to it by Massop. Unlike most hoodlums at the time, it must be stated that Jim Brown was a cut above the rest; street smart and literate - traits that served him well on his rise to the top of the food chain.

With Brown ushered into the fold by non other than the top-man himself, Claudius Massop, and him already having a reputation of not being a walk over, plus surviving multiple gun shot wounds - his respect came somewhat naturally and with him being the man he was, he capitalized greatly.

Jim Brown was an intellect, at least when it came to criminal activities-ahead of most of his peers by leaps and bounds. According to some, he always had a plan, a *vision*, even if it meant spilling some blood along the way, but be that what it may, or may not have been, there is no denying that none-the-less, Jim Brown was a thinker.

Known originally as 'Ba Bye', those who knew him say he was a tough, no-nonsense type of man, who fought tooth and nail for his party's honour, once he had signed on to their philosophy. His commitment however led to accusations, and like Massop, Coke was soon nabbed by agents of the state, thrown behind bars and slapped with a murder charge. But just like Massop, after a few months in jail, Coke was eventually freed after the main witness to the murder turned up dead.

It was after that release from jail that Coke shed the moniker 'Ba Bye' and took upon himself the nickname 'Jim Brown', after the hall of fame American football player, whom he felt was the perfect representation of who he thought he was; *a larger than life aggressor*.

It is said that Coke honed his skills as a steel-nerved and feared enforcer during the politically turbulent 70s, when the rules of engagement in politically volatile areas demanded that the enemy be pushed back.

Such a scenario provided the perfect breeding ground of evolution for Coke and others of his ilk. Coke was responsible for keeping his political rivals at bay, who would wish to attack his community and inflict violence upon its citizens; a Sentry of sorts. But regardless how one may feel about Coke, one thing cannot be denied, like many before him, he too was the product of a divisive political system created by both the times, and some of Jamaica's early political leaders who were desperate for power after independence from Great Britain.

Enforcers back then were a dime or less a dozen - expendables- and Jim Brown was determined to change the dynamics of that scenario, because unlike Massop and Mitchell, Coke was smart enough, *early enough*, to wean himself off the breast of political nutrients, and perhaps could be described as the first political enforcer to free himself from the economic shackles foisted on him and others of the same kind by political power brokers of the day.

After the JLP's victory in 1980, Jamaica, which was one of the major suppliers of marijuana to the United States, Canada and the United Kingdom, evolved into a major transhipment port for the deadly drug, cocaine. The JLP had chosen to align themselves with the US in the Cold War, and at that government's request, embarked upon a major ganja eradication campaign throughout Jamaica.

The anti-marijuana initiative caused economic fallout between the growers and traders of the illegal crop in Jamaica, and literally forced drug traffickers to seek alternative means (alternate drugs) to make their money. Cocaine commanded a much higher market value than ganja and soon proved to be the perfect substitute for drug traders who quickly diverted their skills to satisfying an overwhelming demand for the white substance [cocaine], primarily in the United States.

It was during this time that it is said, Coke; along with his confidante, Vivian Blake, developed a massive drug-running empire, with bases of operation in Florida, New York, New Jersey, Philadelphia, Chicago and other parts of the United States.

However, unknown to them at the time, operations of such magnitude are like magnets to law enforcement – they draw attention, and it didn't take long for the spotlights to come on, with United States federal authorities paying full attention to not only their activities in the illicit drug trade, but also paying full attention to the brutal *modus operandi* of these Jamaican gangsters. **NOTE:** The Shower Posse was not the only perpetrator at the time with Jamaican roots – there was also the likes of the notorious Spanglers Posse – who incidentally were bitter enemies of the Shower Posse: The Spanglers Posse's original members hailed from Matthews Lane, (almost a literal stone throw from the Shower Posse headquarters in Tivoli Gardens) and other nearby areas affiliated to the PNP (People's National Party).

The Shower Posse, so called [it is alleged] because of their *predilection* to spray their enemies with bullets, was so feared by their rivals, and created so much havoc abroad that the US Government was forced to allocate a budget to facilitate a massive counter offense aimed at destabilising the gang in the 80s.

The Shower Posse may've been brutal, but so were their rivals, the Spanglers Posse, who when it came to violence, were not *lackeys* – equally brutal in their own right. In retrospect, except for negative, just like their archenemy, little else can now be said about their actions, which all seemed fixed on making the suicidal climb to the summit of stupidity - mainly centering around the importation of the political violence, that *had been bred in Jamaica since the 1940s*, to the streets of North America; a move that literally made no sense, outside of stroking personal egos.

While Blake was known as the brain behind the empire, Coke was known as the muscle and the provider thereof, and in the process, became so wealthy that he could literally ignore political handouts which to him were being dispensed in too little portions by the powers that be.

Money and power however didn't change Jim Brown, he was still adamant about his political duties, just as when he was broke. One 1984 incident made that point clear: REPORTEDLY, Coke led a team of men from his stronghold of Tivoli Gardens into Wilton Gardens, also known as Rema, then a JLP-aligned community, ran by orders from the bosses in 'Garden' (another name for Tivoli). For years Rema was regarded as a sort of bastard cousin of the more developed and powerful Tivoli Gardens. But Rema had itself spawned fierce street warriors who were hardened in the art of criminal warfare from their daily experiences - living in an area which was the first line of defence against PNP thugs who launched repeated attacks from Arnett Gardens.

A disagreement between persons from Tivoli Gardens and Rema had prompted Coke and his gang's expedition into Rema, and when the gang left Rema, seven men laid dead. The dispute was said to have been over weapons belonging to Tivoli Gardens, but which were in the hands of men from Rema, who refused to return them.

Shortly after the incident the police arrested Coke and charged him with seven counts of murder, but Coke was again freed after no one came forward to testify against him.

On the day of his release, heavily-armed men celebrated openly in downtown Kingston; firing a barrage of gunshots in the air directly in front of the Supreme Court; an act that sent police officers, court staff and civilians scampering for cover, shaking in fear. It was all smiles as he [Jim Brown] emerged from the Courthouse and was held high by the crowd, before being whisked off to his fortress in Tivoli Gardens like a King after a victorious crusade.

Soon after, then Prime Minister and Member of Parliament for West Kingston, Edward Seaga, along with other JLP officials, visited Rema and appealed to the residents to *'let bygones be bygones'*, a request that was hard to fulfil with lives lost, but for whatever the reason, eventually it was.

With his legal troubles in Jamaica behind him and his political connections rock solid, Coke now had time to continue his illegal quest to acquire wealth. In 1986, federal authorities in the United States reported that the Shower Posse had spread their wings to over a dozen US cities and were raking in a substantial portion of the estimated 25 percent of the billion dollar illegal drug trade that Jamaican gangs earned.

But as the Shower Posse grew in stature, so did the federal investigation into their activities, and in November of 1988, 53 Shower Posse members were arrested in New Jersey on drug distribution charges. A month before, a federal grand jury indicted 34 members of the Shower Posse, including, Coke, Blake and Blake's two half-brothers, Errol Hussing and Tony Bruce.

Coke however managed to remain a free man until the beginning of the 1990s when international police investigations, which had become like a noose around the Posse's neck, began to tighten.

Richard 'Storytella' Morrison, a leading posse member, was 'captured' in Jamaica by US authorities and illegally whisked abroad to stand trial.

In February 1991, Coke was arrested by the police in Jamaica and locked up at the General Penitentiary, now called the Tower Street Adult Correctional Facility, after the US Government requested that he be extradited to that country to answer to murder and drug trafficking charges.

Coke's bid to acquire a *special leave to appeal* was rejected by the United Kingdom Privy Council and after a year of legal wrangling the writing was on the wall.

BUT WHEN IT RAINS IT POURS:

Exhibit B

The Florida-based website, www.emergency.com, posted this report in August, 1992.

Miami, FL. A drug gang war that started in Kingston, Jamaica, early in 1992 may have recently spilled over into the streets and bars of Miami. Reportedly, an early Saturday morning nightclub shooting of twenty-two (22) people involved members of the Jamaican "Shower Posse." Gang crimes officers of the Broward County Sheriff's Office say that the nightclub killings may have been retribution for the February killing of Mark Coke, a leader of the Jamaican "Shower Posse" drug gang. The "Shower Posse" supposedly gets its name from the "shower" of lead it shoots at rival gangs.

An agent of the Bureau of Alcohol, Tobacco, and Firearms says that Saturday's shootings "had all the earmarks" of a Jamaican "Posse" hit. Special Agent Joe Vince was quoted by the United Press International as saying, "the posses are the most vicious organised crime group in the United States today."

Capt. Al Lambeti of the Broward County Sheriff's Office said that the shooting was a "...perfect textbook example of how the posse does business".

The younger Coke's murder was rumoured to stem from a dispute between Shower Posse members and members of the Black Roses Crew, which was then led by William 'Willie Haggart' Moore, who would eventually be killed in a drive-by that has spawned many rumours until this day. Popular dancer, Gerald 'Bogle' Levy, [Haggart's right hand man] was reportedly doused with alcohol during the dispute, which occurred at a weekly dance called 'Beachline' held at the Hellshire Beach in St Catherine. The dispute was however diffused by police officers who were on the scene before it could escalate.

Three weeks later, the very day his son was buried, Jim Brown, who was now in the custody of the Jamaican authorities, was burnt to death in a mysterious fire inside his cell.

Unconfirmed reports suggest that the notorious gangster committed suicide because he realised that he would be handed over to the US authorities, but this claim has been refuted by others who say his death was as a result of a botched escape attempt. Still others say Coke was murdered to keep him from spilling the beans to the Americans.

The killing of Coke's son sparked a new round of political bloodletting, and in the weeks that followed, shootings occurred in Hannah Town, Arnett Gardens, Denham Town, Rose Lane and Matthews Lane, prompting then Prime Minister Michael Manley to call for a meeting with Seaga. The violence also sparked a march by a group of churches through the affected communities, but the violence merely paused, and eventually was even exported beyond local shores.

BUT WAIT, THERE IS MORE:

BECAUSE TO FULLY UNDERSTAND JIM BROWN THE MAN, UNDERSTANDING THE TIME LINE AND WHAT HE DID, WITHIN THAT TIME FRAME, IS PARAMOUNT. Let's remember that in 1966 he was a mere teenage athlete and an apprentice, but by the mid 70s [by the time DUDUS WAS ABOUT 5 or 6 years old] his power had escalated greatly; beyond the imagination and comprehension of most!

Always a street smart quick witted thinker, Jim Brown learnt early the importance of supply and demand, and with his childhood friend, Vivian Blake now in New York hustling [selling drugs], it didn't take long for him [Jim Brown] to create a pipeline that funnelled marijuana straight from Kingston to New York City.

This was the 70s, so airport security was literally nothing to speak of, so the transportation of the illegal substance was almost like a literal walk in the park and Jim Brown made millions from this deal.

With Vivian away and Jim in Jamaica, it was a literal match made in heaven. Vivian needed product, [marijuana] and Jim needed money. One was the brain of the operation, and the other was the muscle, with a reach so far, Jim Brown singlehandedly maintained order on the streets of the United States and elsewhere, all the way from his fortress in Jamaican.

With an over six-foot presence that shouted intimidating from the moment of sight, and with the backing of his cronies, Jim Brown was in full flight. He may not have been the top-man, but it didn't make much of a difference, he lived the part to the fullest; and with him being the one responsible for the New York connection that was bringing in major revenue, his respect was galvanized even further.

By the time the reigns of Tivoli Gardens were in Jim Brown's hands, Jim Brown was already a well groomed man for the position.

With Jim Brown stepping into the position of power right before the JLP's victory in the 1980 General Election, and he now in charge of the party's political stronghold...things changed rapidly.

According to retired U.S. DEA, and ATF agents who were active at the time, - 'Jim Brown and his cronies' power was merely legitimized by the JLP's landslide victory in 1980, because they had already infiltrated the United States by the mid to late 70s.' It is said that he [Jim Brown] was buying guns in the U.S like they were going out of style in 1979 and 1980. According to these agents he was entering the U.S. on a visa, and he had plenty of money to spend on his fetish; guns and ammunition. One agent even went on record to say, *"you think it was Jim Brown's money he was spending to bring back guns to Jamaica that were used to kill the opposition? Give me a break. Where did the money come from? Use your imagination on that one."*

Veteran Jamaican journalist Lloyd Williams confirmed the claims of the U.S. agents in an August 1999 GQ article entitled, *The Caribbean Connection*, when he said, *"The Shower Posse's firepower improved dramatically during the run-up to the elections, (1980). M16s, previously unheard-of, were flowing into Jamaica by the barrelful. Even the most powerful Kingston gangs, drawn from the shanties, could hardly afford American cigarettes,"* he said, continuing with, *"Much less automatic weapons, at least in the beginning. These guys, if they'd seen a pack of Camels, they would have fainted,"* he continued. *"So there had to be people supplying them (with the weapons) and teaching them how to use them."*

Those were the realities of the day, and Jim Brown was a key figure in all that was happening, both locally [in Jamaica] and internationally.

One of the most gruesome accounts of Jim Brown's wanton callousness came to life in a Federal Courtroom when Cecil Conner, aka Modeller, [or] Charles 'Little Nut' Miller, a Shower Posse member who turned on the Posse after being busted in Rochester, New York, in February 1985 [on marijuana and cocaine charges], decided to do a tell all. THE CASE WAS THE NOTORIOUS "NICKLE HOMOCIDE":- Modeller testified that Jim Brown was enraged after being robbed of his jewellery at a Miami crack housed in 1984, and with that occurring he was called in to go back there with Jim and others. Modeller testified that he witnessed a pregnant woman pray before she and four others were gunned down by Jim Brown and other Shower Posse members, while he [Modeller] stood guard – THIS WAS ONE OF THE BLOODIEST UNSOLVED MURDERS IN MIAMI'S HISTORY – Until then – Conner conceded that he was asked to go there to cover Jim Brown's back, and he did just that.

The names of the murdered in the above incident were: Gladstone Brightley, Elaine Wooden, Ginnite Brazil, Dora Woods and Larry Patterson; another woman, Tammy Cox, was also wounded in said incident.

THE STORIES ARE MANY, BUT THIS WAS THE JIM BROWN law enforcement knew. In the garrisons of Kingston, he was a key enforcer for former Prime Minister Edward Seaga's Jamaica Labor Party; Seaga himself called Brown the "protector" of Kingston's poor, and was vocal at his demise and even helped lead the don *dadda's* funeral procession. But to local police - who had tried and failed, to pin 14 separate murder charges on him – Brown was the most influential of the city's so called dons.

- **BUT THERE ARE TWO SIDES TO EVERY COIN:** As time passed, and even with all that was happening, Jim Brown still found time to take unto himself a family, a contradictory move when compared to his affiliation and reputation, both as a womanizer and gangster. He sent his children to some of Kingston's most prominent high schools. His eldest son, Mark Anthony Coke, aka 'Jah T', went to Wolmer's Boys School, while Leighton, otherwise called 'Livity', attended Excelsior High. Michael Christopher 'Dudus' Coke, went to Ardenne High.

Moves like these were what set Jim Brown apart, because although he was who he was; like one female who knew him well said; "di dads a di real man, dem man dey tek care a house [the boss is a real man, he takes care of home, meaning family].

There can be no denying that Jim Brown did just that and more, as you may very well imagine, with him being who he was, he could've easily had the best teachers at the Tivoli Gardens Comprehensive High School, (adjacent to the Tivoli

Gardens fortress), at the beck and call of his children, but he instead took them out of their comfort zone, which not only exposed them, but prepared them.

Jim Brown being led away in handcuffs after court appearance

Besides ensuring that his kids attended some of Kingston's most prominent high schools, it didn't take long for Jim Brown to acquire residence fitting for an upper echelon family, miles away from the hustle and bustle of Tivoli Gardens.

Unknown to most, from as early as the mid 80s, Jim Brown's family residence was not Tivoli Gardens, but was actually in the residential suburbs of *Arcadia*, located in upper St. Andrew. This was a far cry from Tivoli Gardens, both in reality and price range, but money was not an issue, and reality was flexible.

DUDUS however was not whisked away to the suburbs like the rest of the children; his mother was Pauline 'Patsy' Halliburton, now 63, not Jim Brown's wife, Bev Brown, who is the mother of most of his other children, including Jah T and Livity, but even with that, he [Dudus] lacked nothing.

By the time Dudus was 16 in 1985; his father was at the top of his

Dudus' mother inside Tivoli Gardens

game and rising. Dudus was the son of the *don*, and lived like one. Name it and if he wanted it, he got it, because with most of Jim's children no longer permanent residents of the Tivoli community, there was no way he could make it seem as though the child that was visible to the community was being slighted in any way, shape or form. Both Dudus and his mother were well taken care of, by both Jim and the rest of the community. This was Jim Brown's son, so the respect that was his from an early stage was only natural.

TO UNDERSTAND DUDUS THE BOY, one must simply focus on Jim Brown the man, because this was what fuelled Dudus the boy, into Dudus the man; what he saw on a day to day basis. Keep in mind, he was the son of a don, [*like father like son*] a man who was the man before the title was even bestowed on him. And also keep in mind that he [Dudus] lived in Tivoli Gardens even when Jim's other children didn't. He was on the front line of all activity. He lived it, heard it and saw it daily, and no doubt was soon aware of the power that was his. He was ghetto royalty, alive and in living colour.

It shouldn't take much of an imagination to see the type of environment that was the incubator for Dudus. His godfathers and uncles were the likes of Claudius Massop, Vivian Blake, (Carl) Byer Mitchell, Curly Locks and a man said to be one of Jim Brown's most notorious henchman, Bitter-Blood, or Blood; a name bestowed on him due to his complexion and his obsession with the life giving fluid.

These were the hands that held Dudus, the voices that instructed him, persons whose actions he would eventually come to emulate. This was his breeding ground; his training ground – Tivoli Gardens, Kingston, Jamaica, under the protection and guidance of some of the most notorious architects of murder and mayhem Jamaica has ever seen.

ONE INTERESTING STORY: It is said that at the age of fourteen, Dudus almost fell victim to his father's 45 pistol, when he got involved in wanton acts of violence, against both males and females – in and around the community - creating unnecessary problems for Brown, who at one stage got so mad that it's rumoured - his effort to reprimand Dudus came at gunpoint.

NOTE: Jim Brown was burnt to death in what has been dubbed a fire of mysterious origin in a maximum-security cell - Brown was within days of being extradited to face murder and drug-racketeering charges in the U.S.: - Suspicions ran high that he was silenced because he knew too much. Some have even gone as far as suggesting that Jim Brown is not dead, but actually still alive – all a part of a grand conspiratorial cover-up. When faced with these arguments in 1992 outside a Kingston courthouse, Jim Brown's lawyer Tom Tavares-Finson [A JLP Member of Parliament at the time] smiled sarcastically behind his racing-driver sunglasses, before responding to the tune of, *"If you believe Jim Brown just burned to death, by accident, in his jail cell, you'll believe in the tooth fairy. The only thing I can tell you for sure is I saw the body - and Jim Brown is dead."*

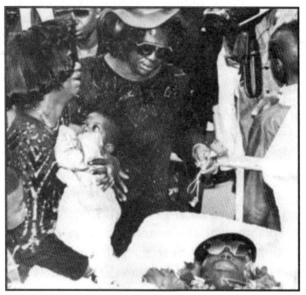

Funeral of Lester Llyod 'Jim Brown' Coke - 1992

INTERESTING NOTE: Edward Sega, then leader of the JLP [Jamaica Labour Party] and Jim Brown's patron, led Lloyd Lester 'Jim Brown' Coke's funeral procession of over 35,000.

• *Dudus – The Man*

Michael Christopher Coke, earned the nickname "Dudus" -- pronounced DUD-us -- because he was known to wear an African-style shirt favoured by Jamaican World War II hero and Cabinet Minister at the time, Dudley Thompson.

Livity vs Dudus

In February 1992, on the afternoon Jah T was being buried, another tragedy hit the Coke family. Jim Brown was dead. He

had died in a mysterious fire in his cell while awaiting extradition to the United States.

With the demise of the father and the apparent heir to the throne; Dudus, [then 22, had been labelled everything from outside son to bastard son, right up to even an adopted son], was chosen to lead Tivoli Gardens over 'Livity', to the latter's displeasure.

Livity, who was older, felt it was his rightful place to lead, but Dudus was seasoned, and Livity, as relevant as he was, was still somewhat removed, at least from the hearts and minds of those that mattered. Sure he was Jim Brown's son, and sure he had the respect of the community, but Dudus had always been there; the people always saw him, some even grew up knowing him. Sure Livity was known, but Dudus was already solidified, and the backing of those that mattered was his; in spite of who had whatever else to say.

PRIOR TO 1992 [as great as such a position may have been], DUDUS was simply the son of a don. His role in Tivoli was minimal, even though he had all the trinkets and respect that came with such a position. Sure he called shots, but nothing of any major significance, and in short, did pretty much what most sons of dons do...Not much.

But according to some, Dudus was already in preparation mode, way before the demise of both his brother and father - from as far back as maybe 1988 or '89. Some say that while Jim Brown was doing major things, on major fronts, and Jah T was handling the other minor infractions, Dudus was already in the process of building his own power base within the power base; one of the key reasons he was able to wrestle power away from Livity so easily. He had his own team of *yes men*, who although from Tivoli, were loyal only to him, and may've been the very source behind what some say was an almost immediate eradication of most of the old guard - upon Dudus' takeover – particularly those who were said to be loyalists of his Father.

A new sheriff was in town, and everyone was going to pay attention...Including his brother, who soon realized that he could not beat him, so his best bet was to join him.

But beyond all that, another interesting story that has left many eyebrows raised is that the rise of Christopher "Dudus" Coke may have had its start with him being overlooked, [snubbed] by the eldest son of reggae legend Bob Marley; Ziggy Marley.

In the early 1990s, soon after Dudus' ascension to the throne and the taking control of the Tivoli Gardens reigns, there was one deal that ignited his rage to the fullest. Reports are that; at the time, Ziggy Marley was building a studio almost on the border of Coke's territory, in an attempt to provide aspiring musicians with a community based source of musical empowerment.

Instead of doing what was customary [filtering the contract to the don], rumour has it that Ziggy broke the unwritten rule and employed outsiders, a move that infuriated the Tivoli don, who quickly decided to make it clear who was in charge of the geographic landmass in question. It is said that a series of message killings sent Marley cowering, and served as a tool of expansion for Dudus' territory, a move which consolidated his rule even further.

This was his method in the early days, brute force and intimidation, traits which he learnt well from the best teachers of the art, and he had no intention of reinventing the wheel – [*if it were good enough for Claudie Massop and Jim Brown, then it was good enough for him*] – it was as simple as that in Dudus' book.

According to authorities, Coke's rise in the underworld was swift and deadly.

His father, Jim Brown - the architect of the Jamaican crime dynasty; The Shower Posse, had set the pace, and he was going to follow – *like father, like son.*

Jim Brown had fashioned his "Shower Posse" - so-named for spraying victims with bullets - into a drug-dealing conglomerate rivalled only by the Columbian Cartels, and Dudus according to some, picked up right where his father left off; he had something to prove.

Some say the loss of his father and brother affected him greatly and then to add insult to injury, he had to basically wrestle away power from his other brother. Maybe those were some of the reasons for all that followed, but should some of the street reports be credited; Jim

Brown was a choirboy in comparison to Dudus. It is said that when Jim would've given an order and step back - in the early days, Dudus would give the order and lead the operation himself.

One of the things that hindered Dudus in the inception of his rise to power was that no one outside of Tivoli Gardens knew him. Everyone knew Jim Brown, and most knew Jah-T, and if they didn't, most had heard of them, and pretty much understood who they were and what they were about, but almost no one outside of Tivoli Gardens had ever heard of Dudus at this time, so at first he wasn't even taken seriously - but all that changed with the quickness.

WEST KINGSTON IN THE EARLY 90s was a bloody scene, as fractions of disenfranchised gangsters fought for control of what some still saw as a vacant throne left by both Jah-T and Jim Brown – totally overlooking Dudus. Not many saw either Dudus or Livity as legitimate heirs: – They may have had the name, but neither had the reputation, and for either to be taken seriously...that had to change – and change it did.

With what has since transpired, in retrospect, it is now clear that Dudus had an unambiguous understanding of the results that violence could produce, and according to some, he used it well – *came, saw and conquered.*

OUT WITH THE OLD AND IN WITH THE NEW: – In a matter of months after taking control of the reigns of power over Tivoli Gardens and surrounding garrisons, bodies started popping up all over Western Kingston; with the most interesting part of all being: Most of those being killed were affiliates of the old guard. The message was clear, the guard was changing, and it was changing with force.

One of the early blatant message killings that left many in shock was that of *Bitter-Blood or Blood, remember him,* [one of Jim Brown's key triggermen] who, it's alleged was murdered by members of the new guard, and given what was then called - *A Western Kingston Burial –*

the callous practice of placing the dead body a-top a handcart, and then leaving it almost immediately in front of the Denham Town Police Station, which is situated right across from Tivoli Gardens.

Incidents like this left everyone in fear. Violence was nothing new, and neither were murders, but this – (the blatant murder of known *top men*), was new, and to make it worst, back when Jim Brown, Massop or even Jah-T in charge, individuals knew who they were dealing with, and on an even lesser extent, knew what to expect, but with this new don in power, who almost no one knew, the game had changed - and no one knew what was coming next.

Just like his father's Shower Posse, who rose to prominence on the strength of fear and intimidation, gaining a reputation for killing at the slightest offense; with the new don in charge, it was as though he had not only read and memorized the book of rules, but had taken the liberty of adding a few chapters and citations of his own.

SEAGA vs DUDUS

Immediately following February 1992; with both Jim Brown and Jah-T dead, Tivoli Gardens became a community in limbo. Their beloved don who was already in jail awaiting extradition to The United States was dead, and the only apparent heir, Jah-T, was also dead, and the Dudus they had all known prior to this dramatic twist of events was definitely not the Dudus in charge...he was a changed man.

Some say he had something to prove, some say he had to do what he did to solidify his position, and still others say he was not responsible or involved in any of what transpired. According to them [those who viewed his hands as clean] all of what took place was due simply to an internal power struggle that developed after the death of the don and his son.

It is alleged that after both Jim Brown and Jah-T's deaths, individuals who were not legitimate heirs to the throne started making claims and moves at it, and this led to the mayhem that followed - open season that quickly became dependent on who could shoot first.

This, according to some was what really happened; men who had been apart of the system from day one, simply refusing to take a back seat to a son or sons who except for DNA, had no right to lead Tivoli or Western Kingston for that matter. They feared Jim Brown and respected Jah-T, but who was Dudus and Livity?

How could they lead Tivoli, West Kingston, and what were now literal remnants of the Shower Posse, both internationally and locally, when there were others who had been around from the days of Massop? This according to some was the real problem, and both sides had their supporters, hence the mayhem that followed.

According to some, Dudus wasn't the perpetrator in this case, but was actually the one who stepped in and brought stability to the situation. First by putting the feud for leadership between him and his brother to an end; a key example that was used to defuse the external conflict even further; at least that's what is said.

"Mi nuh care wha nobody sey, Dudus a di real boss. A him sort out di ting after di dads drop out, an a whole heap a man start gwaan wid one bag a tings, tings wha coulda neva gwaan if Jim did dey bout."
TRANSLATED: I don't care what anyone has to say, Dudus is the real boss. It was he who sorted things out after his father passed, and a lot of other men started to act up, doing things that would have never happen had Jim been around.

BUT AGAIN THERE ARE TWO SIDES TO EVERY COIN:

Others have blatantly disputed those claims, giving a story not only contrary, but actually bloody in scope.

"Yuh a hear me, nutten like dat, di dads a di dads, but a nuh so di ting go. Yea, man an man did a sey how dem lickle yute dey fi run di ting, but di man dem neva a war, di man dem did dun have a understanding, but him also know sey dem man dey was nutten nice, so him mek di first move an get rid a di problem

Edward Seaga being greeted by the residents of Western Kingston

and one bag a talk before it really become a problem to him."
TRANSLATED: Listen, nothing like that. The don [Dudus] is the don, but things didn't go down like that. Yes there were men who were saying that both sons were too young to lead, but there was no war amongst them, they had an understanding, but Dudus also knew that these men, [the same ones who weren't in support] were nothing nice [dangerous], so he made the first move and got rid of the problem and all the talk, before they really became a problem for him.

Regardless which account is true, or which you may choose to believe, one thing that cannot be denied is that a lot of lives were lost and a lot of blood spilled after the throne became vacant in 1992, so much that according to some, it soon got the attention of Western Kingston's then Member of Parliament, Edward Seaga.

If indeed this account is true, it wound not be the first time that Edward Seaga would have intervened in the deadly and bloody politics that the garrisons of West Kingston had been known to produce, and with it directly involving Tivoli Gardens [The Jamaica Labour Party's stronghold], it's not too far fetched to believe that indeed such an incident actually occurred.

The story goes that in a matter of months after leading a funeral procession for Tivoli's strongman, [Jim Brown], which numbered over

35,000, Edward Seaga himself had to pay a visit to the area again, this time to find out what was really going on and try to put an end to the bloodshed.

The bodies were pilling up, and most of those being killed were members of the old guard - some were even friends and close associates of Jim Brown, and many were also said to be well known by Mr. Seaga himself. What was going on, someone was exterminating the old guard, but who would be brave enough to even conceive - let alone execute such a blatant and bare-faced move that not only showed contempt, but disregard for anything that had already been in place for years?

According to those who were around at the time, such acts of aggression not only got Seaga's attention, but got him to act; storming into Tivoli Gardens with bodyguard and feared law man, Keith 'Trinity' Gardener in tow – determined to get to the bottom of what was really happening.

To his surprise, he came face to face with Dudus, a son of Jim Brown, yes, but a son that he wasn't all that familiar with...*Hence the beginning of the legend.*

According to the streets - at first, Dudus wanted nothing to do with Mr. Seaga, simply because, he believed that Mr. Seaga had a direct hand in his father's death, so the younger Coke, now fatherless, was said to have not been too enthused about having audience with the man who may've had a hand in, or was directly responsible for his father's untimely death.

Many say it was a harsh confrontation, with Mr. Seaga spitting venom as he addressed the senseless callousness of the situation, but the young Coke stood his ground, thugs by his side – defiant – he didn't care who was there before, who was senior, or who wasn't. The way he saw it, he had lost both his father and brother in the name of Tivoli

Gardens, and he would be damned if he be pushed out of its leadership; not after such a sacrifice. Plus he was denying any involvement.

According to surviving *elders*, [the term used for older gentlemen in Jamaica]; many were surprised as to how the young Coke handled the situation, especially face to face with the real big man himself – because according to the streets, regardless who is hailed as the don in Tivoli or Western Kingston for that matter, the boss or the real big man, was, still is, and will always be; Edward Phillip George Seaga.

Dudus may've been one of Jim Brown's sons, but he was still a baby when it came to the bigger scheme of things; [at least so was the thought], no one knew him like that; Jah-T, yes, but he was dead too, and here in front of Tivoli Gardens and the entire Western Kingston, and in front of Mr. Seaga himself, stood Dudus – the unknown, untried, untested, claimer of the throne.

No one knows for sure what transpired next, but it's easy to assume that in true diplomatic political fashion, Mr. Seaga, [as he has been known to have done on previous occasions] assisted with the prevailing of good sense. A move that found Dudus, according to many, getting the reluctant backing of Mr. Seaga, which allowed the retaining of the power structure that governed Tivoli Gardens and Western Kingston, to remain within the ranks of the Coke family.

It was either resolve the issue of power struggle or allow the bloodshed to continue, so after all the tough talk and actions to back it up, the issue of who should reign as the Tivoli overlord, was resolved by the Tivoli Gardens architect himself; Mr. Seaga. A compromise was reached - or like one elder puts it, "Blinds sey it, an dat settle it, when Blinds [Mr. Seaga] talks, no dog bark." – **TRANSLATED**: Blinds said it and that settled it, when Blinds [Mr. Seaga] talked, no dog barked - So with Dudus getting the blessing, though reluctantly - the rest like they say, is His-Story.

• *Dudus – The President*

Before Dudus became the President, he was already a don, *born a don according to many*, and with him already gangland royalty, and now ascended to the throne, he did pretty much what all dons do; handle business, squash the competition, intimidate, and so on and so forth. But before we get into all that, there's a bit of info too critical to be ignored; a key discovery that must be noted, is that those who knew Dudus best or were closest to  him, are almost all quick to say that unlike his father, Dudus never really trusted Mr. Seaga, and never came around to fully doing so.

Live and let live...

This bit of information is extremely critical, and in retrospect, also a clear indicator as to why certain precedence was set in place from the inception of Dudus' take over; the type of precedence that facilitated a major power shuffle that left gangland in awe - the type of shift that according to some, found Tivoli Gardens forever out of Mr. Seaga's once gauntlet-like grip of control, and forever into the *President's*.

"Shortman [Dudus] never trus di boss [Mr. Seaga], an everybody did know why, a neva nuh secret, people jus lef dat alone after a while."
TRANSLATED: Shortman [Dudus] did not trust the boss [Mr. Seaga], and everybody knew why, it wasn't a secret, people just left it alone

after a while - stated one aging Tivoli Gardens thug, who claimed to have been a part of the West Kingston inner workings at one time.

And he's not alone in his claim, because according to many who are supposed to be in the know, this was basically the stance that Dudus took when it came to Mr. Seaga. He dealt with him not because he wanted to, but because he had to, and in such, dealt with him from a distance, never once getting close to him like previous dons did.

Then there are others who say it wasn't that Dudus didn't trust Mr. Seaga, *per-se*, they say he just didn't trust anyone - period! Plus with all the unanswered questions and talk, which went as far as suggesting that Mr. Seaga either knew more than he was wiling to admit about his father's sudden demise, and or, all the talk about how he [Mr. Seaga] may've even been directly involved; needless to say, but this was one of the last persons Dudus was interested in getting close to, regardless of who he was.

He [Dudus] was a cautious, sometimes even a suspicious skeptic, with the almost tragic justification that he had every reason to be. But to every analogy there is a counter, and some have credited this type of behaviour to one simple word; astrology.

Born on March 13, Dudus ruled under the sign of Pisces, so according to astrology, he was a natural risk taker, but life had taught him to embrace an entirely different persona, one of immense caution; a characteristic that even saw him becoming a bit of a cynic when it came to his dealings with others; even those closest to him.

This is what those who dealt with him frequently saw, and had trouble dealing with, his constant *Doctor Jekyll and Mr. Hyde* persona; never quite sure what to expect from him on a moment by moment basis.

If not for those casual, occasional instances, Dudus was not by a long shot, the easiest person to deal with. To most who had the brief pleasure of meeting him, they would've never guessed (even if their life depended on it), that he was who he was. He was too polite and articulate, too calm, too smooth, and definitely too quiet, but this was Dudus, a man who learned from early, the power of portraying an image that is counter to your reputation; or at least counter to the one the public clothes you in.

This was who he was, and how things were, and if you were privileged enough to be apart of the inner workings, you simply accepted it; you may not have liked it, but if you were there, you were smart enough, not to be stupid enough, to let your thoughts of displeasure transform into actual words.

To put it simple, Dudus was a challenge from the start. No other don had ever behaved like him. All those before him were seen, *they made sure they were*, but not Dudus, except for his constant games of soccer, it was as though he was in constant hiding.

The list of issues that surrounded him didn't stop there, because in spite of who was in charge, and regardless how tough they may've been known to be, or actually was, in comparison, they were relatively easy to deal with when compared to Dudus; none was as complex as he was, but unknown to all, this was one of the key elements that he used to keep everyone, and the entire organization in line.

Most dons in comparison to Dudus were just happy to be in the positions that they had eventually found themselves, with little thought of much else, and they were not shy about letting it known either, but when Dudus was compared to them, the difference was like that of night, when compared to the rays that illuminate the day. He never seemed happy, instead he always appeared to be skeptic.

Other key traits that separated Dudus from all his predecessors (beyond all that was his by birthright, both biologically and otherwise), were that he was exposed, educated [*by leaps and bounds when compared to all his forerunners*] and talented in more ways than one. A point made clear from early on in his reign – when he answered questions without words to the tune of, *this was not going to be another typical wild west shoot-'em up chapter; -* NO. *His outlook was too different for that*; so much so, that it ushered in a welcomed change that no one could deny if they were to be truthful and facilitated the most peaceful/crime free period that West Kingston and Downtown, Kingston (on a whole) had ever seen.

From the inception Dudus' focus was different, driven by a different type of determination. He was dedicated to a totally different cause, the likes of which it seemed no other don would've even dared imagining at the time.

A calculated risk taker and a master at multitasking; the latter being a skill that propelled his elevation in gangland even further than many would've ever estimated at the inauguration of his reign. This was Dudus, and as time progressed, he got better, or worse, all depending on which side one was witnessing him from.

"Di man [Dudus] did have a style wey him look pon yuh like him a look tru yuh!...Believe mi, a nuff man mi si da look dey bruk dung, widout even seying a word!" **TRANSLATION**: "The man [Dudus] had a style where he would look at you like he was looking right through you...believe me; I have seen that look break down many men, without him even saying a word!"

Calculating and silent...Intimidating...

That was Dudus, the same person he appeared to be before donship, but who after taking control of the reigns of power, simply became a more astute version of what he already was.

67

- *"People who talk too much will eventually... ALMOST ALWAYS, say the wrong thing...Or at least say too much"* – **Christopher 'Dudus' Coke**

A lot has been said and made of the blatant hatred the garrisons of Jamaica have when it comes to informers, [the same as snitches], and the above is exactly what Dudus' outlook was when it came to the matter of verbal exchange. *"Why give a speech when the point you're trying to make is in one sentence?"* – He would say - to the point, short and sweet, say only what is necessary and leave the rest to speculations...Somewhat like a politician...

One individual who claims to have grown up with Dudus makes the claim that, *"the President never inna di whole heap a talking ting from long time, dat neva new, an him never too inna nuh body wha always a talk talk...Is a man who feel like sey, if yuh have a ting fi sey, sey it an dun, wha all di talking fah."* **TRANSLATED**: "The President [Dudus] was never into a whole lot of talking, that was just him, and it never changed, and he wasn't too fund of anyone who was always talking either...He was the type of person who felt like if you had something to say, say it and be done, why keep talking about."

This was his stance, his persona, one of his major characteristics; a man of few words who prided himself as being a good listener, and not much of a talker, but many say this again was another tool he used to intimidate and in-still fear; always seemingly listening to you so attentively, it's as though he was waiting to catch you in a lie.

From all accounts, Dudus had always been a quiet individual, always seemingly in deep thought, and with his elevation to the top of Tivoli Gardens food chain, such a persona was galvanized even further. Some say he became withdrawn, and very, very suspicious of almost everyone and everything around him, and was almost in a consistent state of paranoia. He saw what others didn't, and what wasn't even there, and heard what others didn't and what wasn't even said, but with him being who he was, it didn't take long for almost everyone under his influence to begin marching to the beat of his drum; regardless how off-key it may've been playing.

You got so close and no more...

Don's had always been the most colourful characters in their realm of power; the loudest, the most arrogant, and in almost every case, they were amongst the most recognized individuals [at least in their own territories], but not Dudus; it was as if this new don didn't even exist. Those who knew him knew him, but not even they were privy to see him at times; he became somewhat of an enigma, but what many didn't know, was that this... Like almost all his moves, was by calculated and sinister design.

Like all dons before him, Dudus surrounded himself with a few handpicked individuals, the only difference was, in comparison to his predecessors, the handpicked individuals were no longer from the old guard, like they usually were, and to the surprise of many, some weren't even from Tivoli Gardens or West Kingston for that matter – a move that was as unorthodox as unorthodox could get when it came to gangsterism that was known to govern territories such as Tivoli Gardens at the time. And if that wasn't enough, he was empowering them, and in some cases, it was as though he was literally deputising them!

What was Dudus doing? That was the private question of many, who dared not voice their discontent until now. He was breaking all the rules... Rules that were apart of the entire fabric of West Kingston from day one, and to add insult to injury, this was Jim Brown's son. He above everyone else should know better, so what was he doing, how could he be letting strangers in the fold?

Members of the community at the time, had concerns, but what they didn't know was that Dudus saw what they didn't, *he wasn't tunnel versioned, his blinkers were off,* because the same rules that so many were so adamant about upholding had failed miserably and led to deaths... The deaths of his father and brother to be specific, so why should he [Dudus] hold on to any of those so-called rules?

He was going to make his own rules.

He had seen the end results of many a don before him. Their mistakes were his to analyze and learn from, and he refused to make the same mistakes they did, so his entire approach to donship was different – **ONE KEY EXAMPLE:** The introduction of strange faces. What many didn't understand at the time, was that these new faces to the mix [Tivoli Gardens' inner circle] created a smoke screen that was to Dudus' benefit. With not many knowing him, the influx of influential and beneficial strange faces, who all seemed to have the power of donship, suddenly made things confusingly interesting, with no one outside the circle actually knowing who the don really was... Another thing this unorthodox move did, was that it kept everyone else in line without even making the attempt to, because with strangers around - loyal only to Dudus, it also showed that his power-source was not limited to just those around him, unlike all his predecessors: – These strange moves kept everyone on edge, talking, guessing, wondering, and while they did... Dudus thrived.

A New Dawn...

Dudus was heard of, but rarely ever seen. He was known to call the shots, but was never ever seen firing one; and in a matter of time, became somewhat of a *Phantom.*

So much mystery surrounded Dudus that he even became the subject of folklore, with some stories so fantastic, if one didn't know better, one may believe that they were talking about some noble saint or a celestial being of some sort, but to almost all mystery; there's a reasonable and often times pretty simple explanation, and when it comes to Dudus being not only elusive, but almost invisible, the explanation is relatively simple.

Dudus was cautiously scared...

No, Dudus wasn't a coward, but at the same time, he wasn't *'brave-heart'* either; he was cautiously scared, and had every right to be.

To understand this, first you have to at least make the attempt to get inside his mind, and then at least try to understand where he was mentally; in, around and after February, 1992.

DUDUS – in, around and after February 1992:

Petrified: *adjective* **1.** terrified, horrified, shocked, frozen, stunned, appalled, numb, dazed, speechless, aghast, dumbfounded, stupefied, scared stiff, scared shitless *(taboo slang)*, terror-stricken.

- *Petrified*, is without doubt where Dudus was mentally, before, around and definitely by February 1992. Recently out of his teens, Dudus was merely twenty-two [22] years old, and as much of a don as he was by birth and notwithstanding how much training he had derived from just being him, and overseeing his team of *yes-men*; by no means was he anywhere near ready for the shoes that he was about to fill and this was in spite of how adamant he seemed when he and Livity [his brother] had faced-off regarding the leadership of Tivoli Gardens and its enclaves. **THE REALITY OF THE SITUATION WAS**, his [Dudus'] father was dead, his brother was dead, and so was his sister, all in one, tragic, bloody and rapid succession; a reality that without doubt came with major mental pressure

71

and a lot of anguish and uncertainty, the likes of which eventually led to the inevitable - relocation to a constant **petrified** state. With so many related deaths in the air, Dudus was no doubt concerned about his own mortality, and to keep that vulnerability subdued or hidden, [which he literally had to, he couldn't let anyone see him sweat] he became what he eventually became; *a suspicious and calculating individual.* Dudus' transition to top-man was no easy task, and came with way more challenges than most may have realized, and way more than he was letting on. He may've been Jim Brown's son, but not everybody was on his side, and that was clear out the gates, [hence the bloodshed that commenced immediately over control after Jim Brown and Jah-T's demise] so with that being the issue it was, how could Dudus not be concerned? It was only natural. Then to make matters even more complicated, there was the already fruitful drive to dismantle what once seemed like the impregnable Shower Posse; [Vivian Blake, *almost like an uncle to Dudus*, and the head and brain of the operation was under Federal indictment for the last four years; (at the time, since 1988 to be exact), and he [Vivian] was also on the run. Then there was the unthinkable; snitching in the ranks of the very posse that was known to have zero tolerance for informers. Things were unravelling - along with Blake, the Federal Indictment had 34 other names, and it was getting worse by the minute. Several posse members, including, Shower Howie, Banana, Foodhead, Sugar Belly and Snowman, *all notorious Shower Posse members*, were already either arrested, brought up on charges, doing lengthy prison sentences, dead or on the run; while still others were already deported or had made their way back to Jamaica in a bid to avoid prosecution. The organization was unravelling, crumbling, and the normalcy at which things once operated, alongside the normalcy that he, Dudus himself once knew, was suddenly becoming no more, and couple all this with everything that was happening on the ground - around him - up close and personal - and the reality is apparent; it was enough to put anyone in the mental state that Dudus eventually had little choice of residing in - the state of being consistently *Petrified*!

Paranoid: *adj* **1.** (Psychiatry) of, characterized by, or resembling paranoia **2.** (Psychiatry) *Informal* exhibiting undue suspicion, fear of persecution, etc.

- This was yet another key characteristic that marked Dudus' arrival at the coveted position of power; he suspected everyone and everything, near and far! But then again, who could he trust?... Definitely not the members of the *old guard*, he had seen how things were handled in his father's absence and he had heard all the talk and whispers, so his trust level for them was next to zero! Then there was the '*if he could do it factor*,' a factor that came to life with Charles '*Little Nut/Modeler*' Miller; the once high profile posse member, who turned on them and spilled the beans to the Federal Authorities in a bid to save his own skin. This was one of those cold hard facts that would've been hard to deal with for anyone, let alone Dudus, a person, born and reared on the teachings of *Garrison Gospel*, where one of the *ecclesiastical* laws were; *no informing*!...This was one of his father's key associates, one who, he had no doubt seen countless times, known from he was a mere youth, and even lived amongst at one time, when Modeler resided in Tivoli Gardens –late 70s to the early 80s. This was an individual who literally considered family; keep in mind that Modeler was not from Tivoli Gardens to begin with, but he was however looked at as an honorary resident, given somewhat of a *Green Card* by the dons themselves; Jim Brown and Vivian Blake - but even with all that, here it was, he was one of the first ones to roll-over and sing like a *Canary*. So with that in mind - *if he could do it -* it left little to the imagination - the issue of trust was almost non-existent when it came to the reality of Christopher 'Dudus' Coke – in, around, and after February 1992.

But even so, Dudus was no fool, he knew he couldn't do it alone, he had to trust someone, and this state of paranoia led him to form a circle so tight and influential, even to this day, it still bares signs of impregnability.

Skeptic:–noun 1. a person who questions the validity or authenticity of something purporting to be factual. 2. a person who maintains a doubting attitude, as toward values, plans, statements, or the character of others. 3. any later thinker who doubts or questions the possibility of real knowledge of any kind.

- And again, this was Dudus in all his infamous glory, a *skeptic* of the highest order. The meaning of the word *skeptic* is basically self-explanatory, and speaks volumes when it comes to the man in question. He was what he was, a skeptic, but on the flip side of the coin, he was a skeptic with reason. He wasn't delusional, he wasn't imagining things. What he feared and was concerned about was real; his life could be snuffed out at any given moment. His issues of trust were also real, if he were to tell it, his father was betrayed by those closest to him, and those who were once trustworthy had proven that there was indeed *no honour amongst thieves*. And with this, Dudus questioned everything and second guessed everyone. The old guard was out, he literally wanted nothing to do with them; a new don was on the throne, and his *young guns*, who viewed the old guard as mere elders whose time had passed - warriors who apart from the elders' respect, were worthy of nothing more. And then to top all that, it wasn't a secret that Dudus didn't trust them, too many of them were suspected of moving *off-key*, so needless to say, they [the young guns] weren't too inclined to either side with or follow them [any member of the old guard]. Plus the young guns also wanted their share of the pie, and what better way was there to partake of this than to side with the new don, and eliminate those who you know he wanted eliminated, even if he wasn't saying it out loud or directly?... The young guns may not have known the depths of what they were getting into, but they lined up behind Dudus with quickness, and in no time were all more than willing to prove their allegiance to the don. Dudus' scepticism and paranoia were known to be deadly, and with no one wanting to fall under his microscope of analysis, it produced a contagious rush to show just how loyal one truly was, which most times took the form of extensive, senseless and grotesque blood letting.

One senior resident, originally from Tivoli Gardens community, [*displaced due to what she claims was the accusation of a top-man, regarding the questionable acts of a member of her family*] whose desire was to remain nameless; made this claim about the early days of Dudus' reign: *"yuh a hear mi, mi nuh have nutten bad fi sey bout di don still eunh, but mi nuh too have nutten good fi sey bout him fren dem, cause dem a evil! A dem same time dey, 92, 93, di yute dem start draw card and kill off nuff a di big man dem inna di place, 'cause dem know sey Shortman never trus di man dem, so anything dem sey di man dem sey or do, whether dem did dweet it or not, dem know sey him woulda believe."* **TRANSLATED**: "Listen, I have nothing bad to say about the don, but when it comes to his friends, there is not much good that I have to say, or that can be said about them, because they are evil! It was around that time that some of them started to cast accusations in a bid to justify their killing of those who where there before them. They knew that Shortman [Dudus] didn't trust them [the older heads], so whatever was said about them that was suspicious, be it true or not, they knew he [Dudus] would believe, hence justifying their behaviour."

Petrified, Paranoid and Skeptic; these are the three main characteristics that laid the foundation for what was to come- the inauguration of the President.

Filling the shoes of a great man
- From The Shower Posse to The Presidential Click-

By 1992 The Shower Posse was *already marked for death*. No longer were they under the radar, they had outgrown that years ago, catching the attention of The US Federal Authorities so much that task forces were created just to focus on their activities, after extending their bloody and illegal influence and activities throughout the United States and Canada; reaching into Cities and States such as Anchorage, Detroit, Kansas, New York, Rochester, Daytona, Ohio, Toronto and Montreal. They were under the spotlight, and had been for years, and with Jim Brown dead, and Vivian Blake on the run, the light had gotten only brighter as Dudus took control of the reigns of the community, which was the literal source that was responsible for creating and replenishing such a notorious organization.

This was also a very fickle time in the ranks of law enforcement, both locally and internationally when it came to anything posse related, and with Jim Brown dead, the international law enforcement agencies were fuming, *biting at the bits*, so this was definitely not the time to be identified as the head of such an organization, and Dudus was quite aware of that, and made every effort to disassociate himself and his affairs from anything Shower Posse related; a development it is said which led to the creation of a new entity; *The Presidential Click.*

Dudus had lived throughout his father's reign as Tivoli Gardens' top-man, and he had seen just how things worked, up close and personal, and except for Jah-T, he was actually the closet son to the action. He had also seen just how the people revered him, (his father) and what it had taken to maintain this level of respect and admiration, and he not only desired it, he was determined to maintain and enhance it.

The way he saw it, (according to those who were around at the time of the conception of *The Presidential Click)*, when it came to donship, there was no higher to go than Jim brown, and Dudus was not trying to replace Jim in terms of just a new don, replacing an old one. No, that was not Dudus' intention, his intention was to actually keep the legend alive, especially with chatter circulating that Jim Brown might not really be dead; but that the fire incident was an elaborate hoax; staged for one reason and one reason only...To make sure he [Jim Brown] never faced prosecution in the United States. **NOTE:** Arguments of this nature have become the substance that folklores are made of, because even though there has never been any evidence to support such a theory, in certain circles, this is still believed to be true; Jim Brown is not dead!

None of this was news to Dudus, he knew all that was being said and then some, and he simply decided to make it all work to his benefit. He was the new don, but he would go by a different title, one that would sever old alliances, show his status, but at the same time, leave the memory and calibre of his father in tack.

This was his perception, and with his father already considered, *the don of all dons*, (even though it was said that he was a don who answered to an even more powerful don - Mr. Seaga), from the inception, Dudus was having a problem with Mr. Seaga. Not only was the title he decided to take on supposed to distinguish him from all his predecessors, but by taking on such a title as *The President*, he clearly indicated his defiance towards Mr. Seaga's authority, because according to those around him, the way he [Dudus] saw it, the entire power of the Jamaica Labour Party [JLP] relied on them [Tivoli Gardens and West Kingston], not on them - the Jamaica Labour Party and its politics; if Dudus should tell it, ***Things had changed.*** Another factor that must also be highlighted here is that the whole *President* thing also came about because of what was viewed as the powerhouse-like effect that the Tivoli Gardens' organization [The Shower Posse] had in The United States, which made the influence that he [Dudus] had inherited, seemingly way more than that of Jamaica's ultimate power source...The Prime Minister himself, and if more powerful than the Prime Minister, what more befitting title was there than that of *The President?*

Political reality of the day: Tivoli Gardens was the JLP's political stronghold, led by Mr. Seaga, and what was said in Tivoli had reaching effects right across the Island, and was even able to influence developments oceans away; that was just the way it was, and everyone knew it...Everyone including Dudus.

And with this bit of awareness, Dudus not only became defiant...He had a plan.

FROM DAY ONE it was clear that Dudus was going to be a don unlike his father, and way different than Massop ever was. The usual *modus operandi* of dons before Dudus was that the don always had a dozen or so men around him all the time [*bodyguards, triggermen, associates and hangers-on, who in most cases would all give up the ghost if they had to on his behalf*], and then to make it even more complicated, although he [the don] was the one in charge of almost everything around them and the final *say-so* in all matters, there was no, and could not be any open door policy; you couldn't just want to talk to the don and it happened, unless you were someone in the mix, higher echelon in the streets, some business interest of his or of some calibre when it comes to common political affiliation. If you weren't any of those, and at times, even if you were, there was still a system of stringent scrutiny in place, which at times involved, but was not limited to, the relaying of messages to one or several lieutenants before getting to speak to the don directly.

With Dudus, not too much changed in this area, if anything it got more stringent, but as was established before, he was no fool; he saw the mistakes and accomplishments of those before him, it was as if he had the manual of all manuals to read from when it came to garrison gangsterism, and just like when he attended Ardenne High School, Michael Christopher Coke, was an astute student.

In the inception of his take over, Dudus was leery, but he couldn't seem scared. He was about change, but he also knew that too much change, too fast, can become extremely detrimental, especially when dealing with individuals of a certain background and mentality. And with this in mind he made what was the equivalent of a power move in the corporate world; Dudus craved up the underworld, empowered his lieutenants in the real sense of empowerment, while still maintaining ultimate control over all. A power move that propelled him even further in the hearts and minds of the masses, as he inched closer and closer to his ultimate desire; what he viewed as the presidency of the underworld: – *He was in campaign mode.*

Donship, it seemed was desired by most youth in the ghetto who were trapped in the depressing reality of their day to day existence, and if not donship, they at least desired respect and a piece of the pie; even if that piece of the pie meant nothing more than a new pair of shoes or a few pieces of trendy apparel every now and then, and add a few dollars to the mix and they were sold.

Dudus realized the importance of this simple principle of garrison philanthropy from early in the game. He knew that the simplest expressions of generosity in the ghetto could mean the difference between life and death, loyalty and disloyalty. It was just what it was, and he had seen this principle at work many times before, both from a political standpoint and from a donship standpoint. The desires of individuals were the same, and the results the same if those desires were ever met - Dudus had a plan.

Empower them, so they can empower themselves, while also empowering him in return, while at the same time, without even realizing it, become loyal subjects in the process; this was Dudus' plan, simply *Machiavellian* in nature, and it worked like a charm.

He was from a different school, a different era, so it was only natural that his approach was different. Unlike previous dons who had relied mostly on brute force, Dudus' approach was actually political, much like he had seen the real possessors of power work...His approach may not have been political in the true sense of what politics really entails, but regardless, his move to galvanize his power-base was straight from the pages of what seemed like the Jamaican parliamentary handbook.

Dudus knew that most fractions in varying garrisons who were aligned with the JLP, were simply that, fractions. They were weak and disorganized, but at the same time, they all had the potential to be extremely loyal if given the opportunity; maybe even more than those he had known all his life. He also knew that most of these fractions not only looked up to Tivoli Gardens, but would be forever indebted if they were ever given a coveted endorsement...So he gave it to them; gave them what they wanted, while taking what he desired. They wanted association and he wanted soldiers for his army, the more the merrier, and the farther and wider they were, even better. Unlike previous dons, Dudus' aim was to use a common cause and extend the empire he had inherited to unimaginable heights.

His nifty power move brought about the creation of multiply handpicked dons from various communities, in and around Jamaica's capital, but it didn't stop there. His reach was eventually extended all over Jamaica, reaching as far as the tourist capital of Montego Bay. Needless to say, but all these inductees [*dons who were invited to be apart of the newly formed criminal brotherhood*], were all more than eager to form an alliance with Jim Brown's son, the heir to the Shower Posse throne, and from their prospective, quite possibly the most powerful don that there could ever be.

The President kept it simple, giving them what they all desired at the time, a direct link to, and the backing of Tivoli Gardens and all therein. With Tivoli Gardens now behind them as one unified force, the Dudus influence came naturally. He not only now controlled Tivoli Gardens and Western Kingston as a whole, he now directed activities in other areas, in a way that has never been done before, and made whatever it was that they [dons from outside] were doing in their realm of control that much stronger, and they in return, made him mighty!... The blueprints were in hand, and he was now the new architect in charge of the project, and almost instantly Dudus embarked on what can be described in no uncertain terms as, the creation of mini replicas of what has been dubbed, *The Mother Of All Garrisons; Tivoli Gardens,* all over the Island...more to his advantage than to anyone else's.

With him being who he was, almost all were eager to line up and play *do as I say,* but Dudus was different in everyway; he was about way more than just issuing political commands. The truth be told, he wasn't even all that enthused by politics, because the way he saw it, it made no difference who was elected, what mattered was that he was in power; an entirely different outlook from that of all his predecessors.

JLP – Political billboard – late 70s

KEY POINT: The Jamaica Labour Party, in 1992 had not been in power for the last three years, [they lost the general election to the PNP in 1989], and they [residents of Tivoli Gardens and members of the Shower Posse], were still able to do as they pleased, so in Dudus' book, it didn't make that much of a difference who was actually elected – this was beyond politics, this was business, and all he had to do was maintain and build on what was already in place.

One of Dudus' key sayings and also what eventually became somewhat of a principle in his life was the adage; *money over war*, a simple sentiment that made all the sense in the world to almost everyone who heard it, and with him not only sounding good as he uttered those words, but backing them up with actions that brought forth monetary results, this just made his followers even more eager in their analogous quest.

The newly endorsed dons loved Dudus, not only was he who he was, if he said it, then that settled it; a straight shooter who didn't have to say it twice to make his point. **KEEP IN MIND:** This was 1992, and almost everything that was said to be illegal could be found in Tivoli Gardens, [this was the headquarters] and Dudus was in charge, that simply meant he had plenty to dispense as he saw fit, and he did just that. What was once reserved for only Tivoli Gardens residents, was now finding their way into other politically like-minded communities, and the dons loved every moment of it.

Name it, and if Tivoli Gardens had it or got some, best believe if you were apart of the mix, yours was on the way, and it didn't matter what it was either: - guns, clothes, motorcycles, whatever; that was just how Dudus ran his operation, and the dons loved him, and imposed his desires on those under their authority, with *authority*.

The mindset of this regime was different, making it so much easier to follow, especially with them [the now endorsed dons] answering only to themselves in their realm of power. *Dudus rarely interfered*, and with them now having the backing of such a force, and with them now empowered in their respective zones, they had no problem answering only to one outside of their realm; especially with that one being Dudus himself.

Such moves and achievements not only elevated Dudus in unheard of ways, but it also solved his problem of having to be too visual and feeling too vulnerable; and in short, gave him a new and extended arm of protection that went way beyond the borders of Tivoli Gardens and its environs; a system which, (to him) if were in place to begin with, may have been just what was needed to save both his brother and sister's life.

NOTEWORTHY FACTS: The death of Dudus' brother, Jah-T led to an eruption of violence that left almost 20 dead in its wake. Interestingly enough, this flare-up of violence all started in the emergency room of The Kingston Public Hospital, when residents from Tivoli Gardens decided to avenge the death of their don who they felt was not given the needed assistance by doctors and nurses to save his life. The enraged mob at the time threatened to kill at least 50  nurses and doctors for the don's demise; and within hours of word spreading about Jah-T's death, Jamaica was again gripped with a headline of a *grotesque* magnitude, when gunmen from Tivoli Gardens invaded the neighbouring PNP community of Hannah Town, unleashing their fury on the residents with a barrage of gunfire, rape and pillaging; all in the name of taking vengeance on behalf of their fallen don - Mark Antony *'Jah-T'* Coke.

ADDITIONAL FACTS: Approximately three weeks after Jah-T was killed, he; like all dons before, was given the traditional state-like funeral, with all the theatrics and pageantry that could be imagined. Mr. Seaga [leader of the opposition party – the JLP] himself led the 20,000 plus mourners, mostly young men and women dressed in the trendiest fashions of the day that money could buy, and adorned with what appeared to be hundreds of thousands of dollars worth of gold jewellery. Jah-T's girlfriend, popularly known as Foxy, was seen walking beside Mr. Seaga, looking *foxier* than ever in a tight fitting black dress, which left little to mourn over. Jah-T was sent off to the hereafter looking mighty dapper himself, decked out in a regal looking black velvet suit with a white stained shirt inside; and according to some, never looked better alive. His casket, black with silver handles, cost a then whopping JA$40,000; a handsome sum by any estimation in 1992. Mr. Seaga was lambasted in the local press for not only attending, but leading the funeral procession of a well known thug, but what was done was done.

TRAGIC IRONY: ON THE VERY AFTERNOON that Jah-T was buried, his father, Jim Brown was burnt to death in his cell under what has since been the subject of much debate - questionable circumstances. He had lost his extradition fight, the British Privy Council had denied his extradition appeal, and U.S. DEA agents were already on the ground, in Kingston, waiting to put Brown on a jet, bound for Miami. Brown had vowed that should he was extradited and had to stand trial in the U.S. he would tell all that he knew, not only about the Shower Posse, but about Mr. Seaga and the Shower Posse; which was rumoured to have actually been the brainchild of Mr. Seaga himself.

- **IT IS ALSO SAID** that the very name *'shower,'* [in this particular case] was coined by Mr. Seaga himself in the bloody run-up to the general election of 1980, which some say found the JLP shooting its way to power, which again is also another element that adds an unholy mysticism to the origin of the posse's name, as it is also said that *'Shower'* was a declaration of what they [JLP henchmen] would do, or did to their enemies; *shower them with bullets.*

Jim Brown's cellmate and several other inmates have made claims that on more than one occasions they heard him utter the now infamously chilling words, *"mek dem gwaan man, dem mek a sad mistake if dem feel sey a me alone a go dung,"* **TRANSLATED:** "it's all good, but they've got it twisted if they feel I am the only one going down,' – a statement which is said to have had quite a few individuals shaking in their boots. No one was ever charged for setting the fire that killed Brown, and according to the official report, it was simply a fire of unknown origin that claimed the life of the don, but that's the official report. According to the streets, both Vivian Blake [who was at the time on the run] and Mr. Seaga, who it is said was the real architect of the posse, would've wanted Brown dead at such a critical moment, and according to the streets, both had the money, power and influence to get it done; while still some say it was all a big hoax; organized right on time to use the body of his son, Jah-T, (who was really dead), to cover the elaborate escape plot; hence the whole burning of the body so identification would be hard if indeed there was a switch, - which would actually make sense in a conspiratorial sense, especially with Jah-T and Jim Brown bearing so many similar features; size and all.

ACCORDING TO OFFICIAL REPORTS, Jim Brown died of *Pulmonary Edema*, [which is the abnormal build up of fluid in the air sacs of the lungs], which eventually leads to shortness of breath or suffocating – or in Brown's case, his death was caused from smoke and flame inhalation. **FIREMEN WHO WERE CALLED TO THE THEN NAMED GENERAL PENITENTIARY, WHERE BROWN WAS BEING HELD, CLAIMED** that when they arrived, they were not taken to Brown's cell, but instead became witnesses to a heated argument, already in progress, between police officers, members of the army and prison warders, about whether or not the body of the man on the ground, [who was said to be Brown], which was also already out of the cell, and had even fallen off the stretcher that it had obviously been on, was to be taken to the hospital or not.

The firemen also claimed that they were there for over an hour before the body was moved to the hospital, which in real time - is less than ten minutes away.

Fig. 3 Entrance to the then named, General Penitentiary

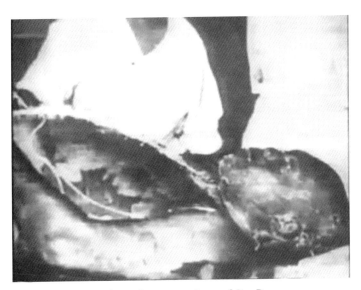

Fig. 4 Officially released autopsy photo of Jim Brown

SHOWER POSSE HIERARCHY

Lester Coke   Vivian Blake   Mark Coke

Richard Morrisson   Maxell Bogle   Kirk Bruce

Dudus and Arms

'Without its own arms no principality is secure'
Niccolo Machiavelli 1469-1527

No one knows for sure if Dudus ever read Machiavelli, although according to reports, investigations and from those who knew him best, Dudus was a well read and a very well informed individual, but whether he read Machiavelli or not aside, there is little question as to whether he made the above principle real in his life. He had to; that was what it was, what the position he was in called for - the reality of being a don.

The Shower Posse [Dudus' inheritance] was literally birth out of the barrel of the gun, and with the posse's wealth reaching in the hundreds of millions of dollars [according to DEA estimations] during the drug dealing and bloody 80s, and they acquiring unthinkable firepower both at home and abroad; Dudus not only became a don in 1992, he also became the gate keeper of an arsenal of firepower that in reality was enough to start a mini revolution.

HISTORY LESSON: Violence has always been common place in ghettos all across Jamaica, and no other place was it more prevalent than across the politically tense regions of Jamaica's Western Kingston during the 1960s. Even before there was a Tivoli Gardens there was a don or an area leader as they are also called. Many have come and gone; individuals like Alvin George Gordon, Micky Jacques, Desmond Paige, George 'Rock' Dinall, Donovan Jones, Left Hand and Hutch, are just a few names that may get mentioned in a conversation of this nature, but regardless who is mentioned or who isn't, when it comes to the *Notorious Hall of Fame*, many older Western Kingston residents all agree that the linage has to start with Zackie, the 'High Priest', the first notable top-ranking [as thugs were also called back then] from Western Kingston to be affiliated with the Jamaica Labour Party. His reign, like most to follow was violent and short; Zackie was killed in the political eruption that was fostered by the 1967 general election, which saw the JLP claiming victory, walking away with 33 of the 53 parliamentary seats. Zackie was also the mentor to Claudie Massop or Jack, as Zackie affectionately called him. After Zackie's demise it was time for the young Massop, his protégé to take over, who eventually, like Zackie, became a victim of his own handiwork – violence – Massop's death gave way for Carl 'Bya' Mitchell, who quickly gave way to Lester Lloyd 'Jim Brown' Coke, who gave way to his son, Mark Anthony 'Jah T' Coke, ultimately arriving at the door steps of the oval office to the *President* himself; Michael Christopher 'Dudus' Coke.

The road that led to *The Presidency* was one littered with violence and intimidation; disputes, disagreements, shouting matches, stabbings, choppings/hackings, shootings, fire-bombed houses, rapes, tortures, robberies, extortions, murders, and overall mayhem, but within all this, one of the lessons learnt by almost all residents of the ghetto was just how powerful of a tool a gun always seem to be, regardless of the conflict that may arise.

Dudus too learnt from an early stage *the power of the gun,* but unlike many, he also knew that the power of a gun does not lie only in its usage, but also, and at times even more so, in the intimidating factor that it possesses just by being present.

Dudus knew this better than most, he had seen the power he had achieved by just having access to these instruments of death, without ever having to use them from an early age. He also saw that others were willing to use them on his behalf, if he was able to supply them and with his ascension to the throne, he decided to put into effect a lesson he had learnt - tested and proven to be true over the years.

Dudus' plan was simple, he knew he couldn't be seen everywhere with a dozen or more men around him; this would make him an automatic target, and then again, the operation had evolved beyond that years ago, so he would be silly to hold on to a principle whose time had passed. He also knew that he couldn't monitor everything himself, so instead of always having a dozen or more men around him, constantly on the move, and constantly screening people, Dudus decided to go about it in an entirely different way, instead of just mere men, his intention was to have a dozen or more *dons* under his control, answering only to him, and doing for him what he really wanted nothing to do with anyway - the whole pettiness that came with the expanding territories now under his control.

Dudus knew the desire of almost every man was the same when it came to power; *the urge to rule resides in all*, and with this reality realized, his plan worked like a charm. The don was willing to share power, [at least so it seemed] not just give commands, and with this perceived reality accepted by all those who were handpicked to be apart of the newly formed *alliance*, they became ecstatic, never once realizing that what they were given power over was always high on the list of things Dudus cared little or nothing about.

It was all a ploy, an act of masterful manipulation on Dudus' part, and became yet another power move that enforced the type of loyalty that is still said to be alive and well, in the very place of its birth; *Tivoli Gardens*.

Being educated separated Dudus from the start, [most of his peers were high school drop outs or worse, their education level stopped somewhere around the sixth grade or middle school] so his views were way different from theirs. He saw what the others didn't, and he also saw the mistakes of those before him. He also had enough time to devise a plan to capitalize, which is exactly what he did.

Every man was a *boss* in his own right, at least so it's believed, and in the circles that are being discussed in this volume, regardless how much of a *boss* a man may believe he is or proclaim to be, if he was going to say anything and be taken serious in the ghetto, often times it took the addition of a gun to solidify that position; and with Dudus being the new don, he had plenty of both - *guns* at his disposal and plenty of *men* who wanted to solidify their proclaimed or desired positions.

After the influx of illegal weapons into Jamaica starting in the late 70s and escalating into the early and mid 80s, coupled with the elevation of the Shower Posse's wealth and their fetish for guns, by the time Dudus came to power, it's believed that Tivoli Gardens was operating like a well oiled militia; *guns a-plenty* and *guns a-ready*; so to put it simply, there was an excess of weapons at Dudus' disposal, and according to sources, like the *general* he now was, he distributed them to an all too willing cast of recruits.

Arm them, instruct them, intimidate them without seeming to, and leave them with the promise of swift retaliation if there is any deviation from the plan. Whatever arises in your territory, deal with it, if you can't, we will, and if we have to come and deal with it, then you have just compromised your position of power:

This was the often times, *unspoken*, but generally known and understood rule of Dudus' expansion project, which also came with an undertone of death, a reality that no one wanted to face, and worked overtime not to – a development that led to what could be termed, *'blind loyalty'*.

A point that needs not to be overlooked here - is that regardless of how *intricate* and deadly these individuals may've seemed when they left headlines bloody and readers grappled by fear; the truth was, intricacy was actually very limited - if anything, simplicity would've been the better adjective to use to describe the *modus operandi* of these men, but regardless how simple their structure of operation may've been, it was simple enough to work - and in no time links were being made, and a network that came to blanket the city of Kingston and eventually other areas of Jamaica was formed.

With the appointed and endorsed dons from each territory eager to play, *do as the don of all dons said* - at the drop of a dime - and in return reap all the fringe benefits that came from being apart of such an infamous syndicate, it didn't take long for Dudus to have literal robots at his disposal – acting on his every command.

The alliances and affiliations may've finally been under one umbrella, but truth was; Dudus was playing politics - the perfect politician of sorts, even more so than the real politicians themselves. With him being who he was, from day one he had inside information, so he was quite aware that the link did not stop at the borders of Western Kingston, but in the same breath, he also knew that beyond the borders of Western Kingston was where the power structure weakened. One of the key factors which he felt contributed to Jah-T's death - [he wasn't safe outside of his zone]. And with his newly formed alliances, Dudus was *hell-bent* on changing that.

Western Kingston has always been the backbone Constituency of the Jamaica Labour Party and Dudus knew that. He also knew the power that had been garnered with the rise of the *Shower Posse*, and like it was once said in the streets back then, *"everybody want di garden link;"* [Garden – another name for Tivoli Gardens]. Dudus was also quite aware of this. He had seen many outsiders come to Tivoli Gardens for favours of all sorts, and had also seen the benefits, which granting such favours yielded in return. And like the true businessman he was, he was ready to capitalize, but just as with everything else; on an entirely different level.

In many circles Dudus is viewed as or held in the esteem of being some sort of *wizard* when it comes to gangsterism, but what many fail to realize, is that as calculated as all he did may've seemed, all he was doing was making an admirable attempt to secure himself in the process!

And rightfully so...

NOWHERE WAS SAFE; that was the reality of the day and also Dudus' greatest concern upon taking control of the throne.

His brother was dead, mainly due to an altercation that started miles away from their territory, and ending with him meeting his demise not too far from their power base; something which should never have happened, but it did.

He had also lost a sister [Mumpie] in an even closer proximity to home, and to top all that, it seemed as if not even jail was safe, because his father went in one way, and came out another; and although he was a mere child, he was also quite aware of what many around him had termed the *police murder* of his father's forerunner and mentor, Claudius Massop - within walking distance from his house.

And this issue of *safety* wasn't one sided either, all sides [JLP, PNP and the other] had been counting their casualties; **CASE IN POINT:** Glenford *'Early Bird'* Phipps, area leader of neighboring Matthews Lane, [a PNP stronghold] and once the head of the infamous Spanglers Posse, and also a notable PNP activist, [older brother to Donald *'Zekes'* Phipps – the now incarcerated Matthews Lane don] was also murdered in dramatic fashion; killed in downtown, Kingston while serving in his capacity as supervisor of Metropolitan Parks and Market on Wednesday, July 15, 1990.

Another notable gangster at the time, Wayne *'Sandokhan'* Smith, who was accused of being the mastermind behind the attack on the Olympic Gardens Police Station in the mid 1980s, in what seemed like an early real life prelude for blockbuster movies such as *Assault on Precinct 13.*

This incident [*first of its kind, and still to date, the only assault of this nature with such results*], left three policemen who were on duty at the time dead, and a cache of weapons and ammunition in the hands of obviously, some of the most ruthless that Jamaica had to offer at the time. The incident rocked the nation so much that it is said that Michael Manley, [then leader of the Peoples National Party - PNP] who was out jogging at the time the news broke, immediately jumped in his vehicle and headed to the community; arriving in a stupefied state of shock.

Law enforcement was irate, but as fate would have it, none of the curfews and dragnets produced any results, with an even more head shaking twist to the entire scenario being: The police not having the satisfaction of dispensing justice on him, neither in the streets nor in the courtroom, as Sandokhan, who was said to be bringing too much heat to his cronies, was found dead, believed to have been killed by them in the Tower Hill community of Kingston - 1989.

Then there was Nathaniel *'Natty'* Morgan, another notable gangster who came to prominence the same year that Sandokhan was killed. Like almost all gangsters, he lived and died by the gun, meeting his waterloo shortly after escaping from Jamaica's Gun Court Rehabilitation Center in 1990. He was implicated in several atrocious acts of criminality after his escape; including murder, rape and numerous robberies, but eventually he too was cut down, this time by the police in Lakes Pen, St Catherine, eight months following his impressive escape.

AND NOTE, these were the notables, the *nobodies* were being killed a dime a dozen, everyday, in almost every corner of the city, both by the police and by other forces, so Dudus' concern about *safety* was real, not meritless by a long shot...

NOWHERE AND NO ONE SEEMED SAFE...

Power was great, but what was the sense of possessing such a potent potion and not being able to enjoy it? – It didn't make sense to Dudus, and soon *safety* became a literal obsession throughout his reign.

He had seen up close and personal the end result of the don who got too comfortable, and he refused to fall victim to such level of contentment.

In hindsight, the mistakes of the past were obvious, and almost immediately Dudus set out to rectify what he felt should've been rectified a long time ago.

Dudus may've been bestowed with the title of being a political activist, but a little known truth is that his interest in this arena was actually miniscule. He understood its significance and how manipulatively important it was, *to and for the masses*, but from his personal prospective, [uttered countless times in the presence of many] Dudus viewed politics as a vice whose time had passed. It had served its purpose, the politicians had gotten what they wanted [power] and they [individuals like himself] had achieved their objective [financial independence], and from his new vantage point, he no longer saw what the politicians deemed and preached as important - as significant - why should he, when it wasn't politics that had made him wealthy?

Dudus was much like his father, progressively independent in his thinking, so he already had plans to rid himself and his power-base of political dependence. He saw much more value for those under his command. He had seen it done, and he was ready to duplicate it, but he had to address the issue that was haunting him - *the issue of safety*.

A lot was his for the taking, but a lot was also at stake, and after certain kinks were worked out, the smoke cleared and certain critical pieces thought to be firmly in place, Dudus eventually started to make the moves he had envisioned, mainly to his newly acquired territories, where he was always received like a visitation from some *extraterrestrial* being.

BUT THIS JUST DIDN'T HAPPEN OVERNIGHT: At first it is said that as good as Dudus was talking about spreading his wings and empire, and all the sense he was making, when it actually came down to doing it, even with all the plotting and scheming that he had done and was still doing, he still remained hesitant, even acting at times as if he wasn't even interested in venturing outside of Tivoli Gardens. – *'He just didn't trust all this moving around'* - explained one tight-lipped individual; acting as though he knew way more than he was wiling to add to the conversation. Under the circumstances, behaviour of this nature is understandable, but even so, he still had a theory that needed testing.

Dudus had a plan, he always had a plan, and in this case, it was actually a damn good one, but it was still somewhat of a risky venture. He however knew he had to stick to it to be successful, he couldn't appear like all the others before him; limited to the borders of Western Kingston. If all he was, was a duplicate of his father and a reminder of his brother, then all he was doing was living in their shadows, and he couldn't have that.

His guns and his dons were in place, but still there was an issue when it came to clearing the hurdle of timidity – even with decoys and seemingly un-associated cars and motorcycles always around; ahead, behind and sometimes even beside – *Presidential Style* –

IT TOOK A MINUTE, but Dudus eventually started to make moves, and when he did, they resembled scenes from some big budget Hollywood production. His moves were always incognito, but at the same time, very unorthodox when it came to a don, but this was Dudus, he was going to do it *his way or no way*.

Guns were always around, but Dudus made a rule never to travel in any vehicle that had a weapon in it. There were other vehicles for that; a strategy later replaced by the evolution of secret compartments and elaborate stash spots in vehicles. Then there were always the riders [some of the best motorcyclist are said to come out of Western Kingston], who were always armed and ready for the quick getaway. The decoy cars came next; the vehicles with a few men who looked the part enough to draw attention and distract, but who in reality were never any real threat – they just looked the part; a necessity of sorts for the police who always seem to go after the obvious looking targets. The gunners were however the real danger, *the killer transporters*...Two, three or more, who travelled in front of, behind or alongside Dudus wherever he went – [*This was where the real firepower was*]. *Pilots* were also a part of the detail - those who went ahead - acting totally separate and apart, but who were always there, in the shadows of sorts, just to make sure. It didn't stop there, the final element was the so called double check; another team of men either in heavily tinted cars or on motorcycles, who always just happen to pop up and do a spot check wherever Dudus was, [sometimes discreetly, sometimes not so discreetly] just to make sure all was well. This was Dudus' security detail, which only got better, got more sophisticated as time progressed.

ROOM FOR ERROR... NONE!

Dudus may've been who he was, but truth was, his reality was way different from the reality of a regular youth growing up in one of Kingston's inner city communities. No doubt, his reality had benefits, but it also had its drawbacks, a main one being; exposure to the wider world was limited, and according to many, this was a stumbling block in the early years of his reign.

Except for the areas surrounding where he went to school, Tivoli Gardens and its environs, Dudus wasn't too familiar with too many other places outside of those borders in any real depth. For one, he was the son of a don, who had a whole bunch of enemies, political and otherwise, so he had to be sheltered. So in reality, all that he had taken on as a new don was new in more ways than one, but like almost every single thing in life, time has a funny way of injecting change, and in what seemed like a minute, Dudus was at home in his new role, [at least so it seemed] - upon realizing the magnitude of respect that actually existed outside of Tivoli Gardens for Tivoli Gardens as a whole, and the type of respect that was his, simply because of who he was and the position that he had now inherited.

The fringe benefits that were his for the taking and partaking of in each and every one of these territories were vast and tantalizing – **AND LITTLE JIM WAS IN TOWN** - Men lined up to take orders and women lined up to take whatever it was that the don and his crew felt like issuing at any given moment. Nothing was off limits to Dudus and his crew – there was a don in charge of everywhere he went, a don who controlled all things in that realm, and he [Dudus], was *his* don.

It didn't take long for Dudus to get his feet wet; and was soon laying down the *law* according to the Tivoli Gardens handbook, in regions as close as Fletcher's Land, another JLP stronghold, and as far as Grants Pen, also another traditional JLP stronghold in the upper regions of St. Andrew.

According to some of those who claimed to have accompanied him on these early expeditions - they explain that it took a while, but Presi eventually and actually started to enjoy making those rounds – especially with him able to move around literally unnoticed, unlike both his father or brother - seeing that most individuals outside of Tivoli Gardens didn't know what Dudus even looked like - until recently.

"General is a man wha neva too love di road, but is a man wha wi jus sey watch yah, wi a mek a flex, an is all a next day ting before wi touch

back di base. Is a man wha work offa him vibes, more time road don't even mention, but a next time, a pure trampoose and ends out, especially if is a spot wha gi him a vibes." **TRANSLATED**: "General [another name for Dudus] was not a person that loved the road, but he is the type of person who will just get up and say, let's go, and it might be the next day before we get back to the base [Tivoli Gardens]. He works off his vibes, sometimes mention of the road is not even up for discussion, but another time we would just be out there, hanging out, especially if it's a spot that gives him a good vibe."

BUT YOU KNOW WHAT THEY SAY - IF IT SEEMS TOO GOOD TO BE TRUE, MOST TIMES - IT USUALLY IS:

Inexperience in any field can be critical, and Dudus was no exception. While Dudus was busy getting familiar with his role and all that it entails, (just starting to enjoy the fruits of his labour of sorts), things were busy going contrary to how he had envisioned it; all wasn't well in *Gotham.*

When Jim Brown was around everyone knew who the don was and knew what to expect. With Jah-T it was pretty much the same, but although it was known that Dudus was in charge, with no track record to go by, both *fear* and *respect* were fickle, and soon evolved into actions fuelled by ignorance - motivated by ego and self-centredness.

With no obvious force to reckon with, [*at least so it seemed*] a few independent entities of sorts had a few ideas of their own, and whether Dudus was involved directly or not, the weight of the blame was on his shoulders – it was happening in his territory.

By time 1994 rolled around, Dudus, just somewhat settling in his role, was faced with what could be labelled as his first major crisis as a don - problems were on the rise. The *Shower Posse* was again in the headlines; Vivian Blake, the reputed leader of the *Shower Posse* who had been on the run for over five years was now in the custody of the

Jamaican authorities, and like his co-defendant and Dudus' father, Jim Brown, he was about to start an extradition battle that was to last just around five years and like it or not, the spotlight was again dangling in Dudus' direction.

With Blake now in custody, questions surrounding the Shower Posse started to circulate again, and so did Dudus' name, but if that were all, maybe he would've been fine - Dudus' problems were far greater by now.

NUMBER ONE ON A LIST OF THIRTEEN: Many reasons have been given and speculations have been countless as to why Dudus and Mr. Seaga never really got along like all previous West Kingston area leaders or dons; but whether it was because Mr. Seaga didn't really know him, like he did Jah – T, or because Dudus just simply refused to take any *talk* from him, due to how he viewed him when it came to his father's demise - one thing was for sure, Dudus and Edward Seaga, Member of Parliament for Western Kingston and the leader of the opposition Jamaica Labour Party [JLP] at the time, had never really seen eye to eye, and weren't going to – at least not anytime soon; a general perception of most Tivoli Gardens and Western Kingston residents, at least by 1994.

DEVELOPMENT: At this particular time, there seemed to be what was the equivalent of a flood of guns in the streets of Kingston, which eventually gave birth to a reckless and brutal upsurge of daring robberies, in and around Jamaica's capital city; Kingston. Interestingly enough, although there were and *still are* many armed fractions all around this area - all these acts were said to have been committed by men from Western Kingston; Tivoli Gardens to be more specific, and Mr. Seaga, then Member of Parliament for said community, was *pointing fingers* and *calling names*.

DUDUS DID IT: Mr. Seaga pin-pointed Dudus [Christopher Coke] as the ringleader of these criminal acts. The accusation was that Coke was not only involved, but was also responsible for the crime wave that was wreaking havoc across the city's capital, but it didn't stop there. Mr. Seaga took it a step further, turning over a list of thirteen men from his constituency, (to then Police Commissioner, Trevor MacMillan), whom he claimed were the chief culprits - but to some, all this was, was a list of men, he [Mr. Seaga] simply could not control.

It's believed that Dudus was at the top of Mr. Seaga's list, a claim not too hard to believe, if indeed what is said of Mr. Seaga's actions is indeed true: It is said that Mr. Seaga himself put up a JA$25,000 reward, for the arrest of Christopher *'Dudus'* Coke, who again he claimed was the ringleader.

This many say was the defining moment that made it clearer than ever that this was not going to be the typical Member of Parliament and area leader/don – relationship. And still there are some who believe that the whole list of names drama was all a big publicity stunt on Mr. Seaga's part.

Surrounding the same incident, reports also circulated that Mr. Seaga himself said he had warned the criminals, but was told by the don that since he [Mr. Seaga] did not give them their guns, he could not tell them what to do with them.

The then Commissioner of Police, Trevor MacMillan, however rubbished what he also viewed as a publicity stunt on Mr. Seaga's part, stating that – *'he was not going to, and could not by law, round up men at Mr. Seaga's request, or suspicion, without evidence or charges against them.'*

NOTE: *This list was never made public.*

It is said that the guns Dudus had put on the street were out of control, and that he could not control them. Yet some say that all that was happening was by design and not as random as it was presumed to be, or even as it appeared to be. Yes - there was a string of daring robberies around the time in question, and according to many, *yes*, they all in one way or the other had a lot to do with men form Western Kingston, but contrary to what many have been led to believe, another story goes that the guns weren't out of control as they were thought to be; *they were actually unleashed!*

ALWAYS MORE TO THE STORY: (Briefly referred to on pages 56 and 57) - The story goes that Ziggy Marley, son of Reggae legend and former Trench Town resident, Bob Marley, was building a recording studio almost on the border of Rema and Trench Town. This was an effort of social empowerment on Ziggy's part, who was desirous of providing an outlet for aspiring musicians form the community, but as admirable as Ziggy's effort may've been, this was a piece of real estate that Coke viewed as under his control, and with that, it meant that whatsoever was going on in said territory, [or on this piece of land] had to go through him, which in this case meant, the contract for impending construction was to be his. A reality that Ziggy was either unaware of, or just didn't have any regard for.

Some have even said that the young Marley viewed the demand of the Tivoli men as *presumptuous* and *outlandish*. And rightfully so according to many, because this was Ziggy Marley; Bob Marley's first born, he was building a studio for the community, so how could you infringe on that? He was who he was, and the son of who he was, so who was this Dudus, who no one outside of Tivoli actually knew, feared or had reason to fear?

It is said that Ziggy shrugged off all the talk of retaliation for his *violation* as just idle chatter, not once according to sources, ever taking the situation serious, but what he didn't know, was that he had just made the life shortening mistake of not giving Dudus and his cronies the desire of their hearts and wallets.

Ziggy didn't give the construction work to Dudus and his clique, and they were furious! And this some say became the first test of Dudus' *presidential powers* - activating all the guns that had been distributed, with one intention in mind; sending a very clear message to the *Legend's* son that a new sheriff was in town.

NOTE: *This was also the same year [1994] that Bob Marley was inducted into the Rock and Roll Hall of Fame.*

Retaliation was swift and methods of revenge savage, with a series of killings and shootings that some say left the young Marley petrified with fear.

"Di man dem draw everybody inna dem ting, all people wha don't even like music." **TRANSLATED**: "They involved everyone, even people who weren't into music like that," explained one older Trench Town resident, who still shakes her head when she recalls the horrors that followed the disagreement of forces.

"Di garden man dem jus come and start shoot, anybody and anything, dem shoot up di site, dem shoot up di worker dem, dem just gwaan wid a bag a tings, and one ting jus lead to di next." **TRANSLATED**: "The men from Tivoli Gardens just came and started shooting, anybody and anything. They shot up the construction site [where the studio was to be built], they shot up the workers, and just acted wild and crazy, and one thing led to the next.

This was the general concurrence of most who found themselves on the receiving end of the gun barrels, and Dudus had plenty of those to spare. He was sending a message, [go through me...Not around me] but although it was delivered, a few other things got delivered in-between the constant drive-bys and wanton acts of intimidating shootings.

AND ALSO ADD: Robberies, robberies and more robberies; each one more daring, more barefaced than the last. Dudus was implicated, but truth be told, Dudus was no robber, he had no reason to rob, he had just inherited an empire.

Be that what it was on one side of the coin - on the other, it made absolutely no difference what he inherited or didn't inherit. He was being implicated in acts of criminality, and that's all that mattered. Some have argued that although the sending of the message may've been sanctioned by Coke, he knew nothing about robberies – acts said to have been committed independently by affiliates of the *dons* he had empowered, the same *dons* he had activated, and the same *dons* who all had their own agendas – in one way or the other, and who some say were using this opportunity as the perfect cover to further their causes.

THE HEAT WAS ON: Eyes were on him again, Vivian Blake's capture had opened old *Shower Posse* wounds, Dudus' Member of Parliament had put him at the top of a list of *trouble makers*, and he was getting a crash course in Murphy's Law - *whatever can go wrong, usually does.*

Things were wrong, this wasn't the way he had planned it – he had to regroup – rethink his approach, because so far it was clear that he had taken a path that was leading in all the wrong directions, and he couldn't have that - he had to get it right.

Fig. 5 Map of the Western Kingston area – Tivoli Gardens circled

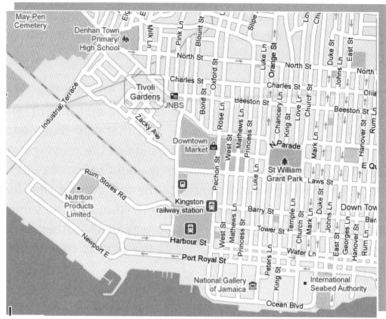

Fig. 6 Aerial photo highlighting the area of West Kingston

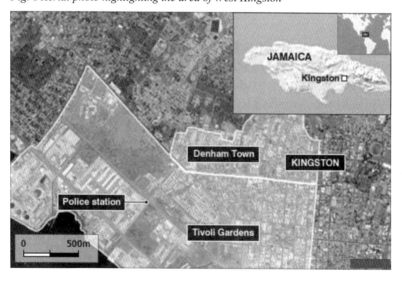

• *Inside Tivoli Gardens:*

-The Dudus reign-

- Act I -

A SIGH OF RELIEF: 1994 was not a good year for Dudus, and he couldn't have felt better than when 1995 rolled around and the dust seemed as though it was settling.

It didn't take much after the incidents mentioned in the previous chapter for Dudus to realize that contrary to prior belief, bullets flying and people dying was not such a great idea after all [in the 80s maybe, but this was the 90s], and that was regardless of the point you were trying to make.

Another interesting development during his time was that Dudus also got a crash course in *the Art of True Power;* an issue he had obviously gotten twisted prior to going up against Mr. Seaga. He could feel how he wanted to, no one was saying he couldn't, but keep it to himself; if he didn't, therein laid the problem. No one was saying he couldn't be the don [even though again, Mr. Seaga wasn't all that familiar with him, nor was he (Mr. Seaga) too enthused about him, (Dudus), someone he didn't really know, except for him being Jim Brown's son, and someone he had no track record of, running his political stronghold] . Anyway, the message was sent, *'never forget that I have the power of the state, and even if what I say is not true, the minute I say it, the lights you have been trying to avoid will come on.'* This was the message some say Mr. Seaga sent Dudus in 1994 with him being on top of his list of culprits. And Dudus got the message – loud and clear and in response, literally became *Mr. Invisible.*

This was a very critical time for Dudus in other ways as well. He knew [although it wasn't official] that he was in the *crosshairs* of law enforcement. A lot had happened, and his name was being called, and fingers were being pointed. The law wanted him, and so did other opposing enforcers in the street, and with Vivian now in custody, and questions again circulating about who was now in charge of the *Shower Posse* – (an issue again that had his name a-top the list) - Dudus was not in the most comfortable of positions.

TIGHT AND TRICKY [1995]: Although it was well accepted in Tivoli Gardens and Western Kingston at large, that Dudus was the new don, and thought to now be in position of the keys to the *Shower* Posse's wealth; contrary to popular belief, things were nowhere near what they were thought to be financially around this time.

What needs to be remembered and understood here, is that in 1994, *Dudus* may've been *Dudus* - Jim Brown's son, but he was not Jim Brown, he was not Vivian Bake either, and he wasn't even Jah-T. He was just *Dudus* – Jim's little son who many believe was taking on too much for his little head, but they [the doubtful] could say what they wanted to – Dudus was there to stay.

OUT OF SIGHT - OUT OF MIND: Both Jim Brown and Jah-T were known to have made visits to the U.S. to check on the operations of the *Shower Posse,* and this alone was a key factor that kept the machinery working like clockwork. Those abroad liked the fact that the *don* wasn't just a *don* in the shadows, but he was also a *don* on the ground, showing up every now and then, not just to be seen, but also to solidify his position of power. Dudus was however different, he had never left Jamaica, had NO SAY-SO WHATSOEVER in the *Shower*

Posse's activities along the way, so how could he now just assume such a vast and (in their world) prestigious position of power? Many were not feeling such a suggestion.

There was no doubt that posse members and affiliates abroad had their own issues to attend to, [the heat was on in the U.S.]. So they weren't too particular about focusing on some *don* that they didn't know, or had a reason to respect - even though they couldn't just ignore him and kick him to the curb, especially with the people of Tivoli already accepting him as their *don*.

To those abroad, Dudus may've been a *don* to the people of Tivoli, but he was no *don* to them; those on the front line in the United States, Canada or the UK. Accepting Dudus as their *don* was hard - they didn't know him in that capacity; they knew Jim, knew Vivian, even knew Jah-T, but very few if any of them, even knew Dudus, and those who did, knew him as a baby – not the *general* he was now proclaiming to be. So with all the familiar figureheads either gone or out of commission, this moment became extremely tricky in the financial arena – **HOW SO**? Because affiliates abroad [on the front line] suddenly weren't too enthused about sending in the tributes that usually flowed in like clockwork; one of the key fuel types that runs the machinery of the garrisons in Jamaica, and specifically, Tivoli Gardens.

THIS IS HOW IT WORKED: Tributes came in to the *don*, and he dispensed them, this was the usual way of operation, but with all that was happening, at this particular moment in time, compared to what would come later on in his reign, money was funny – and the hands were out.

This was not to suggest that around this time Dudus was broke or anything of that nature - that was never the reality. He just wasn't able to access the strength of his power due to a host of issues that neither he nor anyone else had foreseen, and whatever funds he was able to access was not enough to do what a *don* was usually expected to do. Under different circumstances, this is when, according to the tradition [at the time] in Jamaica – that the political representative would usually step up to the plate and add another notch to their belt, but this too wasn't to be: – The *political representative* was Mr. Seaga, and the *don* was Dudus – they didn't see eye to eye. They had differences, so the reality of the situation was although Dudus was the don in name, for a moment, unknown to many, (outside of Tivoli Gardens and Western Kingston), with all that was happening, that's all Dudus was at this time - a *don* in name – a *don* with limited power – a *don* to a throne that he was still yet to ascend to in the real way that *dons* usually ascend – with the blessings and endorsements of most of those who mattered and definitely the blessing and endorsement of the Member of Parliament for the respective Constituency.

Some say that around this time Dudus even contemplated and made attempts to leave the Island - the heat in the kitchen was just too hot. This attempt however had dual motivation behind it, the heat was one, but Dudus also felt as though he wasn't being given the respect he felt was his from those abroad, and this is when those closest, say Dudus started toying with the idea that a visit was overdue, but with him being who he was – *Dudus the skeptic;* there was never any real manifestation in that arena - DUDUS REMAINED GROUNDED.

COUNTER CLAIM: Although it has long been said that Dudus had never been to the United States, officials in the United States tell a different story; claiming that *'Dudus'* once lived in the US for a short period, and unknown to many, was deported back to Jamaica in 1998, after being convicted in North Carolina for possession of stolen property.

If there is actual evidence to support this claim, then the situations change dramatically, because it would also explain his silence during the early years of his reign, especially after being put at the top of Mr. Seaga's list of problem starters.

If what the US have claimed is also true, then Dudus wasn't merely being low-keyed, he had actually left the island, only to return in much disappointment, but with more determination than ever. And last but not least, if the claims of the US are true, it could also serve as the reason behind the generosity and open-handed policy that Dudus was said to extend towards those deported back to Jamaica with just the clothes on their backs.

WHATEVER THE TRUTH IS - WHETHER DUDUS DID OR DIDN'T LEAVE JAMAICA - IS ONE THAT TIME WILL EVENTUALLY UNRAVEL, BUT WHILE THAT AWAITS UNFOLDING, THIS IS WHAT IS CLEAR THUS FAR.

A YAH MI BORN - A YAH MI LIVE:

Tivoli Gardens had always been home from his birth, and if he was going to remain there, he was going to be the *don* that he was born to be, but he had to get back to the drawing board – that by now was obvious.

Education has always been a great divider in any society, and also in any field, and in the world of gangsters and thugs, the difference it made was also the same. Dudus was no run of the mill thug, that has been established and agreed upon by now, he was an educated thinker, well read, even at the time possessing what seemed like a mental scope that was beyond his physical years – a fact that came to life shortly after making a few visits back to the drawing board, which revealed exactly what it was that Mr. Seaga really had over him: –

He had the hearts and minds of the people – This was the edge –

Mr. Seaga had been there for the residents of Tivoli Gardens and Western Kingston for as long as most of them could remember. He had provided for them and protected them – this was what gave him the edge, what had given him their *hearts* and *minds* – Not just their *fear* and *respect*.

DUDUS HAD TO FIX THIS: The fence between himself and Mr. Seaga was broken, but it wasn't destroyed, but according to all accounts, Dudus had no interest in attending to any such repairs. Maybe it was pride, but even with his feet to the fire, it is said that Dudus never sought to solidify his alliance with Mr. Seaga.

Dudus had always said Tivoli and that wasn't going to change, and Tivoli Gardens had always supported the JLP, and that too wasn't going to change; these were the facts and there was no denying them. **AND JUST FOR THE RECORD**: Dudus had no interest in changing any of that either. His grouse wasn't with the party or Tivoli; his grouse was with the party's leader - Tivoli Gardens political representative, and his Member of Parliament.

THE PLOT THICKENS:

- According to a Federal Indictment, starting in 1994, the Shower Posse, with Coke at its head, sold drugs by the ton. Estimations vary, but they all land in the ballpark of thousands of pounds of marijuana - and almost as much cocaine in kilograms – smuggled into the United States by Coke and his organization. We are not privy to say if these accusations are factual or not; that's for a court of law to decide, but what we have uncovered, is that this particular period [1994-1995] was a time when the drawing board became Dudus' best friend, and he came away with what he felt was a master plan – a plan that was now anchored on much more than before. *Fear* and *respect* are good, but he now wanted *hearts* and *minds*. That's what had solidified Mr. Seaga's position and his hold on power. He had the peoples' *hearts* and *minds* – that was the real source of his power, and Dudus wanted all that and then some. He had found the formula – he just had to sell it to everybody else.

TAPPING INTO THE RESERVOIR OF REAL POWER: *'It has always been and will always be about the people; in the people is where true power lies.'* It took Dudus a while, but he eventually realized that, and when he did, he was ready to act.

Almost instantly Dudus embarked on a mission that found him becoming a replica of Mr. Seaga of sorts. If the power he desired nestled in the *people*, then he had to be about the *people*. Dudus' plan was simple, their hands were out, and he was going to fill them.

Reinventing himself; Dudus embarked on a mission that found him literally becoming the community of Tivoli Gardens *everyday* Member of Parliament of sorts... Not just the *don*.

Seaga had provided and protected the residents of Tivoli for most of their lives, and Dudus was going to do just that, just on a level that had never been seen, or even attempted before.

Mr. Seaga had an edge, but Dudus also had an edge of his own. Unlike Seaga, he was there, in the heart of ground zero [Tivoli Gardens] everyday, not just occasionally – and the issues of the people were constant, not sporadic like Mr. Seaga's visits. This was Dudus' edge; he would fill the void left by the Members of Parliament and community Councillors - AND THAT'S JUST WHAT HE DID:

THE ONION RING EFFECT: At this stage Dudus went into what many say resembled full campaign mode - still remaining low-keyed, but elevating head and shoulders above all who were in opposition, with the quickness: – People were actually simpler than he had thought, and so was the purchasing of hearts and minds.

One of his first moves was to start making phone calls – reaching out to those abroad. This was before the days of mobile access as we know them today. Back then most of the calls made to those overseas were done directly from the Jamaican Telephone Company, or made from an entity [now defunct], which was then known as Jamintel [Jamaica International Telecommunications]. The later of the two was located at the corner of North and Duke Streets, downtown, Kingston - adjacent to the community of Fletcher's Land, a known JLP aligned neighbourhood - [which also gave Dudus somewhat of the sense of security that he desired]. Many have testified that it was no strange occurrence to see The President and his crew, (not as deep and loud as they were initially), come through and make a few calls. It was either that or he would have needed a direct line, which he obviously couldn't risk. It was either those avenues or using one of the then many illegal telephone connections that were available all across the city at that time – also another move that wasn't at the top of his *things to do* list.

Dudus may not have been known as the don that Jah-T was, but he was still Jim Brown's son, so he had the respect to at least warrant a listening ear, and upon utilizing the numbers which he had at his disposal - (some say it was Jah-T's phone book) - it wasn't long before he had plenty of listening ears. And with one call after the other producing results, in seconds Dudus had one convert after another.

REGARDLESS HOW ONE FELT OR DIDN'T, this was Jim's son on the other end of the line, not only getting familiar but making his position clear. This was the new *don* calling. One may not have known him, but with both Jim and Jah-T dead, and Dudus assuming the role, accepted by almost all of Tivoli at the time, it didn't take long for others to start paying attention, listening and understanding. And before many even realized what had happened, the support suddenly started to pour in.

"This bigga dan don ting an bigga dan politics, cause wi dun si how dat go already, dem fi dem self, so we affi look out fi our self," – **TRANSLATED**: "This is bigger than donship and politics, because we already see how those things work at times. They [politicians] are for themselves, so it only makes sense that we look out for ourselves also."

This, it is said, was the foundation on which Dudus' sales pitch was built. They were all on the same team, and self-security in every-which-way there was, only made sense. This was his approach, and along with that he also brought the promise of security for the local family members of those who were away. In addition it is also said that this was the time when Dudus got one over on many of those who were abroad. This came in the form of him convincing quite a few affiliates abroad to open their doors to Dudus' own personal, handpicked implants into the United States.

This was a new era, and unlike his father and brother, if he couldn't make the trips himself, hands and feet of his own influence still needed to be on the ground – and Dudus knew that. This was the only way his plan was going to work, he needed to infiltrate with a fresh influx of foot soldiers – **SO IT IS SAID THE THOUGHT WAS**: It will seem like they were there to take over, so the older guard will either line up or act up, either way showing their hands, which would obviously be dealt with accordingly. Dudus knew that with people on the ground who actually knew him [his people, his friends, his guns] who had seen him in action and respected him, things would soon be different. And like a calculated equation solved, Dudus again proved that he was *right on the money*.

And just like he had predicted, with the above mentioned achieved, things changed with the quickness – a clear indicator that those who doubted him had indeed done so without really knowing his full potential. They had underestimated him.

Making what he had work to his advantage was also key for Dudus. And after laying the foundation for ultimate take over, his next mission was to make sure the message he was preaching made its way home - from all possible directions: – **ALMOST INSTANTLY**, there was what could have been seen as a deliberate show of generosity on *Dudus'* part, but no one was the wiser - he was singing a new song, *'money over war,'* and with him being as freehanded as he suddenly became, no one heard anything else. His efforts were all well received by those who benefited, and it also came with the dual benefit of convincing those abroad that this young *don* – who not many knew, was indeed the *truth*:- Dudus needed others to start saying things on his behalf without him saying or even hinting at it. And again just like he predicted - they did.

With Dudus quickly reinventing himself after being labelled public enemy number one by Mr. Seaga; elevating with literally no political blessing, he gained a level of legitimacy that brought him within arms length reach of what he was yearning for even quicker than he had estimated.

He was the new don, and he wasn't just *talking good*, according to all accounts, he was also *doing good*. The streets were also talking, plus the fact that he was even willing to stand up to Mr. Seaga and say what most were said to be thinking in the confines of their minds, but not brave enough to utter from their lips, were reasons enough to make it clear that he was the real deal – he was Jim Brown's son, a real *Coke*.

The *tributes* rolled in, and Dudus did just like he said he would do; gaining the respect of those abroad even more, while all the time getting closer and closer to his goal, the *hearts* and *minds* of the people. He settled every issue, looked out for everyone. He was seldom ever upfront, but if you lived in or around said community at the time, one thing was sure; you knew who was in charge, and in one way or the other, benefited from the trickle down effect.

THEY BOUGHT WHAT HE WAS SELLING and with that things suddenly became easier. Soon there was little hesitation to any suggestion Dudus made – a very welcomed change on his part, which led to developments such as visas being bought either on the black-market or from some other ingenious way devised for his cronies to enter the territories of choice, which in the majority of cases was The United States of America.

Dudus' campaign for the *hearts* and *minds* of the people went into overdrive upon achieving the above, and soon saw him devising ingenious and elaborate schemes that always seemed people orientated, and thus, were in almost all cases funded by his cronies abroad.

– The people were bought –

Dudus went above and beyond what any don had done before, even doing what the people complained that the politicians should have been doing all along, and weren't doing.

NEEDS AND WANTS: Dudus provided both. He held treats for the children, bought books and school supplies, even going as far as creating a school fund that supported every household in Tivoli Gardens at one time or another during his reign – [an initiative that was a literal *no child left behind* effort, which the residents of Tivoli Gardens embraced wholeheartedly]. Efforts like this made life easier for parents, and made Dudus a hero amongst the masses. Taking the burden of responsibility off them (the parents) was like a dream come true in their depressing economic situations, and in what many have labelled their [the people of Tivoli Gardens] stupor of dependence, they bought into the Dudus' philosophy, lock-stock-and-barrel - blinded by ulterior acts of generosity, and their lack of discipline to both refuse and despise the free ride.

There was even a system devised to assist with the basic necessities of all households inside Tivoli Gardens. If you were sick and needed help, there was help; somewhat of an internal insurance fund of sorts. If you were violated you didn't deal with it yourself - you reported it and it was dealt with, involvement on your part was none or by choice. It may not have made national headlines, but to the residents of Tivoli Gardens, there was finally a system in place that made sense, finally a system in place that worked!

Those abroad were pleasantly surprised, and the contributions, support and bond became greater and stronger. Tivoli was working - fuelled by illicit funds sent home from the illegal activities of those abroad, and with the entire community happy, safe and provided for, and Dudus constantly outdoing himself with one community project after another - the likes of which were never faced with objection from the people – the financial tributes flowed in unreservedly, giving Dudus access to a continuous and steady flow of funds, which added to his power *tenfold*.

Dudus orchestrated the accumulation of clothing and footwear in all sizes and styles – constantly - and distributed them throughout the community without prejudice or reservation. When it was Christmas he played *Santa*, when it was February 14, he played *Prince Valentine*, when it's back to school time, he played *mommy* and *daddy*, and even on birthdays or other special occasions, *The President* was there. Nothing was ignored – nothing was left to chance - his plan was working - so much that it even caught the attention of Mr. Seaga himself, but by the time he realized what was happening, the horse was already out the gate. Dudus was in charge, and although Mr. Seaga may not have approved, it was clearer than ever that Jim Brown's baby boy wasn't going anywhere, any time soon. He was the people's choice, and like it or not, he [Mr. Seaga] had to deal with him. There was just no way around it.

Whatever happened next has remained a matter of speculation, but it was at this time that it is agreed upon by most in the know that Mr. Seaga forever lost control of Tivoli Gardens as Jamaica had known it. To those on the outside, the change went ignored, but to those on the inside, a lot had changed, so much that Mr. Seaga's role in Tivoli Gardens was reduced to a mere figurehead, because Dudus was now in possession of the very *titles* to what Mr. Seaga had once been the sole proprietor of; the *hearts* and *minds* of the people of Tivoli Gardens.

Mr. Seaga had always been a master politician, and although his back was against the wall, he sure as hell wasn't going to just sit back and allow Dudus and his cronies to push him out of the very place he had not only built, but conceived and brought to life through blood, sweat and tears.

If he was the people's choice then so be it. This seemed to have been the conclusion that Mr. Seaga arrived at after careful analysis of the situation, says many. He was a politician, so he was quite aware of the rules of engagement, so he knew he couldn't continue to show direct opposition to his don [even though Dudus wasn't his don]. That could spell trouble and wouldn't look good to the wider society and he knew that Dudus was also aware of this. This wasn't Jim Brown or Massop - so like the master politician he was, the allegation is that Mr. Seaga stepped back in order to *save-face* politically, and was soon seen in a capacity that appeared to have been limited to the community's athletic and cultural development. Everything else concerning Tivoli Gardens was said to be under *Dudus' portfolio*.

When Mr. Seaga's reduced role in the community is brought into the discussion, many *pundits* shy away or have suggested that Mr. Seaga was merely giving Dudus enough rope to hang himself, but that never happened. Instead, it seemed as though Dudus was *hanging others*, growing from strength to strength, causing even the eyebrows of Mr.

Seaga himself to rise. According to many, *he* [Dudus] *actually reminded him* [Mr. Seaga] *of himself.*

DUDUS WAS GOOD - VERY GOOD: To the people of Tivoli Gardens and neighbouring environs, Dudus was a progressive don, who not only talked about it, but was about it. He said *money over war,* and he obviously meant it – because money suddenly seemed to be flowing in the streets of Tivoli Gardens again, and there was no war, not even an inkling of it. Dudus needed as little attention as he could get, and should there was violence in the streets, he knew he would be implicated, so like the true strategist he was, in no time he instigated a truce between himself and numerous warring factions – even making allies of some. And if that wasn't enough, Dudus went one further by not only declaring downtown Kingston *a safe, crime free zone,* but he backed up his talk with action: FORGET THE POLICE – THE LAW DOWNTOWN KINGSTON WAS DUDUS:

DUDUS is believed to and has since been credited with – [by even the Mayor of Kingston and St. Andrew], being instrumental in the eradication of certain petty acts of criminality in and around the downtown, Kingston area, which were all common place before his intervention.

It must also be noted that it's widely said and accepted by most Jamaicans, [at least in the region that this book focuses on], that Dudus was the one who made downtown Kingston safe again – for residents, business operators and visitors to the commercial district. He is said to have literally and almost singlehandedly put a damper on crime, doing what law enforcement was unable to do at the time. But this is a claim that has been rubbished and countered with venom by some, who say *all Dudus did, was put a stop to what he himself had instigated in the first place.* All he did according to those who hold this view, *was, call his dogs off and chase off the strays, which wasn't hard to do, with him being who he was in the world of Jamaican criminality.*

Opinions differ like night and day when this topic comes up for discussion, even though it has come from the lips of officials such as Kingston's present Mayor himself **[2011- Desmond Mckenzie]**, but in spite of which side of the fence one finds themselves on, regarding this specific issue; one thing cannot be denied, there was a dramatic reduction in crime in this region of Jamaica's metropolis, and it wasn't due only to the efforts of the Jamaica Constabulary Force.

- Money over War -

IF DUDUS WAS A PREACHER, THE ABOVE WOULD BE THE SERMON HE WOULD MORE THAN LIKELY BE REMEMBERED FOR – BECAUSE HE PREACHED IT RELIGIOUSLY:

THE PRINCIPLE WAS SIMPLE: Every man and woman wanted the same things for themselves, children, family and loved ones - security and stability. Their realities may all be different, but their desires are all the same - *in one way or the other*, and Dudus realized this, and with that comprehension, he devised the self reliant effort of self support and self containment, which worked like this: - *If you operated a shop or store in the community, it was supported by the community, and to avoid unnecessary competition for sales, Dudus even made sure that not every establishment was selling the same products – Everyone had to eat: - If you were a mechanic in the area, all the mechanic work came to you, and others even went out and brought work in. He started a construction company that solicited work from a variety of sources, mainly political, which provided constant work for labourers: - If you had no job but had a skill, it was put to use and you were paid for said services, there were times when individuals were even set up in their own businesses, if The President saw the investment as worthy.*

Gone were the days of random and *petty* holdups, the don would have none of that in his territory, and if anyone dared violated, retaliation was swift and deadly. If money was the desire, there was a variety of ways to achieve such a desire without setting the city on fire, and that's how Dudus was setting the order - and everyone was buying into his philosophy.

It is also said that Dudus was responsible for the opening of establishments such as wholesales, restaurants, and even beauty salons in and around the Tivoli region, basically creating the latter specifically as outlets of opportunities for females who had the skills but nowhere to put them to work.

There was something for everyone, and if you couldn't do anything, the opportunity to learn was there if you were willing to apply yourself. Hope seemed alive and well. All who dealt with Dudus directly or indirectly, attested to his shrewd but fair practices and principles. A refreshing change to such a revered and feared office; and with this, the relationship between him and the people deepened, not only with every act of generosity, but with almost every other move that was made by him – he could do no wrong. The wool was over the eyes of the people, and soon they weren't only loyal admirers and respecters of *The President*, but without even realizing it - they became dependent on him, and like it is said, *once you have gotten a taste of the good life, it's hard to let it go, even if your life depends on it.* This was exactly the kind of position the residents of Tivoli Gardens had found themselves in. And the saddest part of it all was; very few ever realize what had really gone down...Even after it went down.

BUT IT WASN'T ALL PEACHES AND CREAM: With all that has been uncovered, it should not be forgotten here that beyond all the enlightening efforts of Christopher *'Dudus'* Coke, there was also a dark side at work. This was Tivoli Gardens, a place whose reputation was born and resided in the barrel of the gun, so with all the positive moves being made by Mr. Coke, it must not be forgotten that the moulding, creating, training, preparing and then the activating of gangsters, still needed to be a matter of priority on his list. Dudus knew that - and so it was – the dark side of Tivoli Gardens never left; it was just camouflaged, admitted by many, as there have been reports of Tivoli Gardens literally operating as the headquarters of *criminality* in Kingston – quite possible even the entire Jamaica.

Reports are that if you desired anything *illegal*, Tivoli Gardens was where it was or where the connection for it was. This was one of those *in-the-street* facts that those who needed to know, knew. In addition, it is also said that besides Dudus' philanthropy, there was also a steady drive to expand his grip on criminality, which came in the form of (it is said) him dealing in all types of vices, which ranged from the sale of marijuana, right up to the more serious accusations of arms dealing and even murder for hire, and everything in between.

During the investigation for this volume, it was also uncovered that Tivoli Gardens served as a command center of sort for criminality, where thugs from all over were said to frequent for meetings of all sorts, to either plot and scheme or squash their differences. Dudus was a *master*, it is said in this arena, using his status and power to act as a sort of *demigod* over issues that were outside of the law, and needed mediation.

FROM ALL ANALYSES, BY AS EARLY AS 1997 - Tivoli Gardens was operating like a *state within a state*, with even its own government of sorts overseeing the progress: - **[IT'S ALLEGED THAT** if the government of Jamaica had an official office for a portfolio, then Tivoli Gardens had an unofficial office for said portfolio**]**. And in what could be determined as nothing short of a blatant disregard for the authority of the land; Tivoli, under the control of Dudus, went as far as even creating a higher office than the one that actually ran the country of Jamaica, to run their Republic. Instead a Prime Minister - *The Republic of Tivoli* – as many have labelled it, had a *President*. They made their own laws - a fact confirmed by the findings that followed the May 2010 incursion by the security forces in search of Dudus, which exposed the most telling discoveries yet; all confirming that what was once labelled as rumours, were indeed just the opposite. The security forces uncovered what appeared to be a courtroom, equipped with even a gavel, but the even more telling and chilling sightings came in the form of a torture chamber with two hangman's noose, and a burial ground, which is believed was used to bury victims who were killed inside Tivoli Gardens. It sounds gruesome, almost like something out of the movies, but believe it or not, it's real – this was Tivoli Gardens – and the evidence speaks for itself.

'Once in the racket, always in the racket' *Al Capone 1899 – 1947*

THE PRESIDENTIAL CLICK: With the problems of The *Shower Posse* what they were [indictments, extradition requests, etcetera], there was and always remained a vigorous campaign to disassociate himself [Dudus] from anything *Shower Posse* related, and with that, along with the embracing of blatant defiance, Dudus gave birth to what law enforcement has said was nothing more than a new name for an old organization...*The Presidential Click.*

Be that what it may or may not have been, just like the gangsters of the 1950s in The United States after the golden years of prohibition, who had to change with the times and become legitimate businessmen, Dudus had to pretty much do the same, in the ever changing and demanding climate that was leading up to the new millennium – especially with the ever looming possibility of being implicated on a whim.

ONE OF DUDUS' FIRST MOVES ON THE ROAD TO LEGITIMACY WAS a literal taking of a leaf from his father's handbook. Jim Brown may've been known to most as just a gangster, but like all gangster's, beyond the tough persona, there usually lies way more, and with Jim Brown, the case was the same; drug dealer and gangster aside, he was also a businessman.

Jamaica's traditional musical genre, [specifically Reggae and later Dancehall] and the ghettos of Jamaica have always been in cahoots. Most musicians at the time came from depressed communities – financially or otherwise, [still so to date] - so they connected automatically with the people and the reality of the ghetto. The impact of music in the Jamaican culture is paramount and well documented, even coming with interesting undertones and elements that go as far back as the 1950s and 1960s, when local musical expressions were weaved into the fabric of political campaigns, with the aim of bridging the gaps that divided the populace. An effort devised to connect and convey ones message in a format and language that *the powers that be* perceived was palatable to the masses.

Jim Brown had seen and knew the effects of this method all too well, but unlike so many of his affiliates, he also saw the financial benefit from a personal prospective; if indeed he could redirect the flow like he had done with the *Shower Posse*. Jim Brown's love for music was well known in the streets and amongst his associates and peers, so it wasn't strange when he decided that he was interested in acquiring a controlling stake in the entertainment industry, which he was also known to passionately contribute to; patronizing many-a-event. That was Jim Brown's desire, he wanted to add *music/entertainment* to his repertoire of business ventures, a desire eventually realized upon him duplicating what he had seen his mentor Claudius Massop, and his rival, Bucky Marshall themselves orchestrate years before – [The One Love Peace Concert].

REBUTTAL: Jim Brown's love for music may've been one hundred percent true, but what many say is also one hundred percent true, was that his desire and eventual investment in said industry, wasn't about the love for music, it was all about money. He had seen the impact of music, saw how it unified and even divided, and he also saw the business side of it. Some even went as far as saying that his true mission was to use music as a forum to celebrate himself and his exploits, while also making a profit in the process – **AND STILL OTHERS SAY**; Jim Brown venturing into this industry wasn't all that big of a deal to begin with [MOST DONS DID] – **and from all accounts, Jim Brown's entry into said industry was actually very simple and easy** - seeing that most of those involved in said industry at the time, viewed him as more than a don, going as far as even calling him *gods* – which is basically saying that he was the *god* for all *dons*. He wasn't just a *dads* [as dons were also affectionately called around that time], he was a *god* – The *god* for all *dads* and *dons*.

BOTTOMLINE: According to Jim Brown's *antagonists*, this was nothing more than another effort of accumulating wealth on his part; there was no real love for the music *per-se*. He was a hustler, and that's all he was doing upon getting involved in the music industry – *hustling*.

INVESTMENT: –Starting in the late eighties, Jim Brown and his Shower Posse affiliates orchestrated and funded an annual summer concert that showed just how well he had learnt the value of utilizing the financially viable medium of entertainment. His concept was *Champions in Action* - Yes [for those who weren't aware, and may've heard of Dudus' summer production of the same name] this was the same annual summer concert; resurrected by Dudus and his Presidential Click in the summer of 1999.

Jim Brown's Champions in Action was held at The Fort Clarence Beach in Portmore, St. Catherine, and was a literal spectacle of *bravado*. So much can be said about this event, but some of the major facts that shows just how *audacious* Jim Brown and his cronies were – are: *This event was one where gun salutes were no strange occurrence, even in the presence of law enforcement,* - these productions were littered with the best that Jamaican entertainment had to offer, from the likes of the legendary and internationally renowned, Grammy winning dancehall Artiste, Shabba Ranks, and dancehall legend and known dancehall rudeboy, Ninja Man, who; after making his way on stage and seeing the massive crowd of over 15, 000 patrons, (most of who were decked out in the traditional JLP colour of green – a clear territorial maker), was quoted as saying in his 1988 performance: *"Jim Brown shoulda get show fi di year fi dis yah show yah man."* -**Translated**: - *"Jim Brown should get show for the year for this show."* Once again a clear indicator of who this man was, and just how powerful he was, what he had achieved and how he was viewed in the streets of Jamaica, by even the most renowned of artistes of the day: – **AND JUST FOR THE RECORD,** Ninja Man was not the only artiste who went

Ninja Man – Champions in Action –1988

on stage and heaped praises on the head of the man who by now was listed on a Federal Indictment that accused him of being involved in over 1, 400 murders, and the smuggling and distribution of tons of narcotics into the United States.

- **SEE VIDEO CLIP ON YOUTUBE**: http://www.youtube.com/watch?v=RNNz-pSpCGo

NOTE: *Champions in Action under Jim Brown's direction was last staged in 1990 – Brown was arrested in 1991.*

Dudus was smart, but he wasn't a genius as many may have thought. He was just smart enough not to reinvent the wheel. Why should he, when the formula was already tested and proven, and now his to use?

The restaging of *Champions In Action* was Dudus' first move to legitimize himself on a larger and an even more global scale. By restaging this production, he not only solidify what was already his, (the streets), but he was also making a show to those abroad of just how powerful he was – a visual representation of his power, which brought to light the kind of power he obviously had to possess to pull off such a feat. **NOTE**: ALMOST EVERY JAMAICAN DANCEHALL ARTISTE OF NOTORIETY HAS PERFORMED ON *CHAMPIONS IN ACTION* – AT ONE TIME OR ANOTHER [Check the clips on YouTube].

SPECIAL NOTE: It has also been brought to our attention during the research and investigation for this volume that almost all the entertainers on these productions, have either performed for *free* or for a *snippet* of their usual performance fees, and in addition, entertainers have also been known to either reserve or cancel prior dates to facilitate performances on said shows, which if not done, was viewed as blatant disrespect towards *The President* and his cause.

It is said that artistes have even been severely beaten and *or* threatened for not performing on said shows. One story recalls the horrors of a top flight entertainer, who at his peak, claimed to have been too busy for such a performance around 2004 or 2005; a declaration that not only led to him being disciplined like a *baby*, but also came with the ego-deflating effect that has since led to his relocation to the more safer streets of South Florida.

Images of artistes have also been known to be used by the Presidential Click on promotional material without the knowledge or consent of said artistes or artistes' management; as apparently, *it is somehow supposed to be understood* that every year, this particular date should be reserved for The President - basically what some have categorized as the entertainers paying their *dues or presidential taxes.*

FACT: Regardless where one is from in Jamaica, the reputation of Tivoli Gardens is common knowledge. A reputation that has had such a diverse effect on the society of Jamaica and Jamaicans at large, that it is understandable that entertainers, who are mostly from garrisons of one sort or another, and who are knowledgeable of the politics of the streets, would not even make an attempt to resist such an advance and or request to perform on *The President's* shows, whenever such advances were made. So under these circumstances - if what is said is actually true, then such compliance would be very understandable.

DUDUS' *CHAMPIONS IN ACTION* - A Presidential Click Promotion; was a success out the gate, and *The President* was a rock star. Many even say this was when he was *unofficially* inaugurated; solidified by the masses and the entertainment industry at large. A key development that literally set him on course to becoming what many have said was the most powerful man in Jamaica before being brought down.

With the first staging of Champions in Action [*held at the same venue as his father's original production - Fort Clarence Beach – Portmore, St. Catherine*], pulling in an estimated 10, 000 plus patrons, paying JA$1, 000 for general admission; you do the math, that's over ten Million (tax-free) Jamaican Dollars, [a one-night intake] and this is without taking anything else into consideration – example, parking, booths rented to vendors, food, alcohol and other beverages.

...Dudus had arrived:

- Act II -

HIS NEXT POWER MOVE: Success is said to be the best form of motivation, and after the success of *Champions in Action* in 1999, Dudus was motivated. So much that he wasn't done, he was just getting started; again proving the type of don he was - a clear and  razor sharp cut above the rest – made even clearer, when in what could be described in no other way than true *Robin Hood-like* fashion, it is said that Dudus seemingly brought all the spoils of his effort back to Tivoli Gardens for distribution after said show.

This was a summer production, and that meant school was out and would be back in session come September [the start of the school year in Jamaica] - and Dudus knowing the burden such a time of the year usually meant for parents, did what many deemed a blessing from above. He supplied the majority of [and quite possibly all] the children in Tivoli Gardens with assistance to get back to school with all the necessary tools for their progress; *the start of what was to be an annual reality.*

This wasn't a Priest or some other holy man of God who was doing this, this was *Dudus*, a don who was running an organization that was said to be murderously notorious, but still this was what he did; an act that *seemed* both compassionate and caring. A literal unheard of, never before seen feat at the time, which once again, unknown to his now captive audience, was merely an additional instalment on their, (by now), already purchased - *hearts* and *minds*.

In addition to Dudus' own funds being used in this act of philanthropy, he also commissioned the assistance of his affiliates abroad, who again bought into his concept wholeheartedly, even joining in with contributions of their own, coming in both cash and kind.

Everyone got involved in the dons humanitarian effort, and Tivoli Gardens loved it. Critics however say acts such as this were all a ploy to manipulate and keep the masses in a *confused state of dependent stupor,* while a greater agenda was being pursued. Some have even suggested that all he was doing was merely one of those self righteous efforts aimed at feeling good about all the evil he and his cronies were doing.

But regardless which theory is true, one thing is sure, Dudus did do the above for his people; source of funds and reason behind his actions making no difference. According to all accounts, this is what Dudus did for the people of Tivoli Gardens... What no other don had done before.

-:*But Dudus Wasn't Done:*-

WEST KINGSTON JAMBOREE: With *Champions in Action* under his belt, Dudus now seemed unstoppable: - The turn out at his first production was a clear indicator of his power. His affiliates abroad were ecstatic, and as the new millennium inched closer, their support and respect for the don, many still didn't know, grew at a rather astonishing rate. A rate which not only brought in more money and gifts, but it also brought in more support than many may have even realized.

Doors opened and individuals quickly became more susceptible to Dudus' requests and suggestions, which quite often included the updating of *or* the addition of guns to the Tivoli Gardens arsenal, which was said to have been pitched under the guise of community protection [*not that there needed to be any real reason for such weapons anyway, because when it comes to the individuals in question, guns were their passion*]. In addition, and to Dudus' delight, soon more of his implants were being welcomed into the land of opportunity – The United States of America: THINGS WERE BEAUTIFUL. Dudus now had the full support of the masses, [both at home and abroad], the support of the entertainment industry, and at the same time, he had found yet another source to make the kind of money he needed to generate in order to support the status of being a don. And all this without almost *any* real political support; support, which (besides Mr. Seaga not being in Dudus' corner), would've more than likely been nothing much to begin with, since it was common knowledge amongst the Jamaican populace [back then] that he [Mr. Seaga] and the Jamaica Labour Party, were battling for political life, after dismal outings both in 1993 and 1997, when their political rivals, the PNP, [Peoples National Party] in 1993 walked away with 53 of the 60 parliamentary seats, and almost duplicated the same feat again in 1997, when they were again declared winners. This time taking 50 of the 60 parliamentary seats; ALL VAGUE COMPARISONS TO THE GLORY DAYS of 1980, when he [Mr. Seaga] was the captain of the landslide victory which landed his party in the drivers seat, only to outdo himself a few years later [1983] when the [JLP] Jamaica Labour Party WAS DECLARED THE WINNER OF *ALL* OF JAMAICA'S 60 PARLIAMENTARY SEATS – AFTER THE PNP BOYCOTTED THE THEN EARLY ELECTIONS.

BUT AS WAS SAID BEFORE, DUDUS WASN'T DONE: Dudus was now a *believer*. He had seen the kind of respect his generosity towards the children of his community had brought him, and upon quickly realizing that this was one of the key roadways to the *hearts* of the masses – He hastily embarked on a mission to go one step further - this time by playing *Santa Claus*.

The birth of *West Kingston Jamboree* came next – another of Dudus' innovative and (some say), manipulative venture, which again utilized the medium of entertainment.

West Kingston Jamboree was again not an original Dudus idea, but again he was responsible for its growth. In short, *West Kingston Jamboree* was a Christmas treat for the children of Tivoli Gardens, but with Dudus in the drivers seat, he not only redirected the vehicle, but he elevated what was once a small scale community effort, into a Christmas celebration of mega proportions.

Efforts of this nature [Christmas treats] were nothing new to the garrisons of Jamaica, but all these events were usually initiatives driven by political motivation, orchestrated by members of parliament or the community councillors, but with Dudus around, Tivoli Gardens had no need for such political charity or even consideration. They had a *President*, so even though the political party that they [Tivoli Gardens] supported was on life support, there was no need for the people to experience the same fate – such was Dudus' outlook, at least so it was reflected - but again a claim that is countered with a rebuttal to the tune of, '*all he was doing again was pulling one over on the people and increasing his power over them and onlookers in the process*'. THE REBUTTAL CONTINUES WITH ARGUMENTS SUCH AS: It's no enlightened new age realization that western society has set a precedence that has placed Christmas at the pinnacle of festive seasons, and it's also common knowledge that it is the desire of all parents to do for their children at this particular time of the year, in ways that they wouldn't, throughout the rest of the year. This is a reality, and another one of equal proportion is that most parents in the garrisons of Jamaica have a hard time doing for their children what is usually their hearts' desire around this time.

This was what it was, how it is and still is in many Jamaican and other neighbourhoods all over the world, and Western Kingston was no different, but Dudus was going to fix that problem. Again enlisting the assistance of those abroad who were more than willing *this time around* to assist in the (now successful) don's ventures, especially with him singing a song to the tune of; finally giving the children of the community a good Christmas, and doing so without the help of politicians, who never seem to ever be able to get it right anyway. This was the pitch, and since the situation was what it was; *with no real backing from Mr. Seaga,* - common knowledge to those in the know at the time - hesitation to join in and assist was almost none.

What was supposed to be a simple Christmas treat improved and evolved into the *West Kingston Jamboree*: A pre-Christmas event where the children of the community were given what not even many children from more privileged means were granted.

The children of Tivoli Gardens got some of the latest and best gifts being touted for the season, sent in mostly from those abroad, but distributed by Dudus and his Presidential Click. They were on the ground, so naturally the credit was theirs. The contributors abroad however could care less, they were just glad to be affiliated with the don directly, and as some have put it, relieved to be finally able to act as if their illegal and brutal acts really had some higher purpose behind them.

NOTE: In addition to the above mentioned help that Dudus enlisted to make *West Kingston Jamboree* a reality, what also needs to be noted here, is that in true Dudus fashion, [never missing an opportunity] he engaged in what could be termed; *'gentle extortion.'* A practice that was centered around reaching out to businesses, in and around the community for contributions towards the Christmas treat in their backyard. AND WITH THE NEIGHBOURHOOD MAKING THE REQUEST BEING TIVOLI GARDENS - contributions came with relative ease, both in cash and kind. In short, Dudus not only got help from his affiliates to push his agenda, but he also [under the guise of a Christmas treat, along with, and in some cases, a bit of intimidation], got the help of major businesses, who provided most of what was needed on the ground to make this a reality, and with help from abroad added – once again, Dudus was a hero.

This was *West Kingston Jamboree*, a Christmas treat like no other for the children of not only Tivoli Gardens, but West Kingston at large. Yet another deliberate move according to some, to as they say, extend his physical and mental reach with the generosity of gifts, a move which there was no denying - worked like a charm.

Everything was in place for these events: food was abundant, drinks were plentiful, there was an assortment of rides, and they even had a *Santa*. From the outside looking in, it was hard to not tip your hat at the effort. The children loved it, and the parents became Dudus loyalists without even realizing it, but what about the adults? Dudus saw it as only fair that after the children had a great day and got the desires of their hearts, it was time for the adults to have some fun themselves, so he added music - more and more each year. He invited affiliates, [other dons included], entertainers and even *politicians*, so they could all see first hand what he was doing for the community, and with that West Kingston Jamboree became a Christmas party for the underworld, their affiliates and sympathisers.

SHOW & TELL: See video clip on YouTube (link below) - of the 2009 staging of West Kingston Jamboree, where JLP [Jamaica Labour Party] Minister of Information – Daryl Vaz can be seen on stage - standing in the background at the beginning of clip (*with arms folded*) at 0:26 sec.

http://www.youtube.com/watch?v=qCQQhVfUj5U&feature=related

SPECIAL NOTE: This was December, 2009 – this was a *Presidential Click* production - and *Dudus* was already a known wanted man.

Music was an essential part of the setting from the start, and since Dudus already had easy access to entertainers, who were all in awe of him, it's almost as though there was a rush to grace the *President's stage* and perform for the people of Tivoli Gardens and Western Kingston, who had become literal symbols for the downtrodden, who refused to stay down - and just like that - *West Kingston Jamboree,* [a FREE annual event for both children and adults alike, with an impressive line-up of Jamaica's best entertainers to top it off] became what it eventually became...Another production under the belts of *Dudus* and the *Presidential Click.*

Who else could have orchestrated such an event?

PROGRESSIVE EVOLUTION: There was a time when parting downtown was a literal *no-no*, but Dudus changed all that. Tivoli Gardens was a safe zone. Cars were left unlocked and not disturbed, unheard of in any other garrison community. No one got robbed and *or* bothered at these events – one such event being the world famous *Passa Passa* weekly street dance. Dudus had created a Mecca, a Gangster Utopia – but even with this achieved, he still wasn't done.

– Act III –

STRONGER: Every move after that made by Dudus was another that contributed to his increase on, and of power. He was a maverick, he had the Midas touch. He said *'money ova war'* and backed it up: Everything he touched turned to gold. And all this without the usual violence that is often times

associated with Jamaican dons. Dudus had the best of both worlds – he was *feared* and *respected* – and above that, the masses *loved* him.

Almost overnight, Dudus became a magnet of admiration, and association with him was now suddenly desired by many; one such person it is said was local West Kingston businessman, Justin O'Glivie.

At the time of Dudus' rise to power, O'Glivie had been in the business of construction for years, and is said to have been an associate of Dudus' late father, Jim Brown. We were unable to actually confirm such claims, but what we did confirm is of equal intrigue.

For as long as there has been garrisons in Jamaica, dons have always had their hands in the construction and development of both community and private projects, in and around their realm of power; that's just the way it was, and still is to some extent – even though most dons had no formal training in this vocation, and at the same time, most weren't even legal contractors to begin with. Most in this field were mere labourers, so in all truth, this was their *forte*, but even so, that's where their level of expertise stopped, but still they oftentimes than not, ended up being in control of major construction projects, [financially and otherwise] and in West Kingston, it was no different. And this was the capacity it is said that O'Glivie had always operated in, and was determined to continue operating in - as Dudus rose to prominence.

Justin O'Glivie was one of the few contractors in the community that was both skilled and legitimate. He was also one of the *originals* who got along with everyone he needed to get along with, and at the same time, he was no threat. His expertise, along with the influence and force of the dons, who could often times secure these contracts just by showing up or sending a message, was like a match made in heaven – YOU SCRATCH MY BACK AND I WILL SCRATCH YOURS. They [the

Justin O'Glivie [seated-left] of Incomparable Enterprise: - Government contract signing at the Ministry of Transports and Works St. Andrew office - Tues. Dec 23rd 08

dons] needed him [O'Glivie], and he needed them.

O'Glivie like most West Kingston residents and affiliates had seen Dudus at work, and was almost certainly an admirer, but O'Glivie was no groupie, he was a businessman, and instantly saw the potential benefit of permanent association.

From all accounts, O'Glivie liked Dudus' fire, but he also knew it had to be quenched. There were way better ways to approach things. And with him being who he was, it wasn't long before he sought

Justin O'Glivie - in front of one of his many business places located on Spanish Town Road [Said to be joint owned by him and Dudus]

137

audience with the don, (*whose style, it is said he was also a fan of, from a personal prospective*), and just like that, upon securing that meeting, O'Glivie walked away a business partner; becoming one of the key pieces in the jigsaw of Tivoli Gardens and Christopher Coke's power structure.

- **NAME OF COMPANY**: - Incomparable Enterprise.
- **TYPE OF BUSINESS**: - Construction.
- **ADDRESS**: 45 Spanish Town Road, Kingston 14.

NOTE: Unlike his father who was known to be flamboyant, Dudus was the total opposite; of a very low keyed demeanour, very much unlike the dons of his era and was said to be more interested in doing big things, opposed to merely being seen - *as* the big thing.

INTERESTING FACT: Unknown to many, Dudus was very much into subliminal messages and symbolism. CASE IN POINT: *The Presidential Click*: A name which depicted who they thought they were and the office they felt they apparently held. This is also true for his personal title: *The President*. And the same was true with the name he chose for his and O'Glivie's company – *Incomparable Enterprise*. ALL NAMES CLOTHED IN BLATANT SUBLIMINAL EFFORTS OF SYMBOLISIM.

INCOMPARABLE ENTERPRISE was a fruitful partnership from the start. O'Glivie had the skill and the tools, and Dudus had the man power and the influence -aka - the intimidating factor.

The Tivoli Gardens factor got *Incomparable Enterprise* many of its early contracts, but as good as that may've been, it simply wasn't enough; not for Dudus who always had his sights set on more lofty undertakings.

Independent contracts were good, but Dudus had heard and learned of better; *Government contracts* were the way to go - but with their political allegiance out of power, there was a roadblock in obtaining such lucrative agreements. All the contracts it seemed were going to the PNP [People's National Party] affiliated contractors. And with this perception, Dudus embarked on what could've been deemed *a novel quest* at the time: **GETTING THE JLP** [Jamaica Labour Party] **BACK IN POWER**.

According to all accounts, this was Dudus' perception, ultimate solution and eventual aim: If he was in it, he was going to win it, and for him to win like he was sure he could, he had to have his people - or at least the people under his spell - in the positions of power - that really mattered.

POLITICS BECAME A MAJOR ISSUE: Prior to this, Dudus' interest in politics was minimal, but with this new realization, the fashion and pace was dramatic at which all that changed. BUT THERE WAS A PROBLEM - and he had a name – Mr. Edward Phillip George Seaga.

The Jamaica Labour Party may not have been in power for years, but Mr. Seaga was still the leader of the *embattled* party, even though many say, and evidence also suggests that the Jamaican electorate was not interested in re-electing him leader of their country. **EVIDENCE**: The Jamaican populace made their feelings known -*election after election since 1989 at the time* - by the continued choosing of the PNP [People's National Party], even after constant missteps, simply because like many Jamaicans say, they were *the lesser of two evils.*

With Dudus and Mr. Seaga at odds for years, and the political climate in Jamaica being what it was at the time, instead of trying to mend an old broken fence, Dudus; now aware of the importance of political power and backing, was soon forming new alliances within the ranks of the Jamaica Labour Party. A development that created a windfall of changes that eventually led to Mr. Seaga resigning from the party's leadership position; turning over the reigns to the Hon. Bruce Golding [Jamaica's present Prime Minster-2011].

SPECIAL NOTE: In the ranks of the JLP [Jamaica Labour Party], Tivoli Gardens was Tivoli Gardens – a dedicated stronghold where the votes were guaranteed – a reality that was said to be the envy and desire of all political representatives. And in the realm of *dons*, Dudus was also *Dudus*, somewhat of a necessary evil, but one said to have also been envied by most political representatives; his ill repute making very little difference whatsoever.

IT IS SAID that soon after the previously mentioned realization, Dudus embarked on a campaign for ultimate take over of his new goal, The Jamaica Labour Party [JLP], an effort which it is said, included a successful effort to demonize Mr. Seaga amongst his peers – planting seeds that went to the tune of, *'for the JLP to ever win a general election again, they could not do so with Mr. Seaga at the head of the party.'* A suggestion that wasn't too far fetched from reality, if we were to take into consideration a track record of constant electorate defeats that spanned over a decade at the time being discussed. This it is said was the *crux* of Dudus' campaign of demonization – a realistic and almost undeniable assessment, which also came with the stroking of the egotistical desires for leadership, which reside in all politicians, who from a point of analytical *retrospect*, bought into what he was selling with relative ease - *they longed for the taste of power.*

NOTE: *Prior to the JLP's 2007 victory at the polls, their last general election victory at the polls was way back in 1983.*

We have all heard the saying, *'if you can't beat them, join them,'* but with Dudus, there was an interesting twist to his take on the all too familiar adage. With him it was, *'if they don't want to join you, destroy them.'* And that is exactly what it is said Dudus did to Mr. Seaga politically – by forming alliances with other party members who saw his outlook as the way forward. And with this achieved, soon *The Theory According to Dudus* was being heralded as the greatest moment of enlightenment since Galileo's - *Dialogo.*

NEWS REPORTS HAVE CIRCULATED that Dudus was instrumental in the JLP's resurgence as victors at the polls in 07– and from all indications, it appear that these accusations and assumptions do hold some weight, because ACCORDING TO THE STREETS, it was Dudus who was responsible for the reshuffling of the party's cabinet, which ultimately led to their victory in 2007 over the then *incumbent*, Hon. Portia Simpson-Miller.

The general consensus among many Jamaicans is that *Dudus* influenced the key players, by simply showing them what they already knew - the Jamaican electorate was *fed up* with Mr. Seaga, and if they [the JLP] were to win, they needed to reshuffle the cabinet and get rid of Mr. Seaga in the process. Such a suggestion was almost *blasphemous*, this was Mr. Seaga, he had been there from day one, and here it was, the very *don* from his own constituency suggesting that they get rid of him to move forward; this was *preposterous!* However it made sense, especially with most already not seeing eye to eye with the aging leader, and also having their own agendas that were not being realized because of the position of opposition that they were in.

DUDUS WAS MAKING SENSE: His plot was simple, get rid of him [Mr. Seaga] and I will give you the desires of your hearts, not the people *per se*, but their votes – and not just the votes and people of Tivoli Gardens or West Kingston either, but he was offering constituencies that weren't even on the JLP's radar, and in addition, there was also talk of constituencies that had lost the dedicated political luster they were once known to possess. BUT HOW COULD HE DO ANY OF THIS IF THOSE IN THE RESPECTIVE POLITICAL POSITIONS WERE UNABLE TO? THE ANSWER IS SIMPLE: Dudus had the streets, he wasn't just a *don*, he was *The President* - the *man* who was the *man*, even above the other dons from their individual communities. IN THE STREETS, he called the shots – it was that simple, so his proposal wasn't some pipe dream. If he said it, he more than likely could deliver it. That was his reputation, and everyone knew it, accepted it and believed in it.

Dudus could influence what went on in zones not even familiar to him physically – that was no military secret – this was common knowledge in the streets. Then to top all that, Dudus also had the admiration and minds of the common man from all over Jamaica. Everyone had heard of his exploits, he was both feared and revered. Tivoli Gardens had crowned him, and the streets adored him, even if they didn't know him. [*Somewhere on his way to the throne, Dudus became the symbol of every inner-city youth's victory over a system designed to keep them submerged*].

By 2002, Tivoli Gardens was the *envy* of all garrisons - [it was rent free, there were no utility bills, your children were provided for, you did as you pretty much pleased, there was always something to do, and violence and security were no longer issues of concern – THE REGULAR BURDENS OF SOCIETY WERE REMOVED]. And almost everyone, from every garrison, near and far, wanted a piece of the pie, and since Dudus was selling; just like the politicians - all his admirers were buying.

This is what it's said Dudus offered - *himself, his power, his influence* – and from all indicators, it was bought, lock-stock-and-barrel.

SHOW AND TELL: Dudus was selling and almost everyone was buying, but the proof like it is said, *is always in the pudding*, and it wasn't long before the Jamaica Labour Party [JLP] got their first *sample delivery* of what Dudus was selling - when it is alleged that his backing in The Local Government Elections of 2003, led to a landslide victory for the Jamaica Labour Party – convincing everyone, from the politician to the technician, and from the preacher to the teacher - that he indeed wasn't *all bark and no bite*.

LOCAL GOVERNMENT ELECTIONS in Jamaica is just what the title suggests; an election that focuses on putting candidates in place to oversee the portfolio of local duties; ie. Road repairs, social services, etcetera.

In other words, the JLP was finally in the position to facilitate the desires of Dudus' heart; they could now issue the types of contracts that he was yearning to get his hands on: – THAT'S ALL THIS WAS ABOUT FOR HIM – NOTHING MORE – NOTHING LESS.

TIPPING THE ELECTION: It is said that Dudus and his cronies set out deliberately to *tip* the election of June 2003 – (in the JLP's favour) - as a sign of good will, just to show that his proposal wasn't just all talk. This was achieved [the tipping of the election] mostly by voter intimidation, sporadic acts of violence, and the age old formula of persuading the desperate with a few dollars; purchasing votes for *pennies*. It is also believed that this was a personal financial investment on Dudus' part; using *his own money* in this colossal effort. An effort for which the Jamaica Labour Party; much like the people of West Kingston, would forever be indebted.

THE VOTES WERE IN: The JLP may not have been in charge of the country at this time, but they were in charge of enough, at least enough that mattered to Dudus, who is said to have also made another key move that solidified his grip on power even more: It is talked of in certain circles that he got Desmond Mckenzie elected Mayor of Kingston and St. Andrew, an accusation blatantly denied by His Worship, but an accusation which if true, would explain the grip and control maintained on the downtown, Kingston region of the city of Kingston; specifically by residents of Western Kingston.

FACT: *Prior to this appointment [becoming Mayor], Desmond McKenzie - a resident of Western Kingston, was a Councillor for the community of Denham Town from 1977 to 1984, and Councillor of*

Tivoli Gardens from 1990, eventually elevating to the rank of Junior Spokesman of the Opposition in the Senate [2002-2003].

With Dudus' part of the deal upheld, it was time for payback, and according to local published reports, this came in hefty government sanctions:

Exhibit C

Excerpt below taken from local Jamaican report published [May 16' 2010]:

- *Since taking over central and local government administrations, the Coke's company has been awarded over $100 million dollars in state contracts, excluding, the latest contract on Washington Boulevard. Records from the Kingston & St Andrew Corporation and the Office of the Contractor General show that the contracts were awarded after the ruling Jamaica Labour Party took over parish council in 2003, and August 2009.*

  Less than a year after assuming power, the Government awarded the company a number of lucrative contracts, which, by August last year [2009], amounted to approximately $71,754,897.49 in contracts endorsed by the National Contracts Commission.

Contracts awarded to Incomparable Enterprise included one to construct a monument for fourth Prime Minister and former leader of the JLP, the late Hugh Lawson Shearer, at a cost of $4,602,848. This monument was constructed at the National Heroes Circle burial ground for the nation's heroes and statesmen.

There are indications that there is an unofficial policy where contracts for projects in the downtown Kingston area are awarded to that company, which has been awarded close to $30 million by the Kingston

& *St. Andrew Corporation (KSAC) since the Jamaica Labour Party took control of the council in 2003.*

The company was also the recipient of a $16.9 million contract in November 2008 to repair the historic Ward Theatre, also located in downtown Kingston.

In 2008 the National Works Agency (NWA) awarded Incomparable Enterprise a contract for over $28 million to repair the Tivoli Gully, which encircles Tivoli Gardens, where Coke has his headquarters. The OCG 2008 report stated that the company was contracted to do emergency Hurricane Gustav repair work to the reinforced concrete retaining wall and to slab the gully.

A contract for $18.4 million was awarded to refurbish the building and modification including the removal and replacement of fixtures fitting to the canteen at the Ministry of Education. In August 2008, Incomparable Enterprise was awarded a contract for $2.7 million for the lease of heavy-duty equipment.

_____End of Excerpt

NOTE: Monetary figures in above excerpt represented in Jamaican dollars

THE EVIDENCE SPEAKS FOR ITSELF: And with *'The Theory According To Dudus'* now a tested and proven reality, it wasn't long before there was disparity in the ranks of the Jamaica Labour Party, which led to what many have described behind closed doors, as the *ousting* of Mr. Seaga, who ACCORDING TO THE STREETS, was replaced by the handpicked Bruce Golding; handpicked by none other than Christopher Dudus Coke himself; which [if true] was another clear indicator of defiance towards Mr. Seaga, who after being outnumbered, still made one last attempt of being somewhat in control by turning over his constituency to his protégé, Olivia 'Babsy' Grange, [current Minister of Culture, Youth and Sports – 2011]; but according to all accounts - Dudus would have none of it!

He was in-charge of Tivoli Gardens, in-charge of Western Kingston, and he wanted someone of his liking in-charge politically, not a person placed there by Mr. Seaga, and especially not his protégé.

CLARIFICATION: Truth *was* - Dudus wanted someone in charge whom he felt he could control, and by giving that person an electoral seat as secure as Western Kingston; the person being indebted for the rest of his or her political career, was a no brainer, and the deeper in debt he got such a person, the better it was for him. That's all it was about - what worked and benefited Dudus - bottom-line.

2005: The seeds of discontent amongst the JLP members matured, and in 2005, Mr. Seaga released the reigns of the Jamaica Labour Party, reluctantly into the hands of the Hon. Bruce Golding, who two years later [2007], was elected Prime Minister of Jamaica; the first time in over 20 years that the Jamaica Labour Party had won a general election. A vision turned reality, and orchestrated [allegedly] by none other than *The President* himself - he was on top of his world.

RICH AND INFAMOUS: Dudus' *strategic* and *insatiable* traits had made him a very powerful man. His craftiness had enriched him greatly and by the time the man took office, who many say was his handpicked

Prime Minster, [Bruce Golding] Dudus was at the top of his game; *mind on is money and his money on his mind* – constantly.

Things changed rapidly, and everything seemed automatic. The word *wrong* didn't seem as though it was a part of Dudus' vocabulary when it came to the moves he was making. Whatever he did, worked!

HE [DUDUS] INVESTED HEAVILY: Into gas stations, heavy equipment, real estate development, land acquisition, entertainment, the hardware industry, fast food franchise, car dealerships, a security company, massage parlous, restaurants, bars, variety stores, beauty shops and beauty supply stores. He even got into the importing industry [a guise many say was used to smuggle weapons into the island]. There was a loan company, and he even had his hand in the transportation sector, and there were even investments in the agriculture industry and a host of other minor ventures. Still, the most *interesting* of them all, is quite possible his investment in funeral homes.

Dudus was into everything that could make him a dollar. He may not have known anything about a particular line of business, but if you did, and sounded as though you knew what you were talking about - he was always willing to take a chance. THEN AGAIN, he had plenty of money to spare, and he was who he was, so if you had the opportunity to pitch your business idea to him, the rest went without saying. **NOTE**: Businessman, *yes*, but Dudus was still who he was…A don, *The President,* who beyond the seemingly humble demeanour, was said to be one of the world's most notorious drug dealers, who ran his kingdom with a fist of iron. A fact said to be well known in the streets – so playing with him wasn't even a thought for most.

SPREADING OF WINGS: Never one to be flamboyant, except for his personal hillside residence (photo inserted below) and modes of transportation (all inserted on following page), which elevated to high performance motorcycles, BMWs and Range Rovers, even with his new found wealth, Dudus changed very little else in his personal department, but what *changed* was his focus, his drive and his overall aim. With power increased, Dudus now saw more, and what he saw, he wanted. No longer was his vision limited to Tivoli Gardens, West Kingston or even Kingston for that matter, he saw more - way more –

and from all investigations, he not only wanted what he saw, he went after it.

With Dudus able to achieve all he had done in such a short period of time, [when compared to the dons

before him], he appeared and literally felt invincible, and with him already having other dons and community leaders under his spell, it wasn't long before Dudus embarked on a mission that resembled ones made years before by U.S. real estate tycoon; Donald Trump.

Dudus had seen the value of being into construction, but he had also seen the value of being involved in business ventures of varied sorts. It was simply a matter of supply and demand, and since most people everywhere desired much of the same things; duplicating what was already tested and proven, was once again a no-brainer. And with that, it's rumoured that business ventures financed by Dudus and his Presidential Click, were soon popping up all over, and not just in the city of Kingston, but all over Jamaica, namely; Spanish Town, Clarendon, St. Ann, and even as far as Jamaica's second city, Montego Bay.

Soon the *Dudus* influence was everywhere. He had perfected the formula for ghetto survival, and soon his blueprint was being replicated all over, closely reflecting what he had *seemingly* perfected in Western Kingston.

Under *'The Theory According to Dudus'* dons went from being known as mere contrivances of violence, to pillars of communities - reinvented into businessmen by the key architect himself.

-:*Money Ova War:*- This was his cry, and he was backing it up. Dudus saw opportunity in every situation. What others saw as obstacles, he saw as stepping stones, and with this outlook, he bought and remodelled several old and idle structures in numerous communities, and in some cases, he and his cronies just took them over [this was

Dudus and *The Presidential Click*, so who was going to oppose them?]

From all signals, Dudus gradually became very passionate about the business of construction. He now had both the money and vision to create almost any reality that his mind could conceive, and from all the evidence gathered - that's exactly what he did. Most dons lacked the shrewdness that Dudus possessed, plus they were all in awe of him, literally under his spell, so what he said was almost never opposed, plus - with him empowering the dons by giving them the perceived ownership, and - *or* overseeing rights,

there was very little issue - *if any* - with what he decided. And this led to Dudus becoming the shadow owner of several community business developments that included most of what was previously mentioned: Wholesales, restaurants, sport bars, etcetera. There have also been reports where he would inject money into struggling ventures – walking away a *percentage stake holder* in said entities.

<u>INTERESTING NOTE</u>: Just to give a CLEAR EXAMPLE of the presumptuousness of the individuals in question - right across from Tivoli Gardens, on Spanish Town Road, on the very building (commercial space) said to be owned by Dudus and Justin O'Glivie, sits the *Jah-T Wholesale* – blatancy, maybe, but quite possibly another symbolic gesture aimed at keeping the legacy of the Coke dynasty alive. It was neither established nor existed during Jah-T's lifetime.

NOWHERE WAS OFF LIMITS: It is said that Dudus' business interests spanned from the Capital City of Kingston, all the way to, and along the Mandela Highway, stopping in Portmore and the old Capital of Spanish Town, before heading on to the Bustamante Highway, reaching into places such as Clarendon and Mandeville, before continuing along the coast all the way to Montego Bay, with pit stops in Negril, before heading along the newly paved highway that now outlines Jamaica's north coast, and arriving at another one of Jamaica's *pristine* tourist attractions and locations; the world famous, Ocho Rios. The training wheels were off – *The Theory According to Dudus* was everywhere - seeds were planted, roots had dug deep into the earth, and fruits were being produced.

AND THE MORE HE THRIVED, SO DID TIVOLI: It didn't take long for Dudus to become a literal multi millionaire, and he lived the role he had assumed to the fullest - *The President* - but along the way, he never once forgot the people.

According to one female, *"Presi was always for the people, is a man wha wi keep a stage show and carry di whole a di money come gi wey to the people dem, a so dem man dey do dem ting, is always bout di people dem an di yute dem fi dem man dey."* **TRANSLATED**: "Presi was always for the people, he is the type of person who will keep a stage show and take all the money right back here and give it to the people. That's just the way he was, that's how he did his thing, with him it was always about the people and the children."

FROM INVESTIGATIONS, statements of that nature and context were not devised to just cast a shadow of deception over Dudus' reputation and mysticism, as evidence proves that he was indeed famous for such acts of philanthropy. BUT TO EVERY ACT THERE IS AN INTENTION. Although there is no denying the claims of the people, what many did not realize is that when Dudus displayed such acts of mindboggling generosity, he simply did it because he could, and not just because he wanted to. This may've all seemed like an elaborate sacrifice on his part, but regardless of the assumption, or how it might have appeared, truth was, it was NOTHNG TO HIM – AND AT THE SAME TIME – as much love as he professed for the people - evidence and those closest to him, testify to a Dudus that was more self-seeking opposed to being anything but a *Samaritan*.

'Sure he gave to the have nots, and sure he did all that people say he did, but he also did much more, and it wasn't all good, and whenever he did anything, whatever he did was always nothing compared to what he really could have done,' states one obviously bitter Western Kingston resident, who we will call Trevor; -(not his real name)- TREVOR CONTINUES: *"Everybody talk good bout di man, and mi nah sey him nuh do good, 'cause him do good, but at di same time, a him same one responsible fi all di death and destruction wha unuh si gwaan inna Western Kingston and nuff oddah part a Jamaica, so mek wi call a spade a spade."* **TRANSLATED**: *"Everyone talks well about Dudus, and I am not saying that he didn't do good, because he did, but at the same time, he is also responsible for all the death and destruction in West Kingston and other parts of Jamaica, so let's call a spade a spade."*

TREVOR CONTINUES: *"Yuh a hear mi, Presi a politician, dem man dey ting set different, dem man dey care fi self more dan people, him jus* *know how fi mek it look good, cause bigman ting, if di man did care bout wi like him sey, him nuh shoulda deal wid di ting different wha day man...A nuff people drop out enuh mi don, and fi wha?, di people dem still come fi him, so mi nuh know..."* **TRANSLATED:** *"Listen, Dudus is a politician, his thing is just different, but it's about self with him more than it is about people, he just knows how to make it look good, because let's face the facts, if he really cared for us like he said he did, wouldn't he have dealt with things in a different manner the other day, one that wouldn't have come at the cost of so many lives, especially since the people still came and got him, anyway."*

Opinions about Dudus differ like night and day, but when it comes to his philanthropy, such acts cannot be denied. Dudus did do for the people – **BUT ON THE FLIP SIDE,** many are saying that when he did, he did it after he secured himself, or because he had so much - giving at that stage just seemed like the right thing to do. Then there are those who say that his efforts were all manipulative – all for show – he did them to look good – did them to buy hearts, minds and blind dedication. And still there are those who say, *do the math*:- **IF** Dudus was getting multimillion dollar contracts from the government of Jamaica – **IF** Dudus was the arms and drug trafficker his indictment says he is – **IF** Dudus was the don he was said to be, who got all the gifts and tributes from abroad to disperse to his benefit – **IF** Dudus was the businessman it is said he was, making the kind of money it is presumed he did – *IF any or all of the above is true* - was true or remains true, **THEN WHAT WOULD A COUPLE MILLION JAMAICAN DOLLARS BE; DISBURSED AMONG TIVOLI GARDENS RESIDENTS. ESPECIALLY AFTER MAKING SUCH MONIES FROM STAGE SHOWS TO BEGIN WITH, WHICH COULD BE LOOKED AT AS A LITERAL TAKING OF MONEY FROM THE POOR AND GIVING BACK TO THE POOR – SEEING THAT THEY WERE THE ONES WHO PATRONIZED SUCH EVENTS TO BEGIN WITH. SO WITH THAT SAID, THE QUESTION SOME ARE STILL AWAITING AN ANSWER FOR IS: DID DUDUS REALLY DO ANYTHING FOR THE PEOPLE LIKE IT IS PRESUMED HE DID, OR DID HE JUST DISTRACT THEM WITH TRINKETS WHILE ADVANCING HIS OWN CAUSE?**

Act IV

-: *Violence During Dudus' Reign:-*

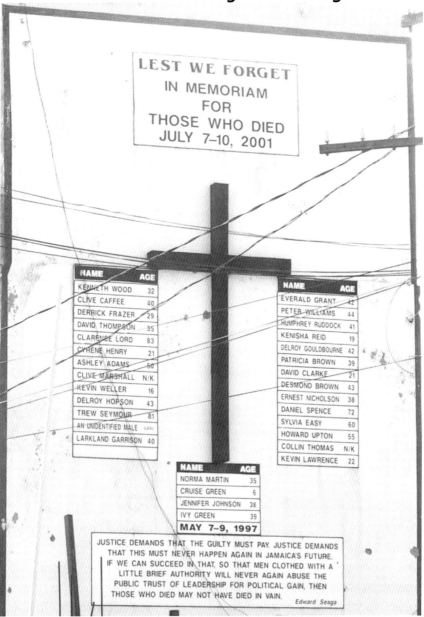

A HUGE BLACK CROSS greets on-comers at the corner of Darling Street and Spanish Town Road in West Kingston; a haunting reminder - (seen in photo on previous page) - which bears testimony to two unfortunate, unforgettable and life-changing events in the history of Tivoli Gardens.

'LEST WE FORGET' is a huge mural imprinted with the names of 31 persons killed in clashes with the security forces during operations in that specific community.

In 2001, twenty-five residents; one soldier and a police officer were killed, after the police and the defence force entered the Tivoli Gardens community in what was explained to the public as a search for guns and wanted men. The stand-off lasted three days, from July 7-10, and was regarded as the darkest spot in the history of West Kingston, *up until* the incursion of the security forces in search of Christopher *'Dudus'* Coke in May of 2010, which left an official report of seventy-four civilians dead.

NOTE: A report blatantly *rejected* by former Member of Parliament of said community for 43 years, and former leader of the Jamaica Labour Party, Mr. Seaga – who was adamant in his claim on national television that the number was actually over one hundred in just *one section*, and maybe even as high as one hundred and fifty in total, if the bodies were ever recovered and counted. Mr. Seaga went on to say in said interview that his account [his opposing number of those killed compared to official reports] QUOTE: *"Is from knowledge that I have, and knowledgeably have."*

- **See Video clip on YouTube:**

  http://www.youtube.com/watch?v=Ua5mi5uOmLY

THE OTHER FOUR RESIDENTS LISTED ON THE MURAL were killed during an operation of a similar nature in the community of Tivoli Gardens - May 7-9, 1997; an incident also referred to by Mr. Seaga in above mentioned interview.

One year after the infamous 2001 shootings, Edward Seaga, then Member of Parliament, said the events *scared the people* of West Kingston.

"It will be difficult for the people to forget or forgive the planner and the executioner of this atrocity," Seaga was quoted as saying.

ADDITIONAL ACCOUNT AND DETAILS ABOUT SAID INCIDENT: On Saturday July 7, 2001, police entered Tivoli Gardens in West Kingston, looking for guns that was said to have killed William *'Willy Haggart'* Moore, the leader of the nearby Arnett Gardens' [a People's National Party stronghold], Black Roses Crew. Moore's death had led to weeks of intermittent gang violence between supporters of both parties in the West Kingston, Hannah Town and Denham Town communities. It is said that after finding only one gun during the search of Tivoli, the security forces were asked by residents to leave. The lawmen however weren't too enthused by their request, and according to residents, began shooting up the area. Some residents recall horrifying memories of law enforcement officers – who after locking down the area, started shooting anyone leaving their homes, and at times even shooting into homes – acts which were *said* to be done even with the presence of rolling television cameras. In the first wave of violence it's reported that 20 residents, one cop and one soldier died. Overnight road blocks went up in areas in close proximity to the action, causing somewhat of a ripple effect across the city's garrisons.

Meanwhile, bodies from the warfare mounted and were left rotting on the streets until Tuesday [*two days in between*]. Families and even the Red Cross

Hell breaks loose in West Kingston

were *said* to be prevented from taking bodies to the morgue by shots from what was said to be police sniper fire. It wasn't until a fact-finding mission by *'neutral'* Kingston businessmen entered Tivoli, accompanied by television crews, that the streets became safe enough for people to leave their homes, for the first time in days. Among the bodies collected were those of 4 persons, believed to have succumbed to their deaths, as a result of a combination of fear, dehydration, heart-attacks and hunger, as many had not eaten since the previous Friday when they could last leave their homes. This included children, one of whom was wounded, said to have been shot whilst in her bed; eventually bleeding to death.

The Tivoli Gardens saga is epic – and the evidence is staggering as to how this part of this city was actually ran, and ran under whose orders. The headlines of Jamaica's newspapers are no strangers to reports surrounding Tivoli Gardens and their exploits – as the following excerpt, taken from the local Jamaican tabloid – The Star – May 13th 2005 – will solidify even further.

Tivoli Split

A RIFT HAS reportedly developed in the leadership of the Tivoli Gardens community in West Kingston following last week's killing of three policemen, THE WEEKEND STAR has learnt.

*The rift is reportedly between Dudus, the community's top man and one of his brothers called 'Livity', an area leader, **THE WEEKEND STAR** understands.*

*Residents of the area tell **THE WEEKEND STAR** that the rift developed after Dudus expressed dissent at the killing of the three cops. They say the top man has stated that the killing of the cops was "eediat ting" and was never to have happened.*

Disassociate self

"Yeah man, the dads vex and seh him disassociate himself from wah gwaan," a resident said. "Is like di whole ting treten fi split a whole family."

The residents fear the rift between both men could split the community in two, as both men are well respected in the area, and this is something they say West Kingston cannot afford.

Both men are sons of the late Lester Lloyd 'Jim Brown' Coke, but have different mothers. However, Livity and Christopher 'Chris Royal' Coke, one of the two men killed by police last week for the killing of one of the policemen, share the same mother.

Upset over cops' murders

In the meantime, the residents say they too, like the rest of Jamaica, are upset about the killing of the policemen. "Mi sorry seh dem kill di police because dem nuh do wi nutten," one resident said. Another resident of Tivoli Gardens said the community does not have anything against the police and would not hurt them. "Wi and di police nuh have nutten," he said.

Since the killings, West Kingston has been the target of several police operations as police say intelligence has indicated that the cop killers may have come from that constituency.

Police linked the cops' death to the killing of Chris Royal and Devon 'Zion Train' Griffiths, another leader from the area, who was also shot dead following a shoot out with members of the security forces. Since Griffiths' killing, information was leaked that 15 soldiers and 10 cops would be killed in retaliation.

Police say Royal and the man with whom he was killed, were reportedly making good on this threat when they killed Corporal Hewitt Chandler. When word of Royal's killing reached West Kingston, the Cross Roads Police Station was shot up during a drive-by and District Constable Canute Brown was shot dead.

Not long after, Inspector Lascelles Walsh was shot dead on his way to work. A policeman was also shot and injured by gunmen while doing beat duties in Greenwich Town, St. Andrew. Police have since held one man in connection with Walsh's killing.

_____End of Excerpt

EXCEPT FOR INCIDENTS OF THIS NATURE, VIOLENCE DURING DUDUS' REIGN was limited when compared to other eras and under the leadership of previous dons. This was a time, [first in Jamaica's modern history] that Tivoli Gardens, West Kingston and downtown Kingston at large, experienced relative peace, and it was said that Dudus was the cause of all that.

Guns were around, that was a given, but the guns were under control. *'The Theory According to Dudus'* was simple; *guns needed to be around, but should only be used when it is a necessity that cannot be avoided*:– And add his clincher - *money ova war* - to the conversation, and what you have was a stimulating cocktail of convincing rationale; *'money and blood don't mix.'*

This was a reality that *everyone*, even the most seasoned killers could relate to, and from all indicators, they bought into Dudus' philosophy without a hitch. However *on the flip side of that coin*, it is said that another reason there was relatively no violence in and around Tivoli Gardens during Dudus' reign, was because (although not made public until recently), Tivoli Gardens actually had their own system of justice, and everyone inside that *jurisdiction*, pretty much accepted it; whether by force, or by choice, but once again the evidence gives a chilling idea of the reality *inside* Tivoli Gardens.

Exhibit E

Gruesome Find

The following except is taken from another daily Jamaican newspaper – The Jamaica Observer - June 6, 2010:

KINGSTON - The gruesome discovery by security forces of shallow graves - one with the body of a person who was buried standing - and a suspected torture chamber was shared with journalists covering the ongoing search of Tivoli Gardens on Friday.

The tour was conducted more than a week after gunmen engaged the authorities in three days of clashes that resulted in the

deaths of 73 people, among them a soldier.

Jamaica Defence Force soldiers told the Observer on Friday that they stumbled upon the graves during a search of an area in the community called Rasta City, located off McKenzie Drive.

"The area is believed to be a location where thugs would dump and bury the bodies of people killed in the community of Tivoli Gardens," one soldier told the Observer.

At least six shallow graves were observed by the Observer reporter in a clearing surrounded by thick, overgrown vegetation which made the trek to the spot difficult.

"Look at this," one soldier said, pointing to a hole with the remains of the person who was buried standing.

The soldiers speculated that the person was buried alive.

The strong stench of dead flesh rose from the ground where the soldiers also said they found the decomposed body of a man buried in another shallow grave in an old, abandoned train car.

Police and soldiers also showed journalists what they believe was a torture chamber in a section of Tivoli called Java.

"The 'chamber' is an area where we believe people were dragged to and then tried in informal court sessions by thugs," one member of the security forces said.

A soldier, who declined to give his name because he was not authorised to speak, showed reporters two small buildings from where the authorities suspected that death sentences were handed down.

"The man them [criminals] even had two gavels used in the informal court," said one soldier.

A bloodstained metal baseball bat, two lengths of rope, each tied in a noose at the top of a door, were seen in the suspected torture chamber. Sections of the floor were covered with thick lumps of partially dried blood. The stench of urine hung heavily in the air.

"The find has pushed us even closer to the conclusion that the area was a highly organised criminal den," said one cop.

"The man them even have medical facility in the area," added one soldier. "Our information is suggesting that this is where criminals who are injured in battle could go for treatment."

Tivoli residents denied knowledge of the alleged "torture chamber" or the shallow graves.

"Is lie them telling, nothing don't go so," said one woman who was among a large group gathered in front of the temporary office set up in the community by the public defender.

"Yu nuh see is mek them meking up the stories. Me live here how long and me nuh know of that," said another woman.

However, the police countered the residents' claim, saying that the decomposed state in which several of the bodies were found was clear evidence that they were killed by men in the area days before the security forces entered on May 24.

_____End of Excerpt

SO AFTER ALL THAT'S SAID AND DONE – even with all of Dudus' *Robin Hood-like* gestures and on-going displays of philanthropy, there still laid a dark and almost scary side to the reign of the man so many affectionately called... *The President.*

- *The Accusations / The Federal Indictment*

```
UNITED STATES DISTRICT COURT
SOUTHERN DISTRICT OF NEW YORK
- - - - - - - - - - - - - - - - - -x
UNITED STATES OF AMERICA          :
                                  :
          - v. -                  :     SEALED
                                  :     INDICTMENT
                                  :
CHRISTOPHER MICHAEL COKE,         :     S15 07 Cr. 971 (RPP)
  a/k/a "Michael Christopher Coke," :
  a/k/a "Paul Christopher Scott," :
  a/k/a "Presi,"                  :
  a/k/a "General,"                :
  a/k/a "President"               :
  a/k/a "Duddus,"                 :
  a/k/a "Shortman,"               :
                                  :
                Defendant.        :
- - - - - - - - - - - - - - - - - -x
```

COUNT ONE

(Conspiracy to Distribute Marijuana and Cocaine)

The Grand Jury charges:

1.   From at least in or about 1994, up to and including in or about October 2007, in the Southern District of New York and elsewhere, CHRISTOPHER MICHAEL COKE, a/k/a "Michael Christopher Coke," a/k/a "Paul Christopher Scott," a/k/a "Presi," a/k/a "General," a/k/a "President," a/k/a "Duddus," a/k/a "Shortman," the defendant, and others known and unknown, unlawfully, intentionally, and knowingly combined, conspired, confederated, and agreed together and with each other to violate the narcotics laws of the United States.

2.   It was a part and an object of the conspiracy that CHRISTOPHER MICHAEL COKE, a/k/a "Michael Christopher Coke," a/k/a

1

"Paul Christopher Scott," a/k/a "Presi," a/k/a "General," a/k/a "President," a/k/a "Duddus," a/k/a "Shortman," the defendant, and others known and unknown, unlawfully, intentionally, and knowingly would and did distribute, and possess with intent to distribute, a controlled substance, to wit, 1,000 kilograms and more of mixtures and substances containing a detectable amount of marijuana, in violation of Sections 812, 841(a)(1), and 841(b)(1)(A) of Title 21, United States Code.

3. It was further a part and an object of the conspiracy that CHRISTOPHER MICHAEL COKE, a/k/a "Michael Christopher Coke," a/k/a "Paul Christopher Scott," a/k/a "Presi," a/k/a "General," a/k/a "President," a/k/a "Duddus," a/k/a "Shortman," the defendant, and others known and unknown, unlawfully, intentionally, and knowingly would and did distribute, and possess with intent to distribute, a controlled substance, to wit, 5 kilograms and more of mixtures and substances containing a detectable amount of cocaine, in violation of Sections 812, 841(a)(1), and 841(b)(1)(A) of Title 21, United States Code.

Means and Methods of the Narcotics Conspiracy

4. Among the means and methods by which CHRISTOPHER MICHAEL COKE, a/k/a "Michael Christopher Coke," a/k/a "Paul Christopher Scott," a/k/a "Presi," a/k/a "General," a/k/a "President," a/k/a "Duddus," a/k/a "Shortman," the defendant, and his co-conspirators would and did carry out the narcotics

2

163

conspiracy were the following:

        a.   Since in or about the early 1990s, COKE has controlled the Tivoli Gardens area, a neighborhood in inner-city Kingston, Jamaica. Tivoli Gardens is a "garrison" community, a barricaded neighborhood guarded by a group of armed gunmen. These gunmen act at COKE's direction. COKE arms them with firearms he imports illegally, via a wharf located adjacent to Tivoli Gardens. COKE also distributes firearms to other area leaders of other sections of Kingston, Jamaica.

        b.   The members of COKE's organization, known as the "Shower Posse," and also as "Presidential Click," (the "Organization") reside in Tivoli Gardens, other areas of Jamaica, and in other countries, including the United States. From at least in or about 1994, members of the Organization have been involved in drug trafficking in the New York area, Kingston, Jamaica and elsewhere. The Organization members have sold narcotics, including marijuana and crack cocaine, at COKE's direction and on his behalf. They have then sent the proceeds of the drug sales to COKE in Jamaica, in the form of cash and/or goods. Organization members rely on COKE to assist them in their drug businesses here in the United States and in other countries. Because of COKE's international power and influence, COKE is able to provide protection to Organization members involved in drug trafficking and other illegal activities, in the United States and elsewhere. Organization members in the United States

3

routinely seek COKE's advice and approval for various matters relating to the sales of narcotics, including how to resolve conflicts with other Organization members. The members of the Organization commonly send cash and goods, including clothing and electronics to COKE as "tribute" payments, in recognition of his leadership and his assistance.

c. In addition to providing COKE with a portion of the proceeds from their drug trafficking activities, and "tribute" payments, members of the Organization in the United States supply COKE with firearms in exchange for the assistance that COKE provides, and in recognition of his status and power within the Organization. Organization members purchase firearms in the United States and ship those firearms to Jamaica. Once those firearms arrive in Jamaica, COKE decides how and to whom they will be distributed. COKE's access to firearms, as well as cash, serves to support and increase his authority and power in Kingston, Jamaica and elsewhere.

OVERT ACTS

5. In furtherance of the conspiracy, and to effect the illegal object thereof, the following overt acts, among others, were committed in the Southern District of New York and elsewhere:

a. In or about 1995, a co-conspirator not named as a defendant herein ("CC-1") sold crack cocaine in the Bronx, New York, that was carried to New York from Jamaica at the

4

direction of CHRISTOPHER MICHAEL COKE, a/k/a "Michael Christopher
Coke," a/k/a "Paul Christopher Scott," a/k/a "Presi," a/k/a
"General," a/k/a "President," a/k/a "Duddus," a/k/a "Shortman,"
the defendant.

      b.   On or about April 3, 2007, COKE, the
defendant, had a telephone conversation with three co-
conspirators not named as a defendant herein ("CC-2," "CC-3," and
"CC-4") concerning firearms that CC-2 and CC-3 had delivered to
CC-4 so that CC-4 could ship those firearms from the United
States to COKE in Jamaica.

      c.   On or about April 11, 2007, COKE, the
defendant, had a telephone conversation with CC-2 in which CC-2
and COKE discussed the terms of an arrangement whereby CC-2 would
distribute marijuana for COKE, in the New York area.

      d.   On or about April 12, 2007, COKE, the
defendant, had a telephone conversation with a co-conspirator not
named as a defendant herein ("CC-5"), about the sale of marijuana
pursuant to the arrangement discussed in paragraph c, above.

      e.   On or about April 21, 2007, COKE, the
defendant, had a telephone conversation with a co-conspirator not
named as a defendant herein ("CC-6"), about handguns that CC-6
was trying to obtain in the United States, to be sent to COKE in
Jamaica.

      f.   On or about May 8, 2007, COKE, the defendant,
had a telephone conversation with CC-5 in which COKE and CC-5

5

166

discussed the distribution of numerous firearms provided by CC-2, CC-3, and CC-4 that had recently arrived in Jamaica.

g.   On or about May 9, 2007, COKE, the defendant, had a telephone conversation with CC-6 about CC-2's attempt to collect a drug-related debt from another individual.

h.   On or about May 10, 2007, CC-5 had a telephone conversation with CC-2 in which CC-5 requested that CC-2 send profits of his marijuana business to Jamaica for the Organization and CC-2 asked CC-5 for help in collecting a drug debt from the individual referenced in paragraph g, above.

i.   In or around May 2007, CC-2 attempted to recover the drug debt from the individual referenced in paragraph h, above, in the Bronx, New York.

j.   On or about June 21, 2007, two co-conspirators not named as defendants herein ("CC-7" and "CC-8"), possessed approximately $239,985 in United States currency, given to them as payment for approximately 600 pounds of marijuana previously supplied to CC-2.

k.   On or about August 1, 2007, two co-conspirators not named as defendants herein ("CC-7" and "CC-8"), possessed over 400 pounds of marijuana, which had previously been in the possession of CC-2.

l.   On or about October 29, 2007, COKE and a co-conspirator not named as a defendant herein ("CC-9"), discussed the possibility that they had been indicted and whether they had

6

167

been charged with marijuana or cocaine trafficking.

(Title 21, United States Code, Section 846.)

COUNT TWO

(Firearms Trafficking Conspiracy)

The Grand Jury charges:

6. From at least in or around 1994, up to and including in or around October 2007, in the Southern District of New York and elsewhere, CHRISTOPHER MICHAEL COKE, a/k/a "Michael Christopher Coke," a/k/a "Paul Christopher Scott," a/k/a "Presi," a/k/a "General," a/k/a "President," a/k/a "Duddus," a/k/a "Shortman," the defendant, and others known and unknown, unlawfully, willfully, and knowingly, did combine, conspire, confederate, and agree together and with each other to commit an offense against the United States, to wit, a violation of Title 18, United States Code, Section 922(a)(1)(A).

7. It was a part and an object of the conspiracy that CHRISTOPHER MICHAEL COKE, a/k/a "Michael Christopher Coke," a/k/a "Paul Christopher Scott," a/k/a "Presi," a/k/a "General," a/k/a "President," a/k/a "Duddus," a/k/a "Shortman," the defendant, and others known and unknown, unlawfully, willfully, and knowingly, not being licensed importers, licensed manufacturers, and licensed dealers, would and did engage in the business of dealing in firearms, and in the course of such business would and did ship, transport, and receive firearms in interstate commerce, in violation of Title 18, United States Code, Section 922(a)(1)(A).

7

OVERT ACTS

8. In furtherance of the conspiracy and to effect the illegal object thereof, the defendants committed the following overt acts, in the Southern District of New York and elsewhere:

a. The allegations in Overt Acts b, e and f in paragraph 5 of Count One of this Indictment are re-alleged and incorporated by reference as though fully set forth herein;

b. In early 2007, in the Bronx, New York, CC-2 had a conversation with CC-6 concerning the methods by which CC-6 had sent firearms to COKE, the defendant, in Jamaica.

FORFEITURE ALLEGATION

9. As a result of committing the controlled substance offense alleged in Count One of this Indictment, CHRISTOPHER MICHAEL COKE, a/k/a "Michael Christopher Coke," a/k/a "Paul Christopher Scott," a/k/a "Presi," a/k/a "General," a/k/a "President," a/k/a "Duddus," a/k/a "Shortman," the defendant, shall forfeit to the United States, pursuant to 21 U.S.C. § 853, any and all property constituting or derived from any proceeds the defendant obtained directly or indirectly as a result of the said violation and any and all property used or intended to be used in any manner or part to commit and to facilitate the commission of the violation alleged in Count One of this Indictment.

8

169

Substitute Asset Provision

10. If any of the property described above as being subject to forfeiture, as a result of any act or omission of the defendant -

      a.   cannot be located upon the exercise of due diligence;

      b.   has been transferred or sold to, or deposited with, a third person;

      c.   has been placed beyond the jurisdiction of the Court;

      d.   has been substantially diminished in value; or

      e.   has been commingled with other property which cannot be subdivided without difficulty;

it is the intention of the United States, pursuant to 21 U.S.C. § 853(p), to seek forfeiture of any other property of the defendants up to the value of the above forfeitable property.

(Title 21, United States Code, Sections 841(a)(1), 846 and 853.)

FOREPERSON

LEV L. DASSIN
Acting United States Attorney

9

170

Form No. USA-33s-274 (Ed. 9-25-58)

UNITED STATES DISTRICT COURT
SOUTHERN DISTRICT OF NEW YORK

UNITED STATES OF AMERICA

- v. -

CHRISTOPHER MICHAEL COKE,
a/k/a "Michael Christopher Coke,"
a/k/a "Paul Christopher Scott,"
a/k/a "Presi,"
a/k/a "General,"
a/k/a "President"
a/k/a "Duddus,"
a/k/a "Shortman,"

Defendant.

SEALED
INDICTMENT

S15 07 Cr. 971 (RPP)

(21 U.S.C. § 846; 18 U.S.C. § 371,
922(a)(1)(a))

LEV L. DASSIN
Acting United States Attorney.

A TRUE BILL

Foreperson.

• *The Extradition Saga*

IN AUGUST OF 2009 an extradition request was sent to the Government of Jamaica from the United States of America. The extradition request was for one Michael Christopher *'Dudus'* Coke, the reputed JLP [Jamaica Labour Party] strongman from Western Kingston, and son of the late *Shower Posse* leader, Lester Lloyd *'Jim Brown'* Coke, who was also requested to be extradited to the United States to face similar charges of drug trafficking and arms smuggling, back in the early 1990s.

It is said that lightening never strikes twice in the same place, but as fate would have it, a somewhat similar replay of what surrounded his father's extradition situation, also plagued *Dudus*.

With delays and talks of what was said to be issues of legalities, and to some extent remains so to date - March 2011, the likes of which was also said to have caused diplomatic strain between Kingston and Washington – TO THE STAGE OF VISA CANCELLATIONS OF SOME OF JAMAICA'S MOST PROMINENT ENTERTAINERS, AND EVEN ONE OF THE ISLAND'S MOST SIGNIFICANT BUSINESS FIGURES. ALL DEVELOPMENTS ALLEGED TO HAVE BEEN ATTRIBUTED TO THE INTERNATIONAL STAND-OFF BETWEEN THE TWO AUTONOMOUS NATIONS. And then add the local saga of the alleged deliberate involvement and attempts by the JLP to stall the extradition – getting involved in a matter that some say should not have been political to begin with, but seemingly turned out to be very much so. AND WITH ALL THAT BEING WHAT IT IS - a lot has been said and made of the matter, but with all the talk, apart from what has been floating around and what individuals may've embraced due to their personal prospective of understanding, the big question that remains unanswered is: *Does the average man or woman, who can't seem to get this topic away from their lips, really know or even understand the true process of Extradition?*

That is the question, and if the truth were to ever be told, it would be a resounding *no*, because apart from what many have heard or feel, according to the rule of law, and what was mutually agreed upon by two *sovereign* nations, the facts and legalities surrounding this issue remains blurred to the common man. Therefore, it's on that premise that I aim to shed some much needed light on an issue that remains misunderstood, even though it is one of the most discussed topics in Jamaica's *recent* history.

EXTRADITION: - *Extradition is the official process whereby one nation or state surrenders a suspected or convicted criminal to another nation or state - extradition is regulated by treaties.*

NOTE: WHAT FOLLOWS NEXT IS AN OFFICIAL COPY OF THE ORIGINAL EXTRADITION AGREEMENT /TREATY - SIGNED IN 1984 BETWEEN THE *UNITED STATES OF AMERICA AND JAMAICA* – IT MUST ALSO BE NOTED THAT THIS AGREEMENT HAS SINCE BEEN MODIFIED/AMENEDED – AND WAS ONCE EVEN SUSPENDED FOR THREE [3] YEARS – RESUMED IN 1995 – AFTER IT WAS DISCOVERED THAT THE HASTY BEHAVIOUR OF A FORMER MINISTER OF JUSTICE LED TO THE ILLEGAL EXTRADITION OF A JAMAICAN CITIZEN – (*OF WHOM IT MUST BE NOTED)* - WAS NEVER RETURNED TO THE ISLAND, DESPITE SEVERAL ATTEMPTS BY THE JAMAICAN GOVERNMENT TO RESOLVE THE ISSUE. HOWEVER, EVEN WITH THAT SAID, THE POINT HERE IS THAT DESPITE ALL DISCREPANCIES, THE MAIN OBJECTIVE OF THIS TREATY REMAINS IN TACT TO DATE [2011] – AND IS PRESENTED HERE FOR DISCLOSURE, CLARIFICATION AND UNDERSTANDING PURPOSES:

98TH CONGRESS 2d Session	SENATE	TREATY DOC. 98-18

EXTRADITION TREATY WITH JAMAICA

MESSAGE

FROM

THE PRESIDENT OF THE UNITED STATES

TRANSMITTING

THE EXTRADITION TREATY BETWEEN THE GOVERNMENT OF THE UNITED STATES OF AMERICA AND THE GOVERNMENT OF JAMAICA, SIGNED AT KINGSTON ON JUNE 14, 1983

APRIL 24, 1984.—Treaty was read the first time, and together with the accompanying papers, referred to the Committee on Foreign Relations and ordered to be printed for the use of the Senate

U.S. GOVERNMENT PRINTING OFFICE
WASHINGTON : 1984

31-118 O

LETTER OF SUBMITTAL

DEPARTMENT OF STATE,
Washington, April 5, 1984.

THE PRESIDENT,
The White House.

THE PRESIDENT: I have the honor to submit to you the Treaty on Extradition between the United States of America and Jamaica, signed at Kingston on June 14, 1983. I recommend that the Treaty be transmitted to the Senate for advice and consent to ratification.

The Treaty is the first modern United States extradition treaty within the Caribbean region. It will supersede the United States-United Kingdom Treaty on Extradition of 1931 which was made applicable to Jamaica in 1935. The Treaty follows generally the form and content of extradition treaties recently concluded by this Government.

Article 1 obligates each State to extradite to the other, in accordance with the terms of the Treaty, any persons charged with or convicted of an extraditable offense by the requesting State. (Extradition shall also be granted, Article 2 explains, for attempts and conspiracies to commit extraditable offenses, as well as for aiding and abetting the commission of such offenses.)

Article 1 further states that extradition shall be granted when the offense for which extradition is requested was committed outside the requesting State provided there is jurisdiction under the laws of both States for the punishment of such an offense in corresponding circumstances.

Article 2 permits extradition for any offense punishable under the laws of both States by imprisonment for more than one year. Instead of listing each offense for which extradition may be granted, as was United States practice until recently, this Treaty adopts the modern practice of permitting extradition for any crime punishable under the laws of both contracting Parties for a minimum period. This obviates the need to renegotiate or supplement the Treaty should both States pass laws covering new types of criminal activity, such as computer-related crimes.

Article 2 also follows the practice of recent United States extradition treaties in indicating that the dual criminality standard should be interpreted liberally in order to effectuate the intent of the Parties that fugitives be brought to justice.

Articles 3 and 6 state mandatory grounds for refusal of extradition. Article 3 provides that extradition shall be denied when the offense for which extradition is sought is a political offense or when it is established that the request is in fact made for the purpose of prosecuting the person sought on account of race, religion, nationality or political

(V)

LETTER OF TRANSMITTAL

THE WHITE HOUSE, *April 17, 1984.*

To the Senate of the United States:

With a view to receiving the advice and consent of the Senate to ratification, I transmit herewith the Treaty on Extradition between the United States of America and Jamaica, signed at Kingston on June 14, 1983.

I transmit also, for the information of the Senate, the report of the Department of State with respect to the Treaty.

The Treaty is the first modern United States extradition treaty within the Caribbean region. The Treaty will facilitate United States efforts to prosecute narcotics conspiracies by expressly providing that conspiracies and attempts to commit extraditable offenses constitute extraditable offenses.

The Treaty follows generally the form and consent of extradition treaties recently concluded by this Government. Upon entry into force of this Treaty, the Extradition Treaty between the United States and the United Kingdom signed on December 22, 1931, shall cease to have effect between the United States and Jamaica.

This Treaty will make a significant contribution to international cooperation in law enforcement. I recommend that the Senate give early and favorable consideration to the Treaty and give its advice and consent to ratification.

RONALD REAGAN.

(III)

176

VII

Article 19 provides that the Treaty will enter into force thirty days after the exchange of the instruments of ratification.

Article 20 provides for termination of the Treaty by either Party upon six months written notice to the other.

The Department of Justice joins the Department of State in favoring approval of this Treaty by the Senate at an early date.

Respectfully submitted,

GEORGE P. SHULTZ.

VI

opinions or when, for the same reasons, the person sought is likely to be denied a fair trial or punished, detained or restricted in his personal liberty. Article 6 provides that extradition shall be denied where the requesting State's statute of limitation bars prosecution or enforcement of the penalty.

Article 4 states that extradition shall not be precluded by the fact that the requested State has chosen not to prosecute the person sought for the acts for which extradition is requested or has discontinued any pending criminal proceedings.

Articles 3(5) and 5 state discretionary grounds for refusal of extradition. Article 3(5) provides that extradition may be denied for military offenses. Article 5 provides that extradition may be refused when the offense is punishable by death in the requesting, but not the requested, State, unless satisfactory assurances are received that the death penalty, if imposed, will not be carried out.

Article 7 states the obligation of the requested State concerning extradition of its nationals. It provides, in brief, that if extradition is denied on the basis of nationality, the requested State shall, if it has jurisdiction, submit the case to its authorities for prosecution. Extradition shall not be refused, however, if the person sought is a national of both States.

Articles 8–11 specify procedures by which extradition is to be accomplished. The procedures therein are similar to those found in other modern United States extradition treaties.

Article 12 provides that surrender shall be deferred when the person whose extradition is sought is being proceeded against or has been convicted of a different offense in the requested State, unless the laws of the requested State otherwise provide.

Article 13 states that the executive authority of the requested Party shall determine to which country to surrender a person sought by more than one State.

Article 14 expressly incorporates into the Treaty the rule of specialty. This article provides, subject to specified exceptions, that a person extradited under the Treaty may not be detained, tried or punished for an offense other than that for which extradition has been granted.

Article 15 permits surrender without formal proceedings where the person sought agrees in writing to surrender after having been advised by a competent judicial authority of his or her right to a formal proceeding.

Article 16 provides that all property relating to the offense for which extradition is requested may, to the extent permitted under the laws of the requested State, be seized and surrendered to the requesting State. This provision is subject to the rights of third parties.

Article 17 governs expenses in a manner similar to other recent United States extradition treaties. This article further provides that the requested State shall represent the requesting State in any proceeding in the requested State arising out of a request for extradition.

Article 18, like the parallel provision of almost all recent United States extradition treaties, stipulates that the Treaty is retroactive in the sense that it applies to offenses committed before as well as after its entry into force, provided that the offenses were proscribed by the laws of both States when committed.

EXTRADITION TREATY BETWEEN THE GOVERNMENT OF THE UNITED STATES OF AMERICA AND THE GOVERNMENT OF JAMAICA

The Government of the United States of America and the Government of Jamaica,

Recalling the Treaty for the Mutual Extradition of Criminals between the United Kingdom and the United States of America concluded in London in 1931;

Noting that both the Government of the United States of America and the Government of Jamaica have continued to apply the terms of that Treaty; and

Desiring to provide for more effective cooperation between the two States in the suppression of crime and, for that purpose, to conclude a new treaty for the extradition of offenders;

Have agreed as follows:

ARTICLE I

Obligation to Extradite

(1) The Contracting Parties agree to extradite to each other, subject to the provisions of this Treaty:

(a) persons whom the competent authorities in the Requesting State have charged with an extraditable offense committed within its territory; or

(b) persons who have been convicted in the Requesting State of such an offence and are unlawfully at large.

(2) With respect to an offence committed outside the territory of the Requesting State, the Requested State shall grant extradition, subject to the provisions of this Treaty, if there is jurisdiction under the laws of both States for the punishment of such an offense in corresponding circumstances.

ARTICLE II

Extraditable Offences

(1) An offence shall be an extraditable offence if it is punishable under the laws of both Contracting Parties by imprisonment or other form of detention for a period of more than one year or by any greater punishment.

(2) The following offences shall be extraditable if they meet the requirements of paragraph (1):

(a) conspiring in, attempting to commit, aiding or abetting, assisting, counselling or procuring the commission of, or being an accessory before or after the fact to, an offence described in that paragraph; or

(b) impeding the apprehension or prosecution of a person charged with an offence described in that paragraph.

(1)

179

2

(3) For the purposes of this Article, an offence shall be an extraditable offence:

(a) whether or not the laws of the Contracting Parties place the offence within the same category of offences or denominate the offence by the same terminology; or

(b) whether or not the offence is one for which United States federal law requires proof of interstate transportation, or use of the mails or of other facilities affecting interstate or foreign commerce, such matters being merely for the purpose of establishing jurisdiction in a United States federal court.

ARTICLE III

Political and Military Offences

(1) Extradition shall not be granted if the offence for which extradition is requested is of a political character.

(2) Extradition shall also not be granted if:

(a) it is established that extradition is requested for political purposes; or

(b) it is established that the request for extradition, though purporting to be on account of the extraditable offence, is in fact made for the purpose of prosecuting or punishing the person sought on account of his race, religion, nationality, or political opinions; or

(c) the person sought is by reason of his race, religion, nationality, or political opinions, likely to be denied a fair trial or punished, detained or restricted in his personal liberty for such reasons.

(3) It shall be the responsibility of the competent authorities of the Requested State to decide any question arising under paragraph (1). However, it shall be the responsibility of the executive authority of the Requested State to decide any question arising under paragraph (2) or (5) except to the extent that the national laws of that State expressly grant such powers to its Courts.

(4) Paragraphs (1) and (2) shall not apply to an offence which is extraditable pursuant to a treaty or convention to which both Contracting Parties are parties, the purpose of which is to prevent or repress a specific category of offences, and which imposes on States an obligation either to extradite the person sought or submit the matter to the competent authorities for decision as to prosecution.

(5) Extradition may be refused for offences under military law which are not offences under ordinary criminal law.

ARTICLE IV

Effect of Decision Not to Prosecute

Extradition shall not be precluded by the fact that the competent authorities in the Requested State have decided not to prosecute the person sought for the acts for which extradition is requested or have decided to discontinue any criminal proceedings which have been initiated against the person sought.

3

ARTICLE V

Capital Punishment

(1) When the offence for which extradition is requested is punishable by death under the laws of the Requesting State, and the laws of the Requested State do not permit such punishment for that offence, the executive authority of the Requested State may refuse to grant extradition.

(2) In exercising its discretion pursuant to paragraph (1), the executive authority of the Requested State shall give due and sympathetic consideration to any assurance given by the Requesting State, insofar as the laws of the Requesting State permit, that the death penalty will not be carried out.

ARTICLE VI

Lapse of Time

Extradition shall not be granted when prosecution of the offence for which extradition has been sought, or enforcement of the penalty for such an offence, has become barred by lapse of time according to the laws in the Requesting State.

ARTICLE VII

Nationality

(1) Neither Contracting Party shall be bound to deliver up its own nationals but the executive authority of the Requested State shall, if not prevented by the laws of that State, have the power to deliver them up if, in its discretion, it be deemed proper to do so.

(2) Extradition shall not be refused on the ground that the fugitive is a national of the Requested State if the fugitive is also a national of the Requesting State.

(3) If extradition is not granted for an offence pursuant to paragraph (1), the Requested State shall, if it has jurisdiction over the offence, submit the case to its highest competent authorities for decision as to prosecution, in according with the law of that State.

ARTICLE VIII

Extradition Procedures and Required Documents

(1) The request for extradition shall be made through the diplomatic channel.

(2) The request for extradition shall be supported by:

(a) documents, statements, or other evidence which describe the identity and probable location of the person sought;

(b) a statement of the facts of the case, including, if possible, the time and location of the offence;

(c) a statement of the provisions of the law describing the essential elements and the designation of the offence for which extradition is requested;

4

(d) a statement of the provisions of the law prescribing the punishment for the offence; and

(e) a statement of the provisions of the law prescribing any time limit on the prosecution or the execution of punishment for the offence.

(3) A request for extradition relating to a person who is sought for prosecution shall also be supported by:

(a) a copy of the warrant of arrest issued by a judge or other judicial authority in the Requesting State; and

(b) such evidence as would justify the committal for trial of that person if the offence had been committed in the Requested State.

(4) When the request for extradition relates to a convicted person, in addition to those items required by paragraph (2), it shall be supported by a certificate of conviction or copy of the judgment of conviction rendered by a court in the Requesting State. If the person has been convicted and sentenced, the request for extradition shall also be supported by a statement showing to what extent the sentence has been carried out. If the person has been convicted but not sentenced, the request for extradition shall also be supported by a statement to that effect.

(5) Statements, depositions and other documents transmitted in support of the request for extradition shall be transmitted through the diplomatic channel and shall be admissible if certified or authenticated in such manner as may be required by the law of the Requested State.

ARTICLE IX

Additional Information

(1) If the executive authority of the Requested State considers that the information furnished in support of the request for extradition is not sufficient to fulfill the requirements of this Treaty, it shall notify the Requesting State in order to enable that State to furnish additional information before the request is submitted to a court of the Requested State.

(2) The executive authority may fix a time limit for such information to be furnished.

(3) Nothing in paragraph (1) or (2) shall prevent the executive authority of the requested State from presenting to a court of that State information sought or obtained after submission of the request to the court or after expiration of the time stipulated pursuant to paragraph (2).

ARTICLE X

Provisional Arrest

(1) In case of urgency either Contracting Party may request the provisional arrest in accordance with the law of the Requested State of any accused or convicted person pending the request for extradition. Application for provisional arrest shall be made through the diplomatic channel or directly between the Department of Justice in the United States of America and the Minister responsible for extradition in Jamaica.

5

(2) The application shall contain:

    (a) a description of the person sought;

    (b) the location of that person if known;

    (c) such information as would be necessary to justify the issuance of a warrant of arrest had the offence been committed, or the person sought been convicted, in the territory of the Requested State; and

    (d) a statement that a request for extradition of the person sought will follow.

(3) On receipt of such an application, the Requested State shall take the appropriate steps to secure the arrest of the person sought. The Requesting State shall be promptly notified of the result of its application.

(4) A person who is provisionally arrested shall be discharged from custody upon the expiration of sixty (60) days from the date of arrest pursuant to the application for provisional arrest if the executive authority of the Requested State has not received the formal request for extradition and the supporting documents required by Article VIII.

(5) The fact that a person is discharged from custody pursuant to paragraph (4) shall not prejudice the extradition of that person if the extradition request and the supporting documents mentioned in Article VIII are delivered at a later date.

ARTICLE XI

Decision and Surrender

(1) The Requested State shall promptly communicate through the diplomatic channel to the Requesting State its decision on the request for extradition.

(2) If the request for extradition is denied by reason of any statutory or treaty prohibition against extradition, the Requested State shall provide such information as may be available as to the reason for the denial.

(3) If the extradition is granted, the competent authorities of the Contracting Parties shall agree on the time and place of the surrender of the person sought.

(4) If the person sought is not removed from the territory of the Requested State within the time prescribed by the law of that State, that person may be discharged from custody and the Requested State may subsequently refuse extradition for the same offence.

ARTICLE XII

Deferred Surrender

If the extradition request is granted in the case of a person who is being prosecuted or is serving a sentence in the territory of the Requested State for a different offence, the Requested State shall, unless its laws otherwise provide, defer the surrender of the person sought until the conclusion of the proceedings against that person or the full execution of any punishment that may be or may have been imposed.

6

ARTICLE XIII

Requests for Extradition Made by Several States

The executive authority of the Requested State, upon receiving requests from the other Contracting Party and from any other State or States for the extradition of the same person, either for the same offence or for different offences, shall determine to which State it will extradite that person.

ARTICLE XIV

Rule of Speciality

(1) A person extradited under this Treaty may only be detained, tried or punished in the Requesting State for the offence for which extradition is granted, or—

(a) for a lesser offence proved by the facts before the court of committal, or in the case of extradition pursuant to Article XV, any lesser offence disclosed by the facts upon which the request is based; or

(b) for an offence committed after the extradition; or

(c) for an offence in respect of which the executive authority of the Requested State, in accordance with its laws, consents to the person's detention, trial or punishment; and for the purposes of this sub-paragraph the Requested State may require the submission of documents mentioned in Article VIII or the written views of the extradited person with respect to the offence concerned, or both; or

(d) if the person—

(i) having left the territory of the Requesting State after his extradition, voluntarily returns to it; or

(ii) being free to leave the territory of the Requesting State after his extradition, does not so leave within forty-five (45) days after the first day on which he was free to do so.

(2) A person extradited under this Treaty may not be extradited to a third State unless—

(a) the Requested State consents; or

(b) the circumstances are such that he could have been dealt with in the Requesting State pursuant to sub-paragraph (d) of paragraph (1).

ARTICLE XV

Simplified Extradition

If the person sought agrees in writing to extradition after personally being advised by a judge or competent magistrate of his right to further extradition proceedings, the Requested State may grant extradition without formal proceedings. Extradition pursuant to this Article shall be subject to Article XIV.

ARTICLE XVI

Seizure and Surrender of Property

(1) To the extent permitted under the laws in the Requested State all articles, instruments, objects of value, documents or other evidence relating to the offence may be seized and such items may be surrendered upon the granting of the extradition. The items mentioned in this Article may be surrendered even when extradition cannot be effected due to the death, disappearance, or escape of the person sought.

(2) The rights of third parties in such property shall be duly respected.

(3) The Requested State may impose conditions designed to ensure that the rights of third parties are protected and that the property is returned to the Requested State as soon as practicable.

ARTICLE XVII

Expenses and Representation

(1) Expenses related to the transportation of the person sought to the Requesting State shall be paid by that State. All other expenses relating to the apprehension of the person sought and to subsequent proceedings shall be borne by the Requested State. However, expenses which, in the opinion of the Parties, constitute special expenditures shall be borne by the Requesting State.

(2) The Requested State shall also provide for the representation of the Requesting State in any proceedings arising in the Requested State out of a request for extradition.

(3) No pecuniary claim arising out of the arrest, detention, examination and surrender of the person sought under the terms of this Treaty shall be made by the Requested State against the Requesting State.

(4) Paragraph (3) shall not apply to claims arising out of failure of the Requesting State to comply with conditions imposed pursuant to paragraph (3) of Article XVI.

ARTICLE XVIII

Scope of Applicataion

This Treaty shall apply to offences encompassed by Article II committed before as well as after the date this Treaty enters into force if at the time of the act or omission comprising the offence such act or omission constituted an offence under the laws of both States.

ARTICLE XIX

Ratification and Entry Into Force

(1) This Treaty shall be subject to ratification; the instruments of ratification shall be exchanged at Washington as soon as possible.

8

(2) This Treaty shall enter into force thirty (30) days after the exchange of the instruments of ratification.

(3) Upon entry into force of this Treaty, the Extradition Treaty between the United States of America and the United Kingdom signed at London, December 22, 1931, shall cease to have effect between the United States of America and Jamaica. Nevertheless, the 1931 Treaty shall continue to have effect in relation to any request for extradition made before this Treaty enters into force.

ARTICLE XX

Termination

(1) Either Contracting Party may terminate this Treaty at any time by giving written notice to the other Party, and the termination shall be effective six (6) months after the date of receipt of such notice.

(2) Nothing in paragraph (1) shall affect any request for extradition made before the date on which the termination becomes effective.

IN WITNESS WHEREOF, the undersigned, being duly authorized by their respective Governments, have signed this Treaty.

DONE AT KINGSTON, in duplicate, this 14th day of June, 1983.

For the Government of the

United States of America

For the Government of

Jamaica

Ambassador of the United
States of America

Minister of National Security
and Justice

NOTE: Previously cited document was signed in Kingston, Jamaica (June 14, 1983) between the Reagan Administration and the JLP [Jamaica Labour Party] Administration.

Jamaica is honoured by the visit of U.S. President Ronald Reagan 3rd from right. Deputy Prime Minister Hugh Shearer is at extreme right. Upon the election of the President two years earlier (1981), Prime Minister Edward Seaga was the first Head of Government to have been invited to the White House as a token of "friendly relations".

Prime Minister, Rt. Hon Edward Seaga and Hon. Bruce Golding in discussion with US Vice - President to Ronald Regan, George H.W. Bush.

- ## Introduction to Exhibits (F-N):

The following excerpts are taken from local newspaper articles printed during the *Dudus* extradition saga and are submitted as evidence to give a clear an unbiased account of what actually occurred in Jamaica during that period.

THE DUDUS EXTRADITION SAGA:

Exhibit F

The excerpt below is taken from The Jamaica Gleaner - Tuesday, September 1, 2009

US gov't names Dudus among world's most dangerous drug dealers

West Kingston strongman Christopher 'Dudus' Coke could face a maximum sentence of life in prison if he is extradited and convicted by United States authorities.

The 40-year-old Coke has been named by the US Department of Justice to a list of "consolidate priority organisation targets" which includes persons the US Drug Enforcement Agency (DEA) says are the "world's most dangerous narcotics kingpins".

"The charges against Christopher Michael Coke starkly illustrate the dangerous connection between the international trade in narcotics and illicit firearms," US officials said in a release dated August 28.

Various charges

John P. Gilbride, the United States attorney for the Southern District of New York, and Javier F. Pena, special agent in charge of the US Drug Enforcement Agency's Caribbean Division, have announced that Coke is wanted to answer several charges.

In the release, the US authorities announced that Coke has been charged with conspiracy to distribute ganja and cocaine and conspiracy to illegally traffic in firearms.

"The United States has formally requested through diplomatic channels that Jamaican authorities formally arrest Coke and extradite him to the Southern District of New York on the US charges," the release added.

If convicted on the narcotics charge, Coke faces a maximum sentence of life in prison and a mandatory minimum sentence of 10 years in prison as well as a fine of up to US$4 million or twice the pecuniary gain from the offence.

In addition, Coke faces a maximum sentence of five years in prison and a fine of US$250,000 on the firearm trafficking charge.

Mere accusations

However, in a note of caution, the US authorities said that the charges contained in the indictment against Coke are "merely accusation and the defendant is presumed innocent until proven guilty".

However, The Associated Press reported that Tavares-Finson (Dudus' Attorney) *dismissed the allegations as "hype" from the DEA and said his client was dumbfounded.*

"He can't understand what it could possibly be," AP further quoted Tavares-Finson. "We'll wait and see. I don't know what's going to happen with the Jamaican Government."

_____End of Excerpt

Exhibit G

The following excerpt is taken from The Jamaica Gleaner – Saturday, March 13, 2010

'Dudus' pressure

The pressure on the Bruce Golding administration to send the worrying extradition request for Tivoli Gardens strongman Christopher 'Dudus' Coke to the courts continues to mount.

Three more powerful organisations have applied additional pressure, saying the Government should send the extradition request to court, even as Coke, the man under immense public glare, celebrates his 41st birthday with an elaborate two-day bash in Tivoli Gardens over the weekend.

The Jamaica Council of Churches, the Independent Jamaican Council for Human Rights (IJCHR) and active human rights organisation Jamaicans for Justice (JFJ) have joined the Private Sector Organisation of Jamaica, Families Against State Terrorism and the parliamentary opposition in shooting down the prime minister's decision to keep the issue out of the courts.

Blunt declaration

"The (extradition) matter should go before the courts," was the blunt declaration of the Reverend Peter Garth of the umbrella church group, which usually stays out of such issues.

"The council is troubled by the seeming trend to reduce or curtail judicial authority, and warns that there are constitutional implications," declared the Arlene Harrison Henry-led IJCHR.

"We fully support the position of the IJCHR and believe the Dudus matter needs to be placed before the courts," asserted Dr Carolyn Gomes, executive director of JFJ.

"In fact, we believe that it is a breach of the principle of separation of powers for the executive to assume the duty of the judiciary," Gomes added.

Last week, Golding told the House of Representatives that the surveillance evidence garnered by investigators was in breach of Jamaican laws - specifically, the Interception of Communications Act.

A growing number of organisations and individuals have rejected Golding's explanation for refusing to extradite Coke to the US to face the courts on a range of charges.

The organisations have argued that it was not the prime minister's call, but that of the courts.

The IJCHR contends that the adequacy of evidence, its admissibility, relevance, weight or otherwise, is a matter for the determination of a competent court, established in the Jamaican Constitution and the laws of the land.

The council argues that the courts are the appropriate guardians of the constitutional rights of the Jamaican people.

The IJCHR further insists that the primary duty of the courts is to interpret legislation in an independent and unbiased manner.

To this end, the IJCHR argues that extradition proceedings should be held in open court to facilitate public scrutiny.

"We embark on a dangerous road when the executive authority usurps judicial functions by making decisions about evidence. As such, decisions can only be properly made by the court after a full public

hearing of all issues, and after the hearing of all parties," the IJCHR stated.

Position not changed

Gomes argues that the position of the JFJ has not changed because of the person involved.

"We have always argued that the court is the final arbitrator, and we have sought to defend the rights of all Jamaicans in a court of law," said Gomes.

On the issue of the Mutual Assistance Treaty, which allows the governments of the United States and Jamaica to extradite suspected offenders following a court hearing, the IJCHR says it is necessary for effective governance, as crime is no longer local in origin and effect but transactional and international.

The IJCHR asserts that the reciprocal rights and obligations, which both countries accept, are intended to serve the purpose of bringing to justice those who are accused of committing grave offences in either of the contracting states and those convicted, but have fled from one state to another.

_____End of Excerpt

Exhibit H

The following excerpt is taken from The Jamaica Observer – Sunday, March 14, 2010

Tivoli under satellite surveillance

Americans said to have audio, video recordings of Gov't officials in community

TIVOLI Gardens, the tough West Kingston base of Christopher 'Dudus' Coke, is under satellite surveillance by United States authorities who are determined to have Coke extradited to answer drug- and gun-running charges in New York, the Sunday Observer has learnt.

According to a security expert with knowledge of the operation, the US has powerful audio and video evidence of activities involving Coke, as well as several Government officials, including members of the legislature, inside the Tivoli Gardens community centre.

With the use of Satellite Internet Telemetry System (SIMS) similar to that used to record wildlife activities, the US has captured the make, colour and licence plates of vehicles entering and exiting Tivoli Gardens at specific periods, as well as conversations, the expert said.

The SIMS, the expert said, is very simple to operate.

"Satellite service is available anywhere in the world for the system to operate. The data is transmitted from the Satellite Telemetry System based on programmed time intervals and/or alarms. It is transferred through satellite and Internet to a dedicated web page, and you can monitor and collect that data as long as you have web access," the expert said.

193

"It is very simple. Set your co-ordinates, hook up your sensors, point the antenna to the sky, and turn on your equipment," added the expert, who spoke on condition of anonymity.

"Wire-tapping communication is an insignificant part of the evidence against Coke," said the expert in reference to Prime Minister Bruce Golding's claim that the evidence supporting the extradition request violated the Interception of Communications Act which makes strict provisions for the manner in which intercepted communications may be obtained and disclosed.

Also captured, the expert said, was a gathering of some Government officials, along with individuals from the Tivoli Gardens community making and smoking what appeared to be marijuana spliffs at the centre, on different occasions.

"The United States is making sure that its case against Coke is airtight, and until he is extradited every Jamaican entering the US will be targeted. The US will not relent on this one," said the expert who met with the Sunday Observer on Friday night.

Relations between Kingston and Washington have deteriorated over the extradition request, with the US State Department accusing the Jamaican Government of delaying tactics.

Two Mondays ago, in a scathing Narcotics Control Strategy Report, the Americans questioned Jamaica's commitment to law enforcement co-operation and charged that "Jamaica's processing of the extradition request has been subjected to unprecedented delays, unexplained disclosure of law enforcement information to the press, and unfounded allegations questioning the US' compliance with the Mutual Legal Assistance Treaty and Jamaican law".

The US also said that the Jamaican Government's handling of the extradition request marked a dramatic change in Kingston's previous co-operation on extradition, including a temporary suspension in the processing of all other pending requests.

The US also labelled Jamaica as the Caribbean's largest supplier of marijuana to the United States as well as a trans-shipment point for cocaine entering South America.

"The Government of Jamaica's ambitious anti-corruption and anti-crime legislative agendas announced in 2007 remain stalled in Parliament," said the report.

"Five anti-crime proposals under consideration as part of an extensive agenda to address the widespread crime challenges have yet to be debated by Parliament," added Washington, which noted that Jamaica is a party to the 1988 United Nations Drug Convention.

However, the following day, Golding rejected the US' charges and said that the evidence presented in the extradition request -- made in August last year -- breached Jamaican law.

"The Jamaican Government, rather than summarily refusing the request, discussed with the US authorities the breaches that had occurred which made it impossible for the minister (of justice), being aware of such breaches, to issue the authority to proceed," Golding said in an address to the Parliament.

"In an effort to overcome the impediment... the Jamaican Government indicated to the US authorities that if other evidence existed, the procurement and disclosure of which were not in violation of Jamaican law, the minister would be prepared to accept that evidence and issue the necessary authority to proceed. No such evidence has up to now been presented," he added.

On Friday, the security expert said that American border officials are turning up the heat on Jamaicans who have massive personal wealth *but who have no supporting documentation to show how the wealth was gained.*

A list viewed by the Sunday Observer includes some of Jamaica's well-known officials, as well as business people of both genders. They are described as having "massive personal wealth", which is said to have raised red flags at US borders.

The spotlight on these individuals has not come as a surprise to University of Miami Law Professor David Rowe, who remained consistent in his view that Coke is an albatross around the neck of the prime minister, the Jamaica Labour Party and the Government.

"There is no question that they are being targeted," Rowe said. "Where the individuals have amassed wealth in a short period of time and without any corresponding income to corroborate it is an automatic red flag to the US Justice Department."

Rowe as well as Sunday Observer sources in the US believe that embarrassing times are ahead for several Jamaican business officials at US borders, even if the Government hands over Coke.

Information reaching the Sunday Observer is that several Jamaicans who have amassed large personal wealth but who are unable to provide credible sources of income are currently in detention centres in the US.

Massive unexplained wealth is said to have been the reason behind an upstanding Jamaican businessman being detained in the US for several hours on a return trip to the island in early January.

It is also said to be the reason for the detention without bond -- at Krome Avenue Detention Centre in Florida -- of a Jamaican man of Chinese descent.

The man and another Jamaican/Chinese are said to have arrived in the US on March 2 on an Air Jamaica flight.

The man, whose Alien card number was supplied to the Sunday Observer, was said to have had his Green Card revoked. He did not respond to our request for an interview last Thursday.

Late last week, the influential Economist magazine reported that American authorities have become frustrated at what they see as foot-dragging by Jamaica's Government over the Coke extradition request.

The article, titled 'Seeking Mr Coke: American anger at Jamaica's slowness in handing over an alleged gang boss', said "if the United States' allegations of political links are well-founded, some Jamaican public figures may fear that Mr Coke's arrest would lead to the disclosure of embarrassing information".

_____End of Excerpt

Exhibit I

The following excerpt is taken from The Jamaica Star – Friday, September 4, 2009:

THUGS CALLED IN TO DEFEND DUDUS

Police unaware of plans

Thugs from west Kingston have reportedly sent for reinforcements from other communities as far away as Montego Bay to ensure that the authorities will not have an easy task should they decide to come for community leader Christopher 'Dudus' Coke.

*Information reaching **THE WEEKEND STAR** is that Coke's supporters from areas like Mountain View, Spanish Town, May Pen and several other communities are threatening to rebel should the* security *forces try to take him in. This is in addition to the stance taken by the men from west Kingston, who are bracing for "whatever" as they vow to defend their beloved don.*

The United States has requested Coke's extradition after he was featured on that country's Justice Department's list of the world's most dangerous drug *kingpins. An Associated Press story out of San Juan, Puerto Rico, earlier this week revealed that the United States has asked Jamaica to extradite Coke to face federal drug and weapons charges in New York. He is charged with conspiracy to distribute cocaine and marijuana and conspiracy to illegally traffic in firearms. The charges were revealed in an indictment that was unsealed Friday in the United States' Southern District of New York.*

Pure mad head

Sources in West Kingston say benefits have been promised to those who have joined the cause. "Right ya now a pure mad head from all bout, some man whe nuh have nuttin fi live fear. When it done if dem survive dem ago have summ'n tho," one man revealed.

Preparation activities have already started and include posting men at strategic points within the community and even putting mattresses on top of houses for thugs.

THE WEEKEND STAR *has learnt that some residents have even fled the area amidst the rumours of the possible capture. Others are bracing for the worst. They say Coke is responsible for the "order" in West Kingston. "Look how West Kingston peaceful and now dem waah it end," a 25-year-old thug from Denham Town said.*

Should Dudus leave, one of his relative is expected to take control of the community.

When THE STAR contacted police *in West Kingston, East Kingston and St Catherine, the lawmen collectively said that they were not aware of any organisation of the thugs, nor of areas in their divisions planning to "disrupt proceedings" should an attempt be made to arrest Coke. One officer said that checks would be made and promised a future update.*

_____End of Excerpt

Exhibit J

The following excerpt is taken from The Jamaica Gleaner – Thursday, March 11, 2010

Golding claims US evidence against Coke illegally obtained

PRIME MINISTER Bruce Golding has accused the United States (US) government of using illegally intercepted telephone conversations for the basis of drug and weapons trafficking charges against west Kingston strongman Christopher 'Dudus' Coke.

Golding, in a statement to Parliament yesterday and responding to a scathing report from the US Department of State a day earlier, declared the Jamaican Government would not extradite one of its citizens without being provided with a stronger case.

"I know that perhaps it is politically expedient to say it is Coke. Or it could have been Matthews Lane strongman Zekes (Donald Phipps)," Golding told the House of Representatives. "Or it could be any of these. I am not defending the wrongdoing of any person but, if I have to pay a political price for it, I am going to uphold a position that constitutional rights do not begin at Liguanea."

Liguanea is the base of the US Embassy in St Andrew.

On Monday, the annual International Narcotics Control Strategy Report, released by the US Department of State, said the handling of the August request for Coke's extradition "marked a dramatic change in (the Jamaican Government's) previous cooperation on extradition". The State Department said the delay in extraditing Coke, as well as a temporary suspension in the processing of all other pending requests, raised "serious questions" about the Jamaican Government's commitment to combating transnational crime.

However, Golding yesterday rejected the assertion, arguing his Government could not ignore breaches in the Coke case.

"The Interception of Communications Act makes strict provisions for the manner in which intercepted communications may be obtained and disclosed," the prime minister said. "The evidence supporting the extradition request in this particular case violated those provisions."

He added, "For intercepted communication to be admissible in any criminal proceedings, it must have been obtained, disclosed and used in accordance with these provisions. This was not done in this case. This was highly irregular."

Golding said that, under the circumstances, Attorney General and Justice Minister Dorothy Lightbourne had a duty to protect the constitutional rights of Coke and not extradite him.

"If the minister, having examined it, recognises that it is supported by evidence that was illegally obtained, disclosed or used, but still proceeds to sign it, she should immediately sign one other document - her resignation," Golding said.

The prime minister stressed that since his administration assumed office in September 2007 it has received 26 extradition requests from the US, 16 of which have been signed by the justice minister.

Responding to Golding's statement, Opposition members Peter Bunting and Dr Peter Phillips questioned why the attorney general would not simply sign the document and allow the courts to determine the merits of the Government's concerns.

Phillips said the structure of the extradition law requires that there be a procedural check by the minister with responsibility for justice, but matters regarding the quality of justice should be dealt with by the court, as well as the legality of evidence.

"There is a reserve power usually considered at the end, not at the beginning of the proceedings, to ensure that there is not the risk of prejudicing hearings held in the jurisdiction that is requesting the extradition of the person," Phillips said.

Golding responded that "it was not intended by this Parliament when the legislation was framed that the minister was to be some lubricated conduit through which extradition requests were to automatically pass".

"The minister has to satisfy herself, or himself, that the processes that were used in submitting the request are in conformity with Jamaican law. When the matter goes before the court, the court has the responsibility to determine whether a prima facie case has been made out sufficient to ground the extradition of the subject."

Coke, who is the reputed leader of Tivoli Gardens, a section of West Kingston represented in Parliament by Golding, has been indicted by a grand jury in the United States.

Yesterday, the prime minister noted that the identity of the co-conspirators named in the indictment are unknown. He said statements supporting an extradition request should not be veiled.

He also suggested that the wiretapping of Coke's telephone conversations was not done by the United States, but was instead transported to that jurisdiction to be used against him.

_____End of Excerpt

Exhibit K

The following excerpt comes from The Jamaica Gleaner / Power 106 News [Jamaica] – DATE: 2010-03-02

Golding defends 'Dudus' delay

The Prime Minister Bruce Golding is defiant this afternoon that the Jamaican Government was right when it refused to sign the extradition request by the United States for West Kingston strongman Christopher 'Dudus' Coke.

The matter is gaining increasing international attention since the release of a US Narco report yesterday, blasting the Jamaica Government for what it calls the unprecedented delay in granting the extradition request.

However, Mr Golding says the attorney general and justice minister Dorothy Lightbourne decided against signing the request because the evidence outlined in the extradition request was illegally obtained.

Mr Golding says the Government has refrained from making any detailed public statement in relation about the Dudus issue because of confidentiality.

He said that position was reaffirmed in the several meetings between Jamaica and the United States.

However, Mr Golding in view of the statements contained in the Narcotics Control Strategy Report, he is obliged to speak.

According to Mr Golding, the United States were seeking to extradite Dudus on the basis of evidence that was illegally obtained under the Interception of Communications Act.

However that would not satisfy former national security minister Dr

Peter Phillips.

He believes the decision should not have rested with a politically appointed person.

Mr Golding says the Jamaican Government has indicated to the US authorities that if other evidence exist, and its procurement and disclosure were not in violation of Jamaican law, the minister would be prepared to accept that evidence and issue the necessary authority to proceed.

_____End of Excerpt

Exhibit L

The following excerpt is taken from The Star – Tuesday, March 2, 2010

DUDUS CASE ANGERS US GOVT

Christopher 'Dudus' Coke is wanted in the United States on alleged drug-related charges.

The United States Government has lashed out at Jamaica's handling of the extradition request for west Kingston strongman Christopher 'Dudus' Coke.

In an unusually caustic report on Jamaica in its annual International Narcotics Control Strategy Report, the Barack Obama administration made it clear it was not satisfied with the handling of the extradition request and charged that the Jamaican government was not holding to the rules.

While co-operation between (the) Government of Jamaica (GOJ) and United States Government law-enforcement agencies remained strong, delays in proceeding with the significant extradition request for a major alleged narcotics and firearms trafficker, who is reported to have ties to the ruling Jamaica Labour Party, and subsequent delays in other extradition requests, have called into question Kingston's commitment to law-enforcement co-operation with the US, the report claimed. According to Washington, in the past, extradition requests from its law-enforcement agencies were routinely and timely processed by Jamaican political and judicial authorities.

Serious questions

The report further stated that the GOJ's unusual handling of the August request for the extradition of Dudus marked a dramatic change in previous co-operation on extradition, including a temporary suspension in the processing of all other pending requests and raises serious questions about the GOJ's commitment to combating transnational crime.

*Last night, Minister of Information Daryl Vaz was unwilling to speak on the US report, pointing **THE STAR** instead to National Security Minister Dwight Nelson or Justice Minister Dorothy Lightbourne. Neither could be reached for a comment.*

_____End of Excerpt

Arrest Dudus

- Lightbourne signs extradition order
- Tivoli hunkers down for possible assault

Gary Spaulding
Senior Gleaner Writer

ATTORNEY GENERAL Dorothy Lightbourne has finally affixed her signature to the extradition order against Tivoli Gardens strongman Christopher 'Dudus' Coke, and Director of Public Prosecutions Paula Llewellyn yesterday secured the required arrest warrant.

At the same time, Lightbourne's Senate colleague, Tom Tavares-Finson, has withdrawn as Coke's lawyer.

The Gleaner that the signed order was dispatched to Llewellyn who immediately secured the warrant for Coke's arrest from the court.

Lightbourne signed the extradition order.

COKE

PLEASE SEE **ARREST**, A3

RICARDO MAKYN/STAFF PHOTOGRAPHER

the entrances to Tivoli Gardens in west Kingston which was blocked yesterday amid tension in over the 'Dudus' extradition issue. See related story on A2.

TOO HOT   TOO

Exhibit M

The following excerpt is taken from The Jamaica Observer – Monday, May 17, 2010

Jamaica to sign Dudus extradition request
PM not resigning, promises more action against crime

A deeply apologetic Prime Minister Bruce Golding tonight announced that Justice Minister Dorothy Lightbourne will sign the authority for extradition proceedings to commence against Tivoli Gardens strongman Christopher 'Dudus' Coke who is wanted by the United States to face gun- and drug-running charges.

In an address to the nation a short while ago, Golding begged the nation to forgive him for dragging out the extradition issue and for his involvement in the matter.

"The Minister of Justice will sign the authorisation for the extradition process to commence," Golding said.

Golding's head has been on the chopping block since last Tuesday's announcement in Parliament that he had personally sanctioned his party's decision to seek the assistance of United States law firm Manatt, Phelps & Phillips to negotiate with the Barack Obama administration in the contentious extradition matter.

Calls from all sectors of society for Golding to resign led him to rally his party's top brass to high level talks on the weekend.

"In hindsight the party should have never got involved in the way it did," he said in tonight's broadcast. "I must accept responsibility for it

and the way it was handled and I must express my remorse. I ask for your forgiveness."

_____End of Excerpt

Exhibit N

The following excerpt is taken from The Gleaner – Sunday, March 14, 2010

United States *vs* its 'backyard' - Washington always wins

Police officers escort Colombian Juan Edison Salcedo Ibarra, an alleged member of Colombian drug cartel of Norte del Valle in Quito, on Wednesday, October 21, 2009. Salcedo Ibarra was detained in Manta, 260 kms, some 160 miles southwest of Quito.

THE FACE-off between Washington and Kingston over reputed Tivoli Gardens enforcer Christopher 'Dudus' Coke has revived memories of similar clashes between the United States and countries in this region.

These include the ongoing battle in Honduras, where the US appears to be using every diplomatic weapon at its disposal to express its displeasure at the interim government's refusal to restore ousted president Manuel Zelaya to power.

In Jamaica, the Government's refusal to sign an extradition order that would place Coke in the hands of US law enforcement has put the administration of Prime Minister Bruce Golding in hot water with Washington.

Coke was named last year by US authorities as leader of the infamous Shower Posse, a gang his father, Lester Lloyd 'Jim Brown' Coke, once led.

Dudus is wanted for alleged drug and gun-running between Jamaica and the US.

But the minister of justice has so far refused to sign the extradition request based on what the Government says were "abnormal procedures" in the US request.

This is not the first time the US has had problems getting persons with alleged criminal ties extradited from Jamaica.

Vivian Blake, reputed founder of the Shower Posse, eluded capture for six years before cutting a deal with the 'Feds' in 2000, and did prison time in the US.

Others extradited

Drug traffickers Lebert Ramcharan and Donovan 'Plucky' Williams were arrested by US and Jamaican narcotics agents in 2004.

They were ordered extradited three years later by local courts to the US, where they received lengthy prison sentences.

Other Caribbean territories, including tiny St Kitts, The Bahamas, as well as Colombia in South America, have had similar run-ins with US officials.

In the case of St Kitts, it took 10 years before the Americans got hold of Kittitian nationals Glenroy Matthew and Noel 'Zambo' Heath, who were named as international drug traffickers by the US in the early 1990s.

Matthew and Heath exhausted their extradition rights before finally surrendering to US agents in St Kitts in 2006. They are currently serving lengthy prison sentences in the states.

Another Kittitian drug lord, Charles 'Little Nut' Miller, was a key member of the Shower Posse. After living in the US Witness Protection Programme, Miller fled to his homeland in the mid-1990s and ran a lucrative cocaine trade between St Kitts and Colombia.

A rise in criminality on the islands was blamed on Miller's illicit activities and prompted the government of prime minister Denzil Douglas to work with US authorities to get him extradited.

In 2000, after five years on the run, Miller surrendered to US agents. He is currently imprisoned in that country.

Trans-shipment point

The twin-island state of St Kitts-Nevis has long been a trans-shipment point for drug traffickers.

Under a 1996 extradition treaty, US agents can physically arrest reputed fugitives in St Kitts once the courts there (in St Kitts) rule against them.

The Bahamas was another active space for the notorious 'Cocaine Cowboys' who operated out of Colombia and Miami during the 1970s and 1980s.

In recent years, the Bahamian government has extradited several nationals wanted in the US for trafficking narcotics.

But in January, The Bahamas denied another extradition request by the US for Viktor Kozeny, a Czech-born financier who has lived there since 1995.

Kozeny is wanted in the US on charges of plotting to bribe officials in the former Soviet republic of Azerbaijan in the late 1990s to get favourable treatment on oil deals.

US authorities have been trying to get him extradited since 2005. However, The Bahamas Court of Appeal ruled that he cannot be extradited to stand trial in the US because bribing foreign officials is not a local crime and he is not subject to American anti-bribery laws.

The notorious narcotics trade that flourished in Colombia during the 1970s and 1980s is largely responsible for the American government signing aggressive extradition treaties with Caribbean governments.

For many years, leaders of the infamous Colombian cartels, including Carlos Lehder and Pablo Escobar, used the region as a route for getting their illegal products into Miami.

Because Colombia had no extradition clause in its newly crafted 1991 constitution, drug dealers were able to elude US authorities, but that changed in 1997 when the extradition law was reinstated.

Since 2001, more than 200 persons once tied to the Colombian narcotics trade have been extradited to the US. They include Gilberto Rodriquez Orejuela, a founder of the feared Cali Cartel, who was given a 36-year prison sentence in Miami in 2006.

In Honduras, officials last week claimed that the US had taken away the diplomatic and tourist visas of 16 interim government officials.

Presidential spokeswoman Marcia de Villeda claimed Washington revoked the visas of 14 Supreme Court judges, the foreign relations secretary and the country's attorney general.

Honduran interim President Roberto Micheletti also claimed that his US diplomatic and tourist visas had been revoked, and linked Washington's move to the June 28 coup, which ousted Zelaya.

Sign of pressure

Micheletti said he had anticipated the action and called it "a sign of the pressure that the US government is exerting on our country" to restore Zelaya.

That is a similar story to the one told by students of Haitian history who claim the United States led and organised the 'revolution' which forced Haitian President Jean-Bertrand Aristide into exile.

Aristide, a former slum preacher, was beloved by many of Haiti's poor, but opposition to his rule grew during his second presidential term after he was accused of masterminding assaults on opponents, allowing drug-fuelled corruption, and breaking promises to help the poor.

With the US openly showing its opposition to Aristide, he was ousted and 'forced' into exile in Africa, giving the US victory in that theatre.

Years earlier, 1989, in Panama, US forces invaded and arrested President Manuel Noriega.

At that time, the US claimed that its former allay was involved in drug trafficking, racketeering and money laundering.

That came just over a year after a Senate Subcommittee on Terrorism, Narcotics and International Operations concluded that "the saga of Panama's General Manuel Antonio Noriega represents one of the most serious foreign policy failures for the United States."

_____End of Excerpt

• *May 24, 2010*

The Incursion of Tivoli Gardens

'Justice demands that the guilty must pay. Justice demands that this must never happen again in Jamaica's future. If we can succeed in that, so that men clothes with a little brief authority will never again abuse the public trust for political gain, then those who died may not have died in vain.' - **The Most Honourable Edward Philip George Seaga – O.N. [Order of the Nation], P.C. [Privy Council] – Former Prime Minister and Member of Parliament for West Kingston.**

Those are the words engraved on the previously mentioned mural at the corner of Darling Street and Spanish Town Road in West Kingston (*see page 153*). They were conceived and recorded with the hope that what had occurred in 2001 [the killing of 27 persons during police operations in said community] would never happen again, but as great as the desire was – for not having a repeat of such a calamity; history had a totally different plan.

On Sunday, May 23, 2010, [AFTER A STAND-OFF BETWEEN WASHINGTON AND KINGSTON, REGARDING THE MUCH TALKED ABOUT EXTRADITION REQUEST FOR THE TIVOLI GARDENS STRONGMAN – DUDUS – WHICH EVEN SAW A PUBLIC DEMONSTRATION BY A SEA OF MOSTLY WOMEN DRESSED IN WHITE, ON BEHALF OF THEIR BELOVED DON], all hopes of an incident like the previously mentioned never happening again was lost forever. And with that reality, the burden of another horror even worst than the nightmares of the past would forever be for the people of West Kingston and Jamaica to bear. THIS TIME - 74 PLUS (*THOSE SAID TO BE UNACCOUNTED FOR*) LAID DEAD, ALL IN THE BID TO CAPTURE *ONE* MAN – **WHO IRONICALLY** – *was NOT Wanted in Jamaica* at the time for any *known* crime – *He was Wanted by the US.*

After going over all the facts and rifling through the *evidence*, *speculations* and cries of *foul-play*, I have come to the decision that words in all reality will not suffice, and would actually do injustice in the effort of explaining or even attempting to give a true account of what really happened during the incursion of Tivoli Gardens by the security forces in search of Michael Christopher *'Dudus'* Coke. So instead of trying to do the impossible – *trying to explain and report all that happened* - I have decided [since it is said that a picture is worth a thousand words] to let the images from the horror tell the story of this life altering episode themselves.

A PICTURE IS WORTH 1,000 WORDS:

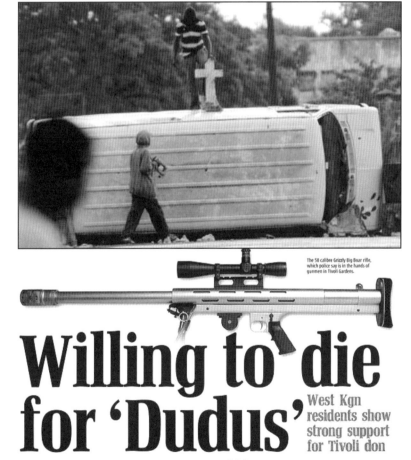

The 50 calibre Grizzly Big Boar rifle, which police say is in the hands of gunmen in Tivoli Gardens.

Willing to die
for 'Dudus'

West Kgn residents show strong support for Tivoli don

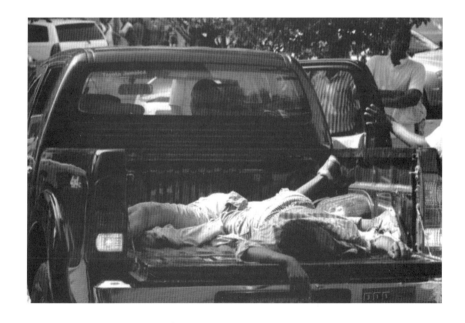

NOTE: *All photos were taken before, during and after the incursion of the security forces into Tivoli Gardens in search of Michael Christopher 'Dudus' Coke, and all directly relate to said incident.*

International Aftermath Report:

Exhibit O

Bodies pile up in assault on Jamaican drug lord Christopher Coke

The following excerpt is taken from the - *Associated Foreign Press* - May 27, 2010

KINGSTON: *Trucks laden with bodies rushed to hospitals in Jamaica's capital yesterday as the government vowed an all-out assault to nab a powerful alleged drug kingpin barricaded by his gang in the teeming slums.*

Hospital sources said they saw more than 60 bodies, although police put the death toll at 27. Prime Minister Bruce Golding warned that the figures would rise, and police later reported several more murders.

Gun-toting troops and police circled the streets into the night as rain descended on Kingston.

Supporters set up tree branches, old cars and abandoned refrigerators to form barricades to seal off the stronghold of Christopher "Dudus" Coke, who is wanted by the US on drug charges. Coke has developed a loyal following among slum-dwellers, who see him as a saviour for offering jobs, education and security. He also has ties with the political establishment.

But after months of stalling, Mr Golding declared a state of emergency to arrest Coke, declaring a battle to rid the nation of its image as one of the world's murder capitals. "The violence that has been unleashed on the society by armed, criminal elements must be repelled," Mr Golding told a heated session of parliament, where opposition members accused him of creating the crisis by earlier inaction.

"The operations being carried out under emergency powers are an extraordinary response to an extraordinary challenge to the safety and security of our citizens."

He pledged to investigate any excesses in the assault, which is being carried out by police and troops backed by helicopters.

"The government deeply regrets the loss of lives of members of the security forces, and those of innocent law-abiding citizens who were caught in the crossfire," Mr Golding said.

With violence turning some of the city's slum areas into a war zone, three trucks loaded with bodies, including a baby, unloaded their cargo at a morgue in one of the main hospital complexes, witnesses said.

Gunfire rattled around the city, as plumes of smoke hung above Tivoli Gardens, which Coke's supporters had barricaded last week to thwart his arrest.

Hospital officials said two trucks bearing "about 50" bodies had been unloaded at the morgue at the Kingston Public Hospital early yesterday.

A third truck was seen arriving full of bullet-riddled corpses, including a baby, later in the day. A nurse said 12 bodies were inside, and they came from a different area to the east of the city called Mountain View.

Police said 211 people had been detained, including four women.

National Security Minister Dwight Nelson told a press conference that Coke, 42, had yet to be captured. "Up to the last briefing I got, the answer is no," he said.

Federal prosecutors in New York last year accused Coke of running an armed network that has been a major supplier of cocaine and marijuana to New York and other US cities.

With rumours swirling among Kingston residents of US support for the effort to arrest Coke, the US and Jamaican governments insisted that the operation was local. State Department spokesman Philip Crowley said the main support offered by the US was bullet-proof vests.

Coke calls himself a businessman. But the battle to capture him threatens dire consequences for an already troubled economy.

Tourism officials have voiced alarm at the damage to the image of Jamaica, where a million tourists each year flock to beaches.

Tourism brings in valuable hard currency to Jamaica. Yet most tourists do not venture into Kingston, long considered the most dangerous part of a country that has 1700 murders a year for a population of 2.8 million.

Britain, Canada and the US all warned their citizens against travel to Kingston. Australia's Department of Foreign Affairs advised travellers to be wary of "domestic tensions" in Jamaica.

_____End of Excerpt

• *On the Run – CAPTURED!*

THE EVIDENCE of the incursion speaks for itself, [*it was tragic to say the least–the closest to a war zone most Jamaicans have ever seen*]**,** but as gripping as that incident may've been, what came next was even more dramatic. DUDUS HAD ESCAPED THE DRAGNET.

The vast majority of Jamaicans thought the effort on the part of the security forces was *too little too late*, because from all assessments, Dudus was not in Tivoli, he was thought by many to have even left the island. It seemed only logical with all the media reports circulating about him being a wanted man, leader of the *Shower Posse*, a looming extradition request, etcetera, but from all indicators, the security forces were right on the money; Dudus was actually in Tivoli.

Exhibit P

The following excerpt is taken from The Jamaica Observer – Monday, June 14, 2010

'Dudus' ran like a 'puss'

FUGITIVE Christopher 'Dudus' Coke took off faster than a cat when soldiers began pounding his West Kingston enclave of Tivoli Gardens early on Labour Day, May 24, an associate of the dethroned self-styled area leader told the Observer.

"The man tek off like a puss when him hear the first bum (bomb) drop," the associate said of his former leader, who has been on the run since May 17 after a warrant was issued for his arrest in relation to an extradition matter.

Coke is said to be leader of the infamous Shower Posse, a gang that has its roots in the United States (US) and which is responsible for the murder of over 1,600 people during the cocaine wars of the 1980s.

Victims were often sprayed with bullets, a practice from which the gang's name was derived, US law enforcers said.

Police and soldiers launched a high profile assault on Coke's Tivoli Gardens base a day after two policemen were killed in the Mountain View area, east of the Jamaica capital, and several police stations either burnt to the ground, or used as shooting practice by criminals who sprayed their walls, windows and doors with bullets.

But Coke, who was in Tivoli Gardens when the clashes began, quickly jumped ship, leaving behind some of his fighters. When the smoke cleared almost three days later, police reported that 73 civilians and a soldier were killed, figures that may be adjusted, according to head of the constabulary, Commissioner Owen Ellington, as investigations showed that some bodies were found outside of Tivoli Gardens.

"Him just tek off so and lef' everybody," the associate said on the weekend. "The man move so fast that not even lightning coulda ketch him."

Asked where he thought 'Dudus' went and which escape route he took out of Tivoli Gardens, the associate said that he was not sure.

"After him move, we no see whey him tun (turn). Him just bolt so," said the man who was among a group of over 500 detained by security forces and processed at the National Arena during the disturbances. He was later released.

The associate insisted that the army bombed sections of Tivoli Gardens, although Jamaica Defence Force official Colonel Rocky Meade has scoffed at the suggestion that bombs were dropped on the community.

Large holes in sections of the Jamaica Labour Party stronghold, as well as two gaping ones in the roof toward the northern section of the busy Coronation Market, across from Tivoli Gardens, did suggest that heavy artillery was used by the military.

The holes in the roof of the Coronation Market were still evident last Thursday when Prime Minister Bruce Golding, along with officials including agriculture minister Dr Chris Tufton, minister with responsibility for local government Robert Montague, Mayor of Kingston Desmond McKenzie and town clerk of the Kingston & St Andrew Corporation Errol Greene, toured it extensively.

Asked if 'Dudus' had let his down his 'soldiers' in crime, the associate said that he was a major disappointment, as he had left the battlefield when things got hot and caused others to fight a war that he started.

"Yeah, me never rate how him do him thing. Him just run way so and a him cause all a dis fe gwaan. It better if him did give up himself, because so much people woulda never dead," the associate said.

_____End of Excerpt

So if we were to believe the words of a captured *alleged* associate; Dudus was in Tivoli at the time of the incursion, but then again, he is not alone in his claim, as similar accounts were also given by others. Another account even suggested that when Dudus, (who was on top of one of the buildings used as a lookout), saw the force with which the armed forces were coming, he panicked, emptied the clip of his MAC 90 assault rifle, tossed it aside and beat a hasty retreat. Except for the fact that rifles of such make and model were indeed found by the security forces after the smoke cleared; this is one of those stories that may very well be true, but simply could not be confirmed.

BUT HOW DID HE ESCAPE?

Tivoli Gardens sits on less than one-hundred acres; not all that big to begin with, and considerably smaller with hundreds of security personnel approaching from all angles, but Dudus still made it out, leaving a community in ruins and confusion, and the efforts of the security forces unfulfilled.

With no Dudus found and so many dead, the uproar across the nation was *instant*, but the security forces were relentless in their effort. TIVOLI AS IT WAS KNOWN WOULD BE NO MORE. In the aftermath the community cried foul, even though this was the same community who had come out dressed in all white, in protest for their don just a few days before, bearing (among others), placards that read, *'We will die for Dudus,'* and *'Jesus died for us and we will die for Dudus.'* These were the same residents who had barricaded the entrances to their community the minute it was clear that the security forces were being mobilized to initiate their search for Dudus. Nonetheless, here it was, now that the battle was brought to them, they were crying foul.

Since the episode that will more than likely live on in *infamy* among the Jamaican populace, [the incursion of Tivoli Gardens], it has been suggested that Dudus' escape was aided by his access to secret tunnels that run beneath Tivoli Gardens, exiting miles away; a suggestion which if true – FOOD FOR THOUGHT – would've had to be a part of the very *blueprint* to begin with. Claims which Mr. McKenzie, Mayor of Kingston and St. Andrew, and Councillor for Tivoli Gardens, flatly denies, maintaining that what was reported as secret tunnels, is nothing more than a longstanding drainage system, which serves to channel excess rainwater from Spanish Town Road and other roadways, and was already known to members of the security forces prior to the incursion. Mr. McKenzie went on to say in his denial of such outlets, *"It is unfortunate that the security forces have sought to misrepresent the community."*

Be that what it may, the exact route of Dudus' escape may never be known, but one thing is for sure, he did manage to elude the security forces during the incursion of Tivoli Gardens, and this is where *the plot thickens.*

A NATION UNDER SIEGE:

That is how one media house reported on the incursion/state of emergency and its after effects. The security forces had moved in on Dudus' stronghold, rounded up a few *hundred* suspects, found a cache of illegal weapons and ammunition, bodies were everywhere, and for the first time in ages according to law enforcement, they were in *charge* of Tivoli Gardens, but as great as that may've been, it was still somewhat of a failed mission. They seemingly had everyone in custody except the man they actually went for - *Dudus.*

IMPORTANT DATA: [AS OF JUNE 2010] *the tally of illegal weapons said to have been found during the joint police-military operation in Tivoli Gardens, West Kingston, stood at 56. The weapons include 29 handguns and 27 rifles. In addition to the guns, a total of 12,020 rounds of ammunition and 84 explosive devices had also been recovered. In its breakdown, the Constabulary Communication Network — the police force's information arm*

— said 9,156 assorted rounds, 1,434 7.62mm rounds, and 1,430 5.56mm rounds were found hidden in the community. The explosive devices included 19 grenades and 31 sticks of dynamite.

NOTE: The above numbers have all since increased dramatically.

THE SEARCH WAS ON

Check points went up all over the city, no stone was left unturned. A *state of emergency* was declared, and law enforcement went on what many say was a rampage and an outright abuse of their power, in their bid to apprehend Christopher *'Dudus'* Coke - but still there was no Dudus.

With no luck in their quest, the efforts of the security forces intensified, bringing with it a trail of tragedy that left the eyebrows of the nation raised, especially when it became clear that the search for the man in question was no longer limited to the garrisons – *Dudus* was way larger than that.

Exhibit Q

The following excerpt is taken from The Jamaica Observer – Friday, May 28, 2010

Search for 'Dudus' results in businessman's death

BUSINESSMAN Keith Clarke was yesterday shot dead as members of the security forces stormed his Kirkland Heights, Red Hills, community in Upper St Andrew in search of alleged drug lord Christopher 'Dudus' Coke.

Clarke, 63, is the brother of former People's National Party Government minister Claude Clarke.

According to the police, Clarke was killed during a joint police/military operation in which four Jamaica Defence Force soldiers were shot and injured.

"A joint police/military operation was conducted in Kirkland Heights, Red Hills, St Andrew at approximately 2:45 am on Thursday 27 May 2010. Four members of the Jamaica Defence Force were shot and

injured and one civilian killed. One firearm was recovered during the incident," the Constabulary Communication Network said in a brief statement.

But yesterday angry relatives, who have called for a full investigation into Clarke's death, said the weapon that was found was licensed to the businessman.

"We are horrified and shocked by the dangerous, unprofessional and outrageous conduct of the security forces in an operation this morning in Kirkland Heights where Keith Clarke was murdered by officers sworn to uphold the law, who forcibly invaded his home and killed him in front of his wife and daughter. The attack was unjustified," relatives said in a statement.

"We expect there to be a complete, full and thorough investigation into this matter and for the officers involved to be held accountable," they added.

Residents of Kirkland Heights said they were awakened by loud explosions minutes to three yesterday morning.

"We heard gunshots for over two hours. Even helicopters were involved in the operation where more than one bus load of soldiers came into the community," one resident told the Observer, adding that after an hour of what sounded like a "war", Clarke was found dead.

"We heard that it was an operation to capture Coke, who is believed to have been in the area, but they shot and killed the wrong person," said another resident.

The shooting angered Carolyn Gomes, executive director of human rights group Jamaicans For Justice, who visited the scene.

"This is wrong; this cannot be allowed to happen," she said and called for the law enforcement agents to be more professional in their approach.

End of Excerpt

CRITICAL DATA: Keith Clarke was Dudus' accountant – Autopsy revealed that he was shot 20 times.

BUT IT DIDN'T STOP THERE:

The hovering sound of Helicopters could be heard all over the city after law enforcement came up empty *handed,* and continued to come up empty *handed* in their quest to find Dudus, who was proving to be every bit of the *elusive don* he was known to be.

But according to many, in hindsight, this was Dudus, not some run of the mill *shotta,* who except for his gun and the few possessions he owned, lacked real resources – so what did they really expect?

Dudus' reach was far and wide, so much that many were of the assumption that he had already fled the island – yet another assumption that proved to be jus that...an assumption.

The search for Dudus was quickly extended beyond the borders of Kingston, with stops in the Sunshine City of Portmore and the old Capital of Spanish Town, where it is alleged that Tivoli had given life to an offspring that went by the name of *Clansman Gang,* but still there was no Dudus.

Talks surfaced about possible departure by boat, and the Coast Guard was put on high alert, but Dudus never surfaced. Treks were made by law enforcement to the properties of prominent residents in places far removed from the action in the city, *locales* such as St. Mary and St. Ann… But still there was no Dudus.

With days gone and still going, and no Dudus on the radar -THE TRAIL SEEMED AS THOUGH IT WAS GOING COLD - and it soon became the general consensus across the nation that he would never be found. Some even suggested that he may've been hiding out at the residence of one of, or was probably in the company of some of Jamaica's most powerful and prominent citizens. Yet another one of those speculations, as great as it sounded, which remained just that… *Speculation.* Truth was, [*except for those who were with him*] no one knew for sure where Dudus was hiding out prior to his capture.

The media was in a frenzy, so was the Internet, with social networking sites such as *Twitter* and *Facebook* going crazy with reports of Dudus sightings, and constant false posts regarding his capture - while talk shows accommodated anyone with a telephone, call credit and the time to spare, freely allowing them to add their two-cents, regardless how little it was really worth in the bigger scheme of things.

What many found to be rather interesting during this interim, was that suddenly it seemed like the police knew everyone they were looking for – and knew them by *legal names* and *aliases* – the likes of whom were all soon flashed across television screens and made public via every radio station across the island, in the form of a list they released of individuals they deemed - *persons of interest.*

NOTE: Most of the listed *persons of interest* were no strangers to law enforcement.

SOME OF THE NAMES RELEASED AS PERSONS OF INTEREST **INCLUDED:**

1. Sandra 'Sandy' Coke [the sister of Christopher 'Dudus' Coke]
2. Danny Banton
3. Orlando Ochoy O'Gilvie [presently Incarcerated after pleading guilty to illegal possession of a firearm, also son of Dudus' business partner, Justin O'Gilvie].
4. Newton McLeod
5. Harold McLeod otherwise called 'Harry Dog'
6. David Heron otherwise called 'Reagie' [said to be the head of the promotional arm of the Presidential Click]
7. Andrew [Leighton] Coke, otherwise called 'Livity' [said to be the head of Live-Up Records]
8. Justin O'Gilvie [business partner to Christopher 'Dudus' Coke] otherwise called 'Stingy'

<u>NOTE</u>: *The US visa of Justin O'Gilvie - friend and business partner of Christopher 'Dudus' Coke, was eventually revoked by the U.S. Embassy.*

From all indications, going public with the list of *persons of interest* created quite a shuffle within the ranks of gangland, and like the *true* gangsters they were, many resorted to the help of the good *ole'* clergy man in assisting them with the burdensome task of turning themselves over to the police. As *un-gangster* as that may sound, that was exactly what most of them did.

<u>Exhibit R</u>

THE PLOT THICKENS: On Saturday, June 5, 2010, local Jamaican tabloid – *The Star* - published a front page headline with the catchy words - *Police seize Dudus BMW coupe.* Newspapers flew off the stands and out of the hands of vendors, but there was a catch to it. The article reported that the police had seized a BMW coupe motor car believed to be owned by Christopher 'Dudus' Coke, the only issue was, he wasn't in it! The article however went on to state that according to the police, a man was seen driving the motor car in Kingston on Sunday and he was stopped and asked his address. He reportedly gave them a Regent Street, West Kingston address. However, upon visiting the address given, only a shack stood there. The man was taken into custody for questioning. It was further reported that the police theorised that the car belonged to Coke and that the man who was driving it was in possession of it for safe keeping.

SCHOOLS CLOSED, AND REMAINED CLOSED. **<u>NOTE</u>: This was also the time when annual CXC (*Caribbean Examination Council*) examinations were being administered across the island - leaving thousands of high school students affected by the civil unrest.**

More and more arrests were being made, but this time the arrests were being made in communities that *startled* many Jamaicans. This may've all began in Tivoli Gardens, but it had long since relocated to more upscale, lavish and quaint communities.

Politicians grappled. The state of emergency lifted slowly and slightly in some parts of the city, while it tightened in others. Businesses slowly opened their doors in the aftermath - owners were timid, but were desperate to pick up the pieces and move on.

A 6:00 p.m. – 6:00 a.m. curfew was enforced in *several* sections of Jamaica's metropolis.

The boundaries of one such curfew area were as follow:

- North along Nathan and Seventh Streets to Asquith Street and Studley Road.
- West along Maxfield Avenue from Spanish Town Road to Nathan Street.
- South along Spanish Town Road from Maxfield Avenue to Industrial Terrace to Marcus Garvey Drive to Port Royal Street.
- East along Slipe Pen Road and Princess Street.

Over 700 persons were detained during the joint police - military operation in West Kingston, with most being processed and released in a couple of days; along with and despite of complains and horrific reports of atrocities, from relatives and almost all those who were eventually released.

BUT EVEN WITH ALL THIS – DUDUS REMAINED AT LARGE, his location was anyone's guess.

IN RETROSPECT: It seems many may've given *Dudus* way more credit than he was actually worthy of, because instead of going out like the legend he had set himself up to be, Dudus - according to many, went out pretty much the opposite - nowhere near what anyone would've expected.

DUDUS CAUGHT!

Those words being used together – *Dudus Caught* - and in the same order was no strange occurrence at the time all this was happening. *Twitter* was blowing up with claims of Dudus sightings and news flashes of Dudus being caught were literally a dime a dozen. All  of which were eventually retracted, turning out to be nothing more than someone having too much time on their hands, or someone having a *Blog* that needed some content. *Facebook* was also going crazy, edited graphics were everywhere, but no one was anywhere near ready for what was to come – not some hoax on the net, but the real, unadulterated deal – *Dudus was caught!*

Exhibit S

The following excerpt is from The Jamaica Gleaner / go-jamaica.com – June 22, 2010

Update: 'Dudus' caught in police spotcheck in Jamaica

Former Tivoli strongman Christopher 'Dudus' Coke is now in police custody in Jamaica.

The Gleaner understands that he was held in the vicinity of Ferry on the Mandela Highway, on the border of St. Andrew and St. Catherine.

The businessman, who has been on the run since the Jamaican government signed an extradition request May 18, was accosted by the police.

The Gleaner understands that he was in the company of the Reverend Al Miller. Miller said he was carrying Coke in to the US Embassy in Liguanea when he was stopped by the police on the Mandela Highway.

The pastor has been instrumental in the surrender of Coke's sister Sandy and brother Leighton.

The one-month manhunt for Coke has stretched from inner city communities in West Kingston to upscale neighbourhoods in St. Andrew. Houses of past and present politicians have also been searched, as the quest to find Coke fanned out to rural communities in Manchester, St. Mary and St. Ann.

The Labour Day military assault on Coke's heavily barricaded Tivoli Gardens stronghold led to bloody clashes which claimed the life of one soldier and 73 civilians.

In their bid to find Coke the police also placed a $5 million bounty on his head.

Coke is wanted in the US on drug and gunrunning charges.

_____End of Excerpt

IT WAS TRUE

DUDUS WAS IN CUSTODY

AND ONCE AGAIN, THE PLOT THICKENS:

Exhibit T

The following excerpt is taken from The Jamaica Observer – Wednesday June 23, 2010 – [APPROXIMATELY ONE MONTH AFTER THE TIVOLI GARDENS INCURSION]

Cops tailed 'Dudus' for hours before pulling over car

- Dudus captured -

CHRISTOPHER 'Dudus' Coke — Jamaica's most wanted fugitive — was captured yesterday afternoon in a police dragnet along the Mandela Highway in St Catherine.

The capture of Coke, who is wanted by United States authorities to answer drug-trafficking and gun-running charges, comes just short of a month after he escaped from his former stronghold of Tivoli Gardens in West Kingston when the security forces stormed the community to execute an arrest warrant on him and restore order after gunmen loyal to him barricaded all entrances to Tivoli and launched unprovoked attacks on the State.

Coke was travelling in a car with the Rev Al Miller when he was held at approximately 4:00 pm at a motor vehicle spot check set up by the police who apparently had information that he would be travelling on that road yesterday.

A cop, who spoke on condition of anonymity, told the Observer that the vehicle in which Coke was travelling was being escorted by two cars carrying gunmen and that police officers were following the convoy for several hours. The cop said the car in front of that in which Coke was travelling was allowed to get away as Coke's capture was their main focus.

"He was the object of our attention and we wanted nothing to interfere with our efforts to nab him," said the cop. "Sometimes we have to weigh our options in matters of this nature," he told the Observer.

When the cop was asked what happened with the third car, which was travelling behind Coke's vehicle, he said the driver sped away on realising that Coke's car was pulled over by the police.

Yesterday, Miller told the Observer that he was taking Coke to the United States Embassy at Coke's request, as the fugitive had expressed his wish to waive his right to an extradition hearing.

Coke was transported to the Spanish Town Police Station where he was held for just over two hours before being transported by Jamaica Defence Force helicopter to an undisclosed location.

The incident caused tension in the town as large groups of heavily armed soldiers and police were called in to man the station and the Prison Oval football field where the helicopter landed.

Last night, a highly placed police source confirmed that Coke was wearing a wig when he was held.

The Observer was also told that Coke, who normally wore a beard, was clean-shaven at the time of his capture.

"When we held him the first thing he said was how he was happy that he was not harmed," a policeman said.

Yesterday evening, during a press conference at his office at Old Hope Road in St Andrew, Police Commissioner Owen Ellington refused to divulge details of Coke's capture.

"The circumstances of Mr Coke's arrest are the subject of an investigation and when the investigation is complete we will inform you," Ellington said.

The police also expressed an interest in interviewing Miller, who was instrumental in handing over Coke's siblings, Leighton 'Livity' Coke and Janet Coke. Leighton Coke was last week charged with shooting after police said he was positively identified by a witness.

"From our standpoint, we believe that he [Miller] needs to come in and speak with us because there are some questions that he needs to answer," Ellington said.

The police also said they were not informed that Coke had expressed an intention to waive his right to an extradition hearing.

"This afternoon before coming down here I spoke to all my senior officers and I asked each individual if they were a party to any discussion or agreement for the bypassing of the legal processes for

Coke to be turned over to US Marshals. Each officer responded negative," Ellington said.

He also said the police would be working with the Office of the Director of Public Prosecutions to get Coke before a local magistrate within 48 hours.

Under Jamaican law, Coke would have to express his wish to waive his right before a local judge before he would be handed over to US Marshals.

The police commissioner appealed to Coke's relatives, associates and sympathisers to remain calm and allow the law to take its course.

Coke's extradition request has been before the Jamaican Government since last August, but was being stalled by the Bruce Golding Administration on the ground that the evidence submitted by the United States was gathered in breach of Jamaican law.

However, faced with mounting pressure to resign after he admitted to sanctioning an attempt by the ruling Jamaica Labour Party to lobby Washington on the Coke issue, Golding announced on May 17 that the Government would sign the order to begin the extradition process.

But his announcement resulted in gunmen loyal to Coke blocking the entrances to Tivoli Gardens. On May 20, mostly female residents of Tivoli Gardens staged a peaceful protest on Spanish Town Road in support of Coke, and then marched through the streets of downtown Kingston. They urged the authorities to leave him alone and many said they were willing to die for him.

On May 24, after repeated appeals for the blockades to be taken down were ignored, the security forces entered Tivoli Gardens but were met with stiff resistance from gunmen who were eventually defeated.

A total of 73 civilians and a soldier were killed in the skirmishes. Two cops were also ambushed and killed by gunmen on the night of May 23 on Mountain View Avenue in widespread violence triggered by other gunmen loyal to Coke.

Since the May 24 offensive, Coke had been on the lam, and the police last Friday increased a $1.2 million bounty for his capture to $5 million.

The US authorities say they have nine co-conspirators who have given them information to build a solid case against Coke, who is the head of the notorious Shower Posse.

_____End of Excerpt

And the rest like it is said; *is history...*

•

Jamaican Adage: *'Long run, short ketch.'*

Photo from the actual stop that led to Dudus' capture

Captured!

AMIDST ALL THE DEATHS AND MAYHEM THAT RESULTED FROM THE INCURSION OF TIVOLI GARDENS, AND AS DRAMATIC AS ALL THE INCIDENTS WERE THAT LED TO EVEN THE CAPTURE OF DUDUS; ONE FIND BY LAW ENFORCEMENT HAS LEFT MORE QUESTIONS THAN ANSWERS AMONG THE JAMAICAN PEOPLE.

Exhibit U

The following excerpt is taken from The Jamaica Observer – Sunday, May 30, 2010.

How did 'Dudus' get extradition papers?

MILITARY and police personnel Friday said that copies of the extradition documents filed by the United States Government against Christopher 'Dudus' Coke were found in his Presidential Click office in Tivoli Gardens after the community was secured by the authorities.

On Friday, two attorneys with whom the Sunday Observer shared the information about the documents expressed surprise, as they said it was not the practice for the subject of an extradition to be in possession of the papers supporting that request.

"It would be very unusual," said one of the attorneys, whom the Sunday Observer will not name.

"My antennae would go up on getting that information," said the other lawyer who explained that extradition documents would only be shared with the subject's attorney after the subject was arrested.

The first attorney also questioned the Judicial Review filed by Coke's lawyers in relation to Justice Minister Dorothy Lightbourne's decision to sign the extradition request, a move that would put Coke before a

Resident Magistrate to determine whether he has a case to answer in the US.

The US Government indicted Coke on arms and drugtrafficking charges last August but the Jamaican Government had refused to sign the document to begin the extradition process.

The Judicial Review is scheduled to come before the High Court tomorrow. Coke's lawyers are arguing that the minister had contended for the past nine months that the US had illegally obtained wire-tap information against their client.

"The reason given for the challenge at this stage is highly unusual," said the attorney.

According to members of the security forces, they also found other sensitive documents relating to the extradition in Coke's office, from which he ran his entertainment company.

They declined to reveal more but were obviously peeved at the discovery which suggested that Coke was the beneficiary of assistance from influential circles.

_____End of Excerpt

Things that make you go……

• *According to the Streets*

'Dem dis Zekes and sell-out Dudus!'

WALK ALMOST ANYWHERE IN JAMAICA, especially throughout the garrisons of Kingston, and if you can get a conversation going about *Presi*, you will almost be sure to hear the above words, either word for word or paraphrased somewhere in that *tête-à-tête*, but regardless

Zekes

how it may be said or even hinted at, what is obviously clear is that there is a great number of Jamaicans that feel as if Dudus got a raw deal. And **NOTE** - this is not a West Kingston or Labour Party *only* opinion either. At this stage, even though Dudus is who he is, the opinions in his favour go way beyond those boundaries.

TRUTH IS, THE REASONS FOR THIS VARY FROM '*A*' TO '*Z*', but in the same breath, what this ushers us into, is the age old reality of what we as people are yet to break away from; *our obsessive love affair with outlaws*: − A fact so

extensively documented over the years, that dispute at this stage in history would make such a stance literally absurd, as the evidence speaks for itself.

Dudus

The public's fascination with outlaws is age old - from the likes of *Bonnie* and *Clyde*, *Pretty Boy Floyd*, *John Dillinger*, *Al Capone*, right down to Mob figure - the Teflon don himself, *John Gotti*, all *media darlings* in their own right, and with the evidence showing what can be described as a literal *raison d'être* when it comes to the public and their obsession with these characters − it must be noted that Jamaica is by no means

250

different; an issue reinforced with so many *Jamaicans* saying much of the same, *'Dem dis Zekes and sell-out Dudus!'* just with different vocal utterances.

So much has been said by almost every Jamaican on this topic, that besides the legalities, I find it imperative to share some of what was said by the people *themselves*. Those close to the action, those observing the action from a distance, and those analyzing it from a presumed – intellectual geopolitical standpoint.

BE WARNED some of the opinions, accounts and suggestions you are about to read range from the reasonable to the ridiculous, right down to the conspiratorial:

- **JAMAICANS SPEAK:**

i. "Dudus anuh angel, but a dem [politicians] create di man dem, and now dem a try distance themselves, but a so dem work, create fi use, and when dem done use, dem refuse, get rid a dem, who dem nuh kill, dem lock up, and now dat di ting get global, dem start dis extradite ting." **TRANSLATED**: "Dudus is no angel, but he was created by the very politicians who are now trying to distance themselves from him, but that's how they work, create to use, and when they are done using, they refuse, getting rid of them in a variety of ways, who they don't kill, they lock up, and now that things are global, they start this whole extraditing bit." – (Elder)

ii. "I is not a Dudus supporter like dat, cause mi nuh know him, have never benefited from him, an mi nuh live nor come from garden, but mi still nuh si how dem fi sey di man wanted inna America, fi tings wha dem a sey a next man sey him do, an some phone argument, wha, a next man coulden use him phone?...An if a even so it go, how you fi tek a man from Jamaica and try him inna a court, inna a country wha him neva go yet? If him commit crime, a Jamaica him dweet, so try him right yahso, nuh mek America dweet, mek America try who dem have an we try who we have, cause dem nah sen nuh body to we fi try, so why we a sen nuhbody to dem, wha, we nuh have nuh justice system?" **TRANSLATED**: "I am not a Dudus supporter like that, because I don't know him, have never benefited from him, and I don't live or come from Tivoli Gardens, but I still don't see how they can say he is wanted in America, for things that a next man is saying he did, with all this talk of wire taps, as if someone else couldn't have used his phone...And even if what they are saying is true, how can you take a man from Jamaica and try him in a court, in a country where he has never been? If Dudus committed any crime he did so in Jamaica, so try him right here, don't allow America to do it, let them try who they have and we will try who we have, because they are not sending anyone down here for us to try, so why should we send anybody to them, don't we have a justice system?" – (Mikey)

iii. "Bruce Golding sell-out Dudus, it simple and plain as dat, sell-out Dudus an garden, Mr. Seaga woulda neva do dat. Him a wicked, after Presi dey yah a hole di order fi him, him sell-out di man an sen police and soulja fi murder wi off – Bruce Golding a wicked!" **TRANSLATED**: "Bruce Golding sell out Dudus, it's as simple as that, he sold-out Dudus and Tivoli Gardens, Mr. Sega would have never done that. He is wicked; even though Presi was here keeping things in check for him, he went and sold him out and then send the police and soldiers to murder us – Bruce Golding is wicked!" - (Tiffany)

iv.   "Same game, different players, Dudus jus another sacrifice, jus like him fadah, everybody know dat." **TRANSLATED**: "Same game, different players, Dudus is just another sacrifice, just like his father was, everybody knows that."- (Wayne)

⚜

v.   "Dudus is a coward like all the cowards before him. His only strength lay in his ability to get people to do his bidding at a price. The wimp probably never even fired a gun in his life. I'll bet that if the security forces grab him he will bawl like a baby begging them not to kill him before he calls for his mama and soils his pants. Why can't we learn? The lout probably had enough to live on with all the luxuries he needed, but he did not know when to call it quits. Power corrupts" - (G. Watson)

⚜

vi.   "Let it be known again that a criminal has no loyalty to anyone but himself. They will sell-out their mothers and children to get their own perceived gratifications. So to all the politicians and business people who align themselves with criminals, you all better take heed. You can't have it both ways." –
(R. Campbell)

⚜

vii. "Coke's strength was always an illusion. Even now many people are still illusionary. He was nothing more than a man living in the shadows of his father. In addition, he had great political coverage being from Tivoli. If Coke was living in the US he would be killed long time by any fryers he contended with. The mask is now off and he is exposed for the coward that he is. Donmanship is nothing but a smoke screen. Look how many of them gave themselves over to the authorities since the fracas – Badman fi who? – Please." - (K. Franklyn)

viii.   The militia fighters that were in The Republic of Tivoli took up arms against The State of Jamaica, which makes them "*enemy combatants,*" and should be treated as such and charged with high treason. The government is too soft with these fools" - (M. Shape)

ix.   "I do hope the police drill Mr. Miller to the max. Why on God's earth would he want to hand over a Jamaican fugitive to the American Embassy instead of the police, and how did he just happen to know where to find Dudus, and all three family members that he was publically known to assist in their surrender to the police. Seems like the Rev was hiding something from the police all along – call me suspicious, but it looks kinda fishy if you ask me."- (J. Cliff)

x.   "The preacher taking the fugitive to the US Embassy, I wonder if he got the reward. Now he is being summoned. That is what happens when politics infiltrate the pulpit – *SEPERATION OF CHURCH AND STATE!*" - (M. Cooper)

xi.   "Was Al Miller doing something legal or illegal? The US Embassy personnel have no police duties in Jamaica. Was Al Miller aiding and abetting a known fugitive? And if Al Miller had indeed made it to the US Embassy with Mr. Coke, wouldn't it be their duty to turn him over to Jamaican law enforcement for due process to take place. So, was Al Miller really taking the fugitive to the US Embassy or was he aiding and abetting the known fugitive? – FOOD FOR THOUGHT." - (P. Lawson)

+

xii. "Thank God Dudus is in custody, I hope he gets the chance to tell it all, so that the Jamaican people and the rest of the world can finally get to hear what was really going on in Jamaica over these years, especially from a political standpoint." – (W. Jones)

+

xiii. "Dudus CAPTURED! Why captured? Why Lord, why? Why not dead and starting to stink? Mind you, I am sure there are a lot of rich and powerful people in JA wetting their pants and skirts – Jamaica, never a dull moment, *the land of wood, water and drama* - the saga continues." – (S. Williams)

+

xiv. "Is it just me, or is it a coincident that just as Bruce is getting ready to attend the G20 summit in Toronto, Dudus is caught? WOW! Now Bruce can face other world leaders without a thick dark cloud over his dead – things that make you go, mmmmmmph." - (S. Mann)

+

xv. "Dudus is the creation of the political system - so even when he reveals all, absolutely nothing will become of the information. In all his evil he protected his people, educated and fed them. What a shame he did more than both governments combined. Do we expect that our politicians and alleged businessmen will be tried and go to prison? No they won't! The same politics will continue with a new spin on the same old corruption. It is the people who will have to make a change, but history has shown that they will continue to vote the same way they have, to get the same election benefits they have always gotten." – (Political Spectator)

xvi. "Dudus in the end you did the right thing. Now he can make the transformation from villain to hero. Tell the world what he knows – and finally show the people that those who live in glass houses must not continue to throw stones. His best bet now is to help Jamaica rid itself of its corruption in high places." – (P. Brown)

xvii. What you all need to understand is that whatever bad Dudus did, he was either ordered or permitted by Jamaica's past and present governments. It's funny how Bin Laden was schooled in the US and supposedly his finances are fueled by secret businesses located in the US, but he is still free to commit crimes and distribute videos to claim responsibility for these acts. I am not defending Dudus at all, but he hasn't done a small *portion* of what some of these terrorists have clamied responsibility for – so help me here – why is Afghanistan (or wherever he is from) not being pressured to hand over Bin Laden, as Jamaica is for Dudus." – (R. Henry)

xviii. "American legal system is different from Jamaica's. I believe Dudus will cut a deal with the US to provide them with all the info they need on other drug kingpins and disappear for good. He could get immunity and be put in the witness protection program, example –Sammy *'the bull'* Gravano, Charles *'Little Nut'* Miller – This is not strange, it happens all the time – Dudus will however never live in Jamaica again – that's for sure." – (A. Williams)

⊥

xix. This is truly amazing the United States Government can demand that the Jamaican Government hand over Christopher Dudus Coke whom they identified as the dangerous narcotics kingpin. But yet nine years after 9/11 and two major wars along with the death of tens of thousands of people, the United States Government has not yet caught Osama Bin Laden, one of the FBI's Ten Most Wanted Fugitives with a 50 million dollar bounty for his capture! But yet the United States Government has been pressing the Jamaican Government for the pass 10 months to hand over Christopher Dudus Coke and the Jamaican Government put a $59,000.00 bounty on Dudus' capture what is wrong with this picture? The United States Government needs to put as much pressure on the Afghanistan Government to hand over Osama Bin Laden." – (G. Ray)

⊥

xx. "All criminal aiders and abettors in Parliament masquerading as legal scholars, should be aware that they may be under investigation abroad for attempting to pervert the course of justice, or obstruction of justice. What is quite apparent with these persons is that they collect a salary from the taxpayers of this country, and at the same time they are working for wanted criminals even against the Country's interest. I say, follow the money – but then again, what's new?" – (C. Emanuel)

✦

xxi.   JA is now DUDUS free, and will be free for a long time. Let's turn the attention to other dons & their Shottas all over JA. Would be Dons, crime doesn't pay. With all the money DUDUS earned from whatever activities, in the end it amounted to nothing – how humiliating for him the don to be caught wearing a granny wig, then leaving with US Marshalls in shackles. If he doesn't get life, when he returns to JA he will be an old man with no money, no friends & no women in white shirts willing to die for him. So what was it all for – Ants fallow fat." – (N. Henry)

✦

xxii.   "Follow the money - there is no doubt that Dudus was what he was, but let's face some facts here, he was a JLP puppet who was (like all those before him) used and then refused. Keep in mind that this is the same person whose company got major contracts from the government, for which he was still owed hundreds of millions of dollars, upon his extradition. Follow the money – and this is also the same person who is said to have handled the party's dirty work in the streets – getting his hands dirty on their behalf, so need I say more?" - (S. Brown)

The people have spoken...

• *Verdict Pending...*

WITH DUDUS IN CUSTODY, JAMAICA HELD ITS BREATH, but in a move that many say was a deliberate attempt on his part to avoid the same fate as that of his father, [*death while in the custody of the Jamaican authorities*] - on June 24, 2010, Dudus waived his rights to fight extradition and departed Jamaica on the same day. Whisked off to the airport like the man he had always said he was...*Presidential style*, even leaving the island like only presidents and diplomats do - Lear jet style, maybe for the last time according to many - too bad all the fanfare surrounding his departure wasn't at his request or design, as almost all things in his life had been. Nevertheless, with all that, Dudus' departure still bore one key element that had always been his to claim; it was *politically orchestrated*, only this time it wasn't at the sole patronage of the JLP [Jamaica Labour Party], but instead, this time such patronage came with the compliments of both the Government of Jamaica and the Government of The United States of America.

DUDUS HAD LEFT THE BUILDING...Blanketed by security to a waiting JDF [Jamaica Defense Force] helicopter...Destination: A private area of the Norman Manley International Airport, where the security was just as heavy as it was at his court appearance, and after the formalities and precautionary checks, the man for whom many had laid down their lives, and who had brought the country to a literal halt, was soon seen being ushered aboard a waiting jet, compliments of the US Marshals.

HOW IT ALL PLAYED OUT:

AFTER Christopher 'Dudus' Coke WAIVED HIS CONSTITUTIONAL RIGHTS TO FIGHT THE EXTRADITION PROCESS IN JAMAICA, he was turned over to agents of the United States law enforcement, and flown to the US within hours of the court hearing. Upon arrival in New York, he was then turned over to the relevant authorities, and was arraigned in a Manhattan Federal court the following day on drug and gun trafficking charges.

Christopher 'Dudus' Coke being led to court by soldiers at the JCF's Mobile Reserve headquarters in Kingston.

Dudus being escorted by law enforcement agents towards a plane at the Norman Manley International Airport, moments before being flown to the United States.

Christopher Coke being helped by Drug Enforcement Administration personnel at Kingston's Norman Manley Airport before jetting off to the US.

DUDUS' EXPLANATION: *Dudus claimed he waived his rights to fight the extradition process because he was fearful of being in the custody of the Jamaican authorities and meet the same fate as that of his father, [Jim Brown] who died in a mysterious fire at the General Penitentiary while awaiting extradition to the US in 1992.*

UPON HIS ARRIVAL IN THE UNITED STATES - the US District Attorney for the Southern District of New York, Preet Bharara, issued a news release which stated that Coke was now in that city *"to face charges of conspiracy to distribute marijuana and cocaine and conspiracy to illegally traffic in firearms."*

Coke was flown out of Jamaica just after 2:00 p.m. (June 24, 2010) aboard a waiting US Marshals service jet, bringing to close quite possibly the most dramatic ten months in Jamaica's most recent history. Coke's departure also brought the curtain down on what many say was an incident which may've had the power to topple the very Government of Jamaica, had it not been brought under control. Some however are quick to rubbish such claims, but the evidence of strained and or damaged diplomatic relations with the United States (now common knowledge) serves as evidence that speaks for itself. And if said incident possessed such power, how far fetched of a possibility is it that said incident also had the power to topple the very government of the land, especially with Coke being who he was, and especially with claims now being made that government official actually suggested that such a development was *very possible* in the privacy of their assumedly *off-the-record* conversations?

SOME CALL IT ARROGANCE, BUT EVEN IN DEFEAT IT SEEMED AS IF DUDUS WAS PLAYING THE DON HE WAS: Issuing a statement through one of his lawyers, one Mr. Tom Tavares-Finson, in which he said that *his decision to forego an extradition trial was in the best interest of Jamaica.*

THE STATEMENT WENT ON TO SAY: *"I take this decision for I now believe it to be in the best interest of my family, the community of West Kingston and in particular the people of Tivoli and above all, Jamaica. I leave Jamaica and my family, in particular Patsy [mother Pauline Halliburton], with a heavy heart, but fully confident that in due course I will be vindicated and returned to them."*

ADDING MORE TO PLENTY: Upon Dudus' *departure* being edged in stone, almost immediately another layer was added to his burdens, when Resident Magistrate Georgianna Fraser, slapped an Order of Restraint on the embattled don, authorising the State to seize his assets, which are estimated to be worth in the hundreds of millions.

RECAP: At approximately 9:55a.m. Thursday, June 24, 2010, Christopher *'Dudus'* Coke, a short, stocky man with receding hairline and a balding scalp, was escorted by three stone-faced members of the Jamaica Constabulary Force into the designated structure being used for his extradition hearing – **located on the premises of** Jamaica's Mobile Reserve Headquarters.

Dressed in a blue and white striped shirt, a pair of Clarks and grey jeans, a gold chain around his neck, white undershirt and leather-band wrist watch, Dudus, who was allowed to walk freely without being handcuffed or shackled, glanced at reporters and nodded his head while making his way to his seat — minutes before the hearing was called to order.

Coke's lawyers — *Mr. Tom Tavares-Finson* and *Mr. George Soutar* — both arrived late, prompting RM Fraser to query whether or not he had legal representation.

RM Fraser: *"Mr Coke, please stand,"* Fraser beckoned. *"Do you have counsel representing you in this matter?"*

"Yes, ma'am," Coke replied in a soft tone, after snapping from his seat in a clear sign of what was his petrified mental state.

"Who?" asked RM Fraser.

"Mr Soutar," replied Coke, who appeared extremely humbled; a far cry from what would've been the norm for a man of his status and calibre.

The lawyers however arrived almost immediately after Mr. Coke gave his answer, and following a rambling apology, Mr. Soutar indicated that his client, Mr. Michael Christopher 'Dudus' Coke wished to waive his right to an extradition trial, prompting the magistrate to ask Coke if this was his desire. To which he replied, *"yes, ma'am."*

Coke was then advised by RM Fraser that he had the right to fight his extradition and that he was also within his right to forego that trial. RM Fraser also informed Coke of the impending charges he would face in the US and outlined the charges to him. RM Fraser then went on to ask if he understood the implication of his decision and if he really wanted to be extradited – to which he replied, *"yes, ma'am,"* in a soft, but yet firm tone.

With the formalities out of the way and Coke's desire clear, he was then given a consent form to which he affixed his signature, in the presence of his attorneys and under the witnessing gaze of two police officers. The process lasted roughly five minutes, and for a second time, Coke again glanced at reporters covering the proceedings, this time, *as many have described it,* with a distant look in his eyes.

With this done, Coke was then turned over to the police for extradition. Shortly before the proceedings came to an end, Coke, through his attorney, Tom Tavares-Finson, thanked the police and members of the Jamaica Defence Force (JDF) for the dignified way in which he was treated, *which he was actually doing for the second time.*

He had done so before; following his capture. Immediately after the proceedings, which ended at approximately 10:15 a.m.; Coke who had seemingly come to grips with his *fate* was whisked away in a dark-tinted blue vehicle, flanked by heavily armed masked security personnel, running alongside on foot.

Those in attendance at the hearing included senior members of the Jamaica Constabulary Force, the Military, and members of the US Marshals. The hearing was not open to the general public and was held at the Mobile Reserve Headquarters [Jamaica's somewhat equivalent of S.W.A.T. (*Special Weapons and Tactics*) in the United States], for fear of security concerns.

In his statement Coke also asked for prayers from Jamaicans and expressed confidence that he would be exonerated when his matter comes up for trial in New York City.

- **IF CONVICTED COKE COULD SPEND THE REST OF HIS LIFE BEHIND BARS.**

In addition to his expressions of confidence about his *eventual* vindication, Coke also expressed remorse over those killed in the mayhem caused by him, which also led to a literally shutdown of the business district of downtown, Kingston - resulting in a reported estimated loss of over $100 million dollars.

DUDUS' WORDS OF REMORSE: *"Above all, I am deeply upset and saddened by the unnecessary loss of lives which could have been avoided, be it of members of the security forces and over...80 residents of Tivoli, or any other innocent Jamaicans that has occurred during this time."*

WHAT HAD BEEN A MONTH LONG RUN, filled with bloodshed, mayhem and drama, was finally over! It had started on May 24, when members of the security forces invaded Coke's heavily barricaded stronghold of Tivoli Gardens to serve an arrest warrant on him and restore law and order. A desire which was met with blatant opposition, when the security forces came under what was described as unprovoked attacks from rampaging gunmen, who had already torched two police stations in Kingston and killed two police officers in separate incidents. – *See page 218.*

CAUSALITY RECAP: One member of the JDF [*Jamaica Defence Force*] was shot and killed during the Tivoli Gardens incursion, and according to official reports, 74 civilians also met their demise. In addition to those numbers, more than 50 civilians and members of the security forces were also shot and injured during said incident.

_____

Coke was apprehended along the Mandela Highway in St Catherine whilst in the company of the locally renowned Pastor; Rev. Al Miller. Miller in a statement said he was accompanying/assisting Coke to the US Embassy, located in a section of the city by the name of Liguanea, where he claimed the fugitive *wanted* to turn himself in to US authorities.

NOTE: *This is the same Reverend who was also instrumental in the surrender of Dudus' siblings (Sandy and Leighton 'Livity' Coke) to the police - who were both on the persons of interest list; circulated after the incursion of Tivoli Gardens.*

BON VOYAGE: Amidst tight security under a light drizzle, at approximately 1:33 p.m. Dudus who was transported via JDF helicopter was landing at the Norman Manley International Airport in Kingston, accompanied by two US Marshals who had been in the island prior to the speedy court hearing, which they also attended.

Upon arrival he was quickly ushered inside a building, where he soon emerged in a blue jump-suit, shackled with waist and ankle chains, before being led aboard the waiting US Marshal Service jet.

By approximately 2:05 p.m., [half an hour, give or take] the jet was airborne; destination THE UNITED STATES OF AMERICA.

- **SEE CLIP ON YOUTUBE OF DUDUS ARRIVING AT WESTCHESTER COUNTY AIRPORT - WHITE PLAINS NEW YORK:**

   http://www.youtube.com/watch?v=b0SUokiopOE&feature=fvwrel

Exhibit V

NEW YORK – FRIDAY JUNE 25, 2010

Christopher 'Dudus' Coke was led into the courtroom on Friday June 25, handcuffed to the back, wearing the standard issued dark blue, jail garb over a brown T-shirt, looking nothing like the drug dealing, gun running don that he is accused of being.

He nodded to some spectators, and after the cuffs were removed, he sat quietly with a court-appointed attorney, Russell T. Neufeld, who spoke with him briefly.

Coke, 41, appeared void of emotions as the judge advised him of his rights and asked whether he wanted to enter a plea of not guilty.

"Yes sir," was his simplistic, non-intimidating response, as he rose out of his seat briefly.

Reporters said the quiet scene in the heavily guarded Manhattan courtroom was a sharp contrast to the violence that was given birth by the very attempt to serve a warrant on Coke, who is accused of being a reputed drug dealer and the head of the notorious Shower Posse gang.

For more than a month, Coke eluded and evaded a furious manhunt by the Jamaican authorities, which left at least 74 people dead and ended in his [Coke's] decision to waive his rights, and be extradited to the United States on federal drug and weapons charges.

Officials in Jamaica said that Mr. Coke had avoided capture by crisscrossing the island and changing his appearance; and that when he was arrested he was wearing a bushy black wig and had shaved off his beard.

Once he was arrested, and his right waived to contest extradition, he was immediately flown to New York [Thursday June 24, 2010] in the custody of federal marshals and DEA agents.

Presiding Judge, Robert P. Patterson Jr. of the Federal District Court, ordered Coke jailed without bond pending further proceedings.

Coke faces charges of conspiring to distribute marijuana and cocaine in New York and elsewhere, and is also charged with the trafficking in, and of firearms. If convicted, Coke could be sentenced to life without the possibility of parole.

Approximately 10 relatives and other supporters of Christopher 'Dudus' Coke attended the hearing on Friday. Among them, according to one relative, were four aunts and four cousins: - One cousin stated that Mr. Coke had relatives throughout the New York area.

After the hearing on Friday, the relatives, although doing their best to avoid clusters of cameras and microphones outside the courthouse, were all adamant in their verbal defence of the man many Jamaicans call Presi or The President.

"They call him the big bad wolf," said one woman sarcastically, who called herself an auntie, who went on to say, "but he's a good person. He's a very good person."

Preet Bharara, the United States attorney in Manhattan, said on Thursday night that he was relieved that Mr. Coke's arrest and transfer to New York were not "marked by the violence that had gripped the streets of Jamaica for so many days."

"We look forward to presenting our case to a jury in a Manhattan courtroom and bringing Coke to justice," said Mr. Bharara.

Judge Patterson scheduled another hearing for Monday, at which the question of whether Mr. Coke will retain private lawyers might be addressed.

Frank A. Doddato, one lawyer who attended the arraignment, said afterward that he expected to be one of several lawyers retained by Mr. Coke, and that they would seek to have him released on bail.

"It obviously will be an uphill fight," Mr. Doddato said, adding that Mr. Coke would seek to be acquitted.

"We're not conceding anything," Mr. Doddato said. "We don't even concede to the time of day."

Women claiming to be Dudus' Aunts arrive at court on June 25th.

A version of this article appeared in print on June 26, 2010, on page A17 of the New York edition. – NEW YORK TIMES

FURTHER DEVELOPMENTS:

Since his first court appearance in June of 2010, Dudus has been back to face the courts on at least three separate occasions to date – [March, 2011]. Nevertheless, as could be expected, the proceedings have already been the scene of high drama, with questions surfacing as to whether funds Dudus intended on using to retain his desired legal team - were tainted. In simple terms, there was concern as to whether or not the funds he planed to use for his legal defence were garnered from his illegal drug trade.

That matter has however since been resolved, and Mr. Coke is now being represented by two high profile lawyers, the most notable being veteran Federal Criminal Attorney, Steve Zissou, (photo inserted)who is known for his work in complex federal litigations. Mr. Zissou has over 25 years experience [admitted to legal practice in 1983]. He is also

known for defending Denver Bronco's, Travis Henry in 2007, and also defending the man implicated in the 1998 US Embassy bombing in East Africa, Ahmed Khalfan Ghailani. It must also be noted that Mr. Zissou is also a former Queens County District Attorney.

Although Coke's last court appearance was Valentines Day, February 14th, there wasn't much love for the embattled don, as more damning discovery was made available by the persecution.

His next pre-trial court appearance is scheduled for April 4, 2011, when it is expected that a further continuance will be sought by *either* or *both*, the prosecution and the defence.

MICHAEL CHRISTOPHER *'DUDUS'* COKE, is presently being held at the Maximum Security **Metropolitan Correctional Center,** in New York City. **MCC** is a Federal Bureau of Prisons remand center in downtown Manhattan, located on Park Row behind the Thurgood Marshall United States Courthouse at Foley Square. It currently houses 750 inmates.

This facility is *renowned* for its history of housing some of the most notable who have ran afoul of the law; individuals including: *Jackie D' Amico*; boss of the Gambino crime family, *John Gotti;* another boss of the Gambino crime family and *Frank Lucas* of the American Gangster fame.

Fig, 7 Metropolitan Correctional Center - where Dudus is being held in New York

Fig. 8 The kind of cell in which Dudus is being held in - at the MCC

THERE IS LITTLE DOUBT THAT DUDUS AND HIS LEGAL TEAM ARE PREPARING FOR THE FIGHT OF THEIR LIVES, but according to published local Jamaican media reports, *Dudus' greatest concern* may still yet be in Jamaica, a fact that had surfaced a few months before the other shoe actually fell.

Exhibit W

The following excerpt is from Jamaica's Sunday Observer – Sunday, March 7, 2010

J'cans give US dirt on Dudus
5 prominent locals on US list of informants

FIVE well-known Jamaicans are among a number of witnesses whose statements the United States Government intends to use against Christopher 'Dudus' Coke, the diminutive and powerful Western Kingston don who has strong family and business connections in the constituency of Prime Minister Bruce Golding.

Highly placed authoritative sources have told the Sunday Observer that included in the five are three well-known underworld figures — one a

convict deportee, another an accused against whom no convictions have been secured so far, and the third an individual currently residing in the US at the pleasure of that country's federal prison system.

According to the sources, two of the three underworld figures are connected to Jamaica's two major political parties — one to the ruling Jamaica Labour Party and the other to the Opposition People's National Party.

The sources also say that both have been granted residency status in the United States in exchange for information against Coke, and at least two of the three are those referred to as co-conspirators in the indictment filed by American authorities against Coke.

The Sunday Observer sources also referred to the fourth and fifth witnesses as "professional informants", meaning that they have given statements in their roles as career professionals.

Christopher Michael Coke, aka 'Michael Christopher Coke'; 'Paul Christopher Scott'; 'Presi'; 'General'; 'President'; 'Dudus' and 'Shortman' was indicted on two counts — conspiracy to distribute marijuana and cocaine, and conspiracy to traffic in firearms.

According to the indictment filed in the US District Court Southern District of New York, Coke and others known and unknown, "unlawfully, intentionally, and knowingly combined, conspired, confederated, and agreed together and with each other to violate the narcotics laws of the United States" in the Southern District of New York and elsewhere.

The alleged acts, the US said, were committed "from at least in or about 1994, up to and including in or about October 2007".

The indictment also accused Coke and others of unlawfully, intentionally, and knowingly distributing and possessing with intent to distribute, 1,000 kilograms and more of mixtures and substances containing a detectable amount of marijuana, and five kilograms and more of mixtures and substances containing a detectable amount of cocaine in violation of Sections 812, 841(a) (1), and 841(b) (1) (A) of Title 21, United States Code.

The indictment also accuses Coke of illegally importing guns into Jamaica "via a wharf located adjacent to Tivoli Gardens" and outlines telephone conversations the US authorities say were conducted between Coke and a number of unnamed co-conspirators regarding the shipment of guns and narcotics.

_____End of Excerpt

BEYOND DUDUS' PRESENT SITUATION: The 5 prominent Jamaicans on the US list of informants might very well be his greatest issue yet, because the million dollar question is and remains, *who are these informants,* what do they know, and what are they going to tell, or what have they told already - OR DOES Dudus have one last trick up his sleeves - a few things of his own to tell?

ONLY TIME WILL TELL: But regardless what we are uncertain of, this is what we are certain of: Dudus is in the custody of the US Government. His stronghold is now under the control of the Jamaican security forces, what once was...Is no more. His once impenetrable network has been penetrated. His lawyers have a gag order imposed on them by *Dudus* himself, while prosecutors are preparing for, quite possibly the case of their lives - the case that many say is *way* overdue in going to trial. The stage is set, and time is at the helm of control, so regardless of how long all this may take to *unfold* and *unravel*, one thing is sure, it won't be long before the *fat lady* starts to sing.

...Stay Tuned

• *Summary...*

AFTER ALL THAT'S SAID AND DONE: According to official reports, 74 Jamaicans died on behalf of, or due to Christopher *'Dudus'* Coke, in what was now clearly a blatant disregard and outright defiance towards the process of law – PERIOD! – The perspective of legalism making no difference whatsoever; be it Jamaican or from the perspective of his key accuser: The United States of America.

SAD REALITY: Regardless how one may want to look at the situation that has unfolded behind the Christopher *'Dudus'* Coke saga, whether it's as a whole or in parts; the reality of the vast extent of loss experienced by Jamaica and Jamaicans is simply one of those irrefutable realities. Financially, Jamaica suffered. Millions of dollars were lost due to the close of businesses in the chaos of what bore resemblances of a nation on the verge of collapse. Millions of dollars in revenue and hours of manpower went to waste; in comparison to what such resources could otherwise be used for - if pursuing Christopher *'Dudus'* Coke hadn't been such a priority.

INTERNATIONALLY, Jamaica was both lambasted and placed under the microscope, and what was uncovered looked *extremely* ugly, so much that it literally had everyone on edge. Internationally, The United States may've been the most vocal, but they weren't the first to sound the alarm; warning their citizens of the potential dangers of being in, or travelling to Jamaica during this *tense* and *uncertain* period.

THE UNITED KINGDOM: On Thursday May 20, 2010, The United Kingdom updated its travel advisory for British citizens in Jamaica.

According to published reports, The British Foreign Office urged their citizens to take extra care when travelling away from their homes or hotels, due to the *"increase risk of civil disorder and street violence in Kingston"* and potentially other urban areas.

CANADA: The Canadians also followed suit, warning their citizens *to "exercise extreme caution in downtown areas of Kingston due to the possibility of civil unrest"*. THEIR WARNING CONTINUED WITH: *"There is a possibility of isolated disturbances, riots, and violence due to ongoing political tensions. The security situation could deteriorate with little or no notice, but the potential for civil unrest and violent clashes remain."*

THE UNITED STATES OF AMERICA: And as expected, the United States wasn't too far behind, issuing a travel advisory that reflected negatively on Jamaica (May 21, 2010). The U.S. State Department travel alert pertaining to the Island of Jamaica cited what it claimed was *unconfirmed* reports of criminal gang members amassing in Kingston and the mobilization of Jamaican defense forces. THE ADVISORY went on to state that *the possibility existed for violence and or civil unrest in the greater Kingston metropolitan areas*. The alert also stated that *if the situation ignites, there was a possibility of severe disruptions of movement within Kingston, including blocking of access roads to the Norman Manley International Airport.*

According to the US travel alert: *"The possibility exists that unrest could spread beyond the general Kingston area.*" The U.S. Embassy in Kingston, Jamaica's capital - went on alert and took extra security precautions after alert was issued, and advised that *American citizens should consider the risks associated with travel to and within the greater Kingston metropolitan areas*. The alert also advised U.S. citizens in Jamaica to monitor local news reports and consider the level of security present when venturing outside their residences or hotels.

- **ALL THIS [*International Cautionary Travel Warnings*] FOR A COUNTRY THAT DEPENDS HEAVILY ON TOURISIM DOLLARS,** which (according to published reports) - in 2009, Jamaica's tourism revenue for the period January to October, was US$1.533 Billion, a figure which was said to have increased in 2010 by approximately 6%.

O—🔑 **THIS WAS NOT AN IRRELEVANT ISSUE:** Another damning factor in this dilemma was that the *Dudus saga* wasn't just confined to Jamaica. This was international news, broadcasted and plastered across almost every major international news network. From the likes of CNN, ABC, BBC, FOX, CBS, and even as far as Aljazeera, who sent a news team all the way from Afghanistan to Jamaica. This effort was not to cover a story on Usain Bolt (three times world and Olympic gold medallist, and also the world's fastest man), the media fanfare wasn't for him or any other local achiever, it was for Dudus – Michael Christopher *'Dudus'* Coke – an internationally accused drug dealer and gun trafficker, a known political activist who was also known as a don in the criminal world, the same *Dudus* who was now also said to be the leader of one of the bloodiest criminal organizations in the history of the United States – *The Infamous Shower Posse* – For this cause, they (the international media) booked flights, packed equipment, booked hotel rooms, arranged for transportation, etcetera. This was the sole motive behind them coming to Jamaica and the reason they all reported. Not because of a great local achiever, but because of a man many have even gone as far as labelling the great *deceiver.*

Maybe what is said about the media is true after all, *'if it ain't bleeding, it ain't leading.'*

- **Jamaica's dirty laundry was being washed in the waters of international scrutiny.**

BUT IT DIDN'T STOP THERE: Death and the garrisons of Jamaica have always been in heavy negotiations, and the incursion of Tivoli Gardens and the Christopher Coke pursuit again proved that the reality of the past was not to be forgotten anytime soon. Death was again in the house, and on a mass scale: Mothers, fathers, uncles, aunts, grandmothers, grandfathers and the saddest of all, children, were left to bear the burden of the loss of family members - and for what? For a man that has been described by his very cronies as a coward? The same man who was arrested in a fashion that strays far from the depiction he was known for. The same man, who after all was said and done, willingly waived his rights to fight extradition and is now housed in a maximum security facility in New York City. Was it all for him, and if the answer is *yes*, with all that's on the table, the next obvious question seems the most logical, was it all worth it? A question to which the answer is a resounding *NO*, now that the smoke has cleared and reality has set in - alongside the visuals, emotional trauma, and the real economic damage that has been like a confrontation with an angry pit-bull – for Jamaica, Jamaicans, and the rest of the world who took time out of their busy schedules to look at what was really unfolding in the *tropical paradise*.

THE REAL LOSERS: In the race of life, the winners are always few opposed to the losers, and the *Dudus* scenario was by no means different, as once again the winners are few and the losers many, and as usual, the victims are all from or related to the same cast of *downtrodden* characters that have been playing the victim role for years… Not the real perpetrators, but those who are labelled as *Collateral Damage* in warfare – average men and women in the streets, who just happen (in most cases) to fall victim to a system that is beyond even their wildest imaginations.

THE PEOPLE LOST: There is simply no denying that. The people were the real losers here, a fact that comes with an undertone of even more disturbing proportions. A fact, which resonates the point that despite what happens to Christopher *'Dudus'* Coke, what must never be forgotten or misconstrued, is that he is *not* the loser here.

Sure he is incarcerated, and sure he may even be found guilty and spend the rest of his natural life in prison, but in the bigger scheme of things, even if that should happen, *Dudus* is still not the loser – BUT INSTEAD - those who suffered the loss of their loved ones on his behalf, or due to *Dudus'* blatant defiance – they (those who mourned for those they lost) are the true losers here; not Dudus, not the government of Jamaica, but those who will now have to live with a part of them missing until they themselves leave this earth.

Seventy Four (74) dead means that there are 74 families who have lost loved ones, who were either providers, protectors or some other essential part of a family structure; notwithstanding how fragile or tremulous it may have been. Fathers died, mothers died, and so did children. Lives were snuffed out, cut short, turned upside down, inside out, shattered, some even demolished – SO AGAIN I ASK, WHO WERE THE REAL LOSERS IN THIS CATASTROPHE?

The answer is no doubt the people, but as one individual puts it, *"why should we even be concerned about them, when they are the same ones who went out demonstrating in support of their beloved don – they supported him all the way to the end, so why change their tune now, when the smoke has cleared and the aftermath is not to their liking?"*

CALLOUS? Maybe, but what is even more surprising, is that as devastating as this incident was, although not voiced openly, statements like the one above is a stance embraced by many Jamaicans, (even with all the support Dudus has gotten) who above all else, feel as if the residents of Tivoli Gardens have gotten a free ride, so if this is the price they pay, then so be it.

When the facts are taken into consideration, such a stance is somewhat justified, because until recently - (*only after the incursion of Tivoli Gardens by law enforcement in search of Christopher Coke*) – Tivoli was considered and looked upon as a rent free community, where NO HOUSEHOLD of the community, (according to published reports in the local Jamaican press), was legally connected to the Nation's power grids, but those same households all had power, which was obtained via illegal connections. A practice which is well known and well documented in Jamaica – a literal ongoing problem for years, - resulting in the loss of billions of dollars in revenue for Jamaica's light and power company – JPS Co.

Although not uttered openly, those are just two of the main reasons behind the view held close to the bosoms of many Jamaicans; garrison residents and otherwise. The same ones who are making ends meet by whatever means possible, without the need or assistance of a *don*.

LET THE DEAD BURY THE DEAD: *Interesting,* and at the same time, somewhat *surprising,* yet another stance held by many Jamaicans who were interviewed for this volume, despite all the deaths and pandemonium produced by the incursion – *let the dead bury the dead.*

In the wake of May 24, 2010, the age old practice of what could be considered the celebration of death has come back to haunt the residents of Tivoli Gardens, because nowhere else in Jamaica are funerals of fallen comrades celebrated like in Western Kingston.

The names of the fallen *soldiers* are too many to mention, but the following facts should paint a very detailed picture of what really is:

Right across from Tivoli Gardens sits the May Pen Cemetery, one of the oldest public cemeteries in the Caribbean. However, as historical as that may sound, this is a place that also serves as evidence of Tivoli Gardens' love affair with death – a practice which is labelled as *honouring* the dead among its residents.

HEROES CIRCLE: In Kingston, Jamaica, there's an officially designated 20 hectare property known as The National Heroes Circle, or National Heroes Park, (the largest open space in Jamaica's capital). As the name suggests, this is the place where national heroes and individuals of national notoriety are interred, but as Tivoli Gardens would have it, they also had and *still* have their own Heroes Circle. IN SHORT, they had and still have their own cemetery, (a section of the above mentioned public cemetery), claimed by them for the burial of those they consider their fallen heroes – the warriors and defenders of their community.

This again by many outsiders is considered another blatant disregard for the authority of the land by the residents of Tivoli Gardens. There is no doubt that the dead must be buried, but what seems to bother many is the way in which Tivoli Gardens and West Kingston have always seemingly celebrated their dead – most of whom were *known* notorious practitioners of evil - the likes of who were always celebrated in style; given what was equivalent to state funerals - with even the Tivoli Gardens Drum Corp upfront at times. There was always a vast turnout of mourners, even from as way back as the burial of Claudius Massop, whose funeral saw a multitude of over 15,000, right up to Jim Brown, whose funeral procession doubled in both fanfare and mourners. And then to top all that, there was the *lavishness of their excess,* even in death was cause for concern; at least among the average citizens of Jamaica, which as was said before, and must be NOTED - are *not* among the majority of the subscribers to such a lifestyle.

Another almost creepy element surrounding the fiasco of death in Tivoli Gardens, was that, although people die everyday, and are buried everyday, *politicians* are not usually numbered among the mourners – that's just not normal, *especially* if the person was of questionable character, but not so with the dead in Tivoli Gardens. Politicians always seemed to be present, political representatives of all calibre always seemed to make time to pay their last respects. From the mere community councillors, mayors, senators, members of parliaments from a variety of offices, right up to even the very *Prime Minister* himself – *and/or* - the nation's *Leader of the opposition* – all *regulars* at funerals in Tivoli Gardens – at one time or another throughout its history.

(Inserted photo – shows Mr. Seaga - *bottom right* - leader of the opposition JLP at the time, leading the funeral procession of fallen accused Shower Posse Leader and known Tivoli Gardens strongman – Lester Lloyd *Jim Brown* Coke - 1992).

EXCESS: The face off with funeral preparations is never easy for most - regardless of who we are, where we live, work or even play. Most times death shows up at the most unprepared-for moments, which often weighs heavily on the scale of ones ability to finance the enormous expense of their loved ones departure, but with the residents of Tivoli Gardens, this never seemed to be a problem, their funerals have always been a display of audacity on parade.

When it came to Tivoli Gardens or West Kingston, especially when talking about persons of *ill-repute*, their coffins are always the best that money can buy. Those in attendance always wore the best, and drove the best; *at least such was the case from their perspective*. Most times than not, the deceased, lying lifeless in their coffin, looked better than they ever did in life – always looking dapper on their way out.

The death of one of their so-called heroes – in what *they* call battle - could be, and at times was, an event that was literally *celebrated* for days, but even beyond that lies what's done after the funeral is over. The headstones used to mark the final resting places are yet another cause for concern. Over the years they have evolved, but despite the era, they have always been elaborate in comparison to markers of other final resting places. In addition, over the years these final resting places have all been well kept, treated like literal shrines to their fallen heroes; fresh flowers laid regularly, weeds removed constantly, restoration done if and when needed, and on and on it continued. This is what happens in this particular neck of the woods, and has left many to look at members of this community in a rather *morbid* light, while at the same time, leaving them with little choice but to embrace the philosophy of *letting the dead bury their dead*, because according to one female from a neighbouring garrison community; *"a fi dem ting dat, dem nuh use to dem ting dey, look how much people dem kill, so wha if di police kill some a dem while dem a do dem job? Dem shoulda tun him ova and none a dat would n' gwaan."* **TRANSLATED**: "That's their thing [death and mayhem], they are used to it, look how many people they have killed, so what if the police killed some of them while doing their job? They should've turned him (*Dudus*) over and none of what happened would've happened."

This may be one voice in the wilderness, or it may be a representation of a wider view across Jamaica, but be that what it is, one thing is sure, Tivoli's love affair with death has come back to haunt them to the point where it's hard for some to even patronize them with sympathy.

The following is a visual example of just how the dead are celebrated in Tivoli Gardens: – AND NOTE, THIS TYPE OF CELEBRATION IS NEVER DONE FOR THE REGULAR RESIDENTS – THIS TYPE OF PRIVILEGE AND FANFARE IS RESERVED FOR THE FALLEN WARRIORS ONLY!

Fig. 9 The headstone for David 'Nunu Puss' Miller, one of their fallen warriors – The last lines on the headstone reads – 'You are a legend,' with fingers below in the form of a V, which is the hand signal used by the Jamaica Labour Party. **NOTE**: *Nunu Puss was a known enforcer whose bullet riddled body was found in 2008 with his throat slashed.*

Fig. 10 The sepulchre (RIGHT) located in May Pen Cemetery marks the final resting place of Lester Lloyd Coke, alias Jim Brown.

IRONIC DEVELOPMENT: It's interesting to note that since the toppling of Tivoli Gardens' strongman, Christopher *Dudus* Coke, there has been legislative moves aimed at addressing the burial practices made famous in Jamaica by Western Kingston. JUST OVER A MONTH after the incursion of Tivoli Gardens, on Friday, July 16, 2010, *The Jamaica Observer* printed an article with the interesting title - *'KSAC bans private vault building at May Pen cemetery'* – an excerpt from the article reads: - *'THE Kingston and St Andrew Corporation (KSAC) has barred private contractors from building vaults at the May Pen Cemetery. The disclosure was made by Mayor Desmond McKenzie during Tuesday's council meeting. He said that the decision was taken after officers observed a vault being constructed at the cemetery on Monday, without any steel.'*

That may be the official explanation, but according to the people in the streets of Jamaica, the problems referred to by the officials as a need for resolve are not new; from all accounts and investigations, the practice of building private vaults is an age old one and no one has ever said anything about their construction, so why *now*? The answer is however very simple, *should* we accept what seems to be an overwhelming opinion by many Jamaicans, which echoes the sentiment that moves of this nature are simply being made at this time, not because they (the authorities) have just become aware of the problems, but because *Dudus* is no longer around. It has also been reverberated that such a *drastic* step is a part of a carefully orchestrated political move aimed at smashing the practice of the *sainthood-like reverence* that has been cultivated around the most notorious of characters in that region.

CORRUPTION IN HIGH PLACES: The history of Jamaica as a nation has proven that there has *always* been, and *still* remains an unprecedented relationship with some elected officials and members of the underworld; a fact that hinges on the doorpost of where the real problem stands. Excuses vary from A to Z as to why this happens, (the climate, the culture, etcetera, etcetera) but the fact that this is so, simply cannot be denied. The men this volume highlights came to prominence with the help of and due to their political affiliation, a reality that simply should not have been so in the first place, but one which has haunted Jamaica even *before* its independence.

The association between politics and the underworld in Jamaica is simply what it is, an undeniable fact, and men like Christopher *'Dudus'* Coke and his father, Lester Lloyd *'Jim Brown'* Coke are just two prime examples of what can go wrong when *power* meets *corruption*; somewhat like what would happen if the Democrats or Republicans were in cahoots with let's say the likes of the Crips, Bloods, MS 13, Latin Kings or even the Mafia. This is the equivalent of what the problem *was*, and to some extent, *still* is in Jamaica, when compared to the wider world – **PROBLEM**: *No separation between politicians and gangsters.* Some are quick to state that there is no real difference to begin with, but that aside, let's face some facts here. The association between the two, on the level that is *common* place in Jamaica, should never be – And therein lies the problem.

Without politics, these men would've been nothing more than mere run of the mill thugs, but with politics, they became *super* thugs. The likes of who grew out of the control of their creators before they even realized what was happening. Maybe Mr. Seaga (former Prime Minster and former Member of Parliament for Western Kingston) said it best on a local television show; IMPACT, aired on Television Jamaica - TVJ, May 2010, when he said in no uncertain terms that when he was Member of Parliament for Western Kingston, *he did not enrich them.* In other words, he knew gangsters were there, but he kept them in check. A clear suggestion that his *predecessor*, (the Hon. Bruce Golding – Jamaica's present Prime Minister - 2011) did just the opposite upon taking the reigns of power, and in doing so, created the kind of monster that Christopher *Dudus* Coke is said to have apparently become.

BUT STOP, wasn't Jim Brown around under Mr. Seaga's reign? He sure was, but then again, maybe Mr. Seaga does have a point, because Jim Brown became rich via illegal means, when what is being alleged, and what the evidence points to, is that regardless what Dudus was involved in prior to Jamaica Labour Party regaining power in 07, his wealth increased by leaps and bounds due to *legitimate* earnings - earnings which came about due to government issued contracts, which amounted to hundreds of millions of dollars.

These are no mere speculations; these are *facts*; undisputed and documented *facts*, which in recent months have become common knowledge — LEAVING ONE QUESTION AND ONE QUESTION ONLY, WHAT IS WRONG WITH THIS PICTURE?

○━┳ There is always going to be those who operate on the wrong side of the law of any land, always have been and always will be, and in the same breath, there will always be politicians, but the line between the two should not be so thin, or in some cases, literally invisible, as was obviously the case in Tivoli Gardens. This is the real problem here, not the after effects, but the root a*nd the very opposite of such action is the solution*, because for any civil society to progress, there must be a *separation* of gangsterism and politics. There must be a separation between the law and the lawless, and this goes not only for Jamaica, but for any progressive thinking democracy. It makes no sense dancing around the issue, because this is the solution if Jamaica is to ever move forward or recover from an image that has tarnished the reputation of this island paradise - far and wide.

THE SOLUTION IS HOWEVER RATHER SIMPLE: The guilty must be held accountable, and those with skeletons in their closets must be exposed, and after that is done, the people **MUST** demand integrity and accountability from those elected to lead. If this is not done, then we all need to get ready for round two, as what we have seen, (if no real changes are implemented) is just a mere forerunner for what's to come under the same *Modus Operandi* – more of the same, carnage and mayhem that will make all previous occurrences pale in comparison.

IN THE AFTERMATH: Dudus is gone, and life goes on – that's just the way it is, but in his aftermath; though thousands of miles away from home and under the jurisdiction of The United States of America, the saga he was responsible for producing continues with repercussions so crucial, they can only be described as devastating.

In one way or the other almost all Jamaicans were affected and to some extent, still are. Many may not have been directly involved, but the psychological burden, strain and damage alone is enough – even without direct involvement.

Sections of Jamaica; namely Kingston and St. Andrew, were placed under a state of emergency equivalent to Martial Law. **CLARIFICATION OF FACT:** A *state of emergency* is a governmental declaration that can also be used if deemed necessary, as a rationale for suspending rights and freedoms of citizens, even if guaranteed under the constitution. Such a declaration is usually issued during a time of natural or man made disaster, during periods of civil unrest, or following a declaration of war or situation of international or internal armed conflict. IN SOME COUNTRIES rights and freedoms may be suspended during a STATE OF EMERGENCY, for instance, freedom of movement, but not non-derogable rights.

This is what happened, what everyone in Kingston and St. Andrew were directly faced with, and what the rest of the nation was faced with indirectly. The wounds are still fresh, and the images of this account remain a literal tattoo on the minds of many, but as dramatic as all that is and may even sound to those unaware of what really unfolded, what needs to be realized, is that the spiral effect of Dudus' world-wind-like impact is like a never ending cycle – with what appear to be like cans of worms being opened, one after another – with damming implications.

SINCE DUDUS' DEPARTURE, one of the most interesting developments is the *blatant*, but still somewhat diplomatic stance of many pubic figures in their bid to distance themselves from the man The United States has labelled one of the world's most dangerous drug lords.

The government-sanctioned 'Dudus', Manatt commission of enquiry was one such platform used to facilitate this effort. Approved in October of 2010, the commission of enquiry was established to clarify the inner ranglings of the entire Dudus extradition saga; including but not limited to the retaining of US law firm, Manatt Phelps and Phillips, to do some level of bidding on behalf of the Jamaica Labour Party and their accused strongman, Michael Christopher Coke.

An excerpt from an article published on Tuesday, October 12, 2010 in the local Jamaica Observer on the matter, entitled: **Gov't approves 'Dudus', Manatt Commission of Enquiry** reads:

Exhibit X

'THE Government has decided to establish a commission of enquiry into the handling of the extradition request for former West Kingston strongman Christopher 'Dudus' Coke and the subsequent engagement of United States law firm Manatt Phelps and Phillips.

Prime Minister Bruce Golding, making the announcement in Parliament this afternoon, said the composition of the commission and the terms of reference will be made public shortly.

The Opposition People's National Party and a number of interest groups and individuals have been calling for a commission of enquiry into both matters which have been fraught with controversy.

Golding initially denied engaging Manatt to lobby the United States government on Coke's behalf, but subsequently admitted that the Jamaica Labour Party, and not the Government, had engaged the firm.'

NOTE: A JA$40 million budget was initially allocated by the Government for the staging of the enquiry, but a figure that was set to rise with the commission seeking an extension. The commission began at the Jamaica Conference Centre in downtown, Kingston on December 6, 2010; when the preliminary sitting took place.

UPDATE: The Enquiry was eventually extended until May 16, 2011, but again not without incident, as the new price tab allocated for said proceedings has since ballooned to almost JA$100 million dollars - a major issue amongst the Jamaican populace.

FROM the commencement of the enquiry, many Jamaicans were left with a taste of *disgust* in their mouths over the proceedings. The commission was viewed by the majority of the pubic as a waste of the tax-payer dollars, and while public officials blatantly danced around questions - needless to say, but the Jamaican public was not impressed. How could they be, when officials like the Minister of National Security, one Mr. Dwight Nelson, took the stand and uttered the words, *'I can't recall,'* when asked questions of a critical and vital nature, and also questions which were directly related to his portfolio. He didn't just respond in that manner once either, he did so several times, and that left many Jamaicans asking; should he be the Minister of National Security if he suffers from *convenient* memory loss?

Then there was the calm and articulate response of Senator Dorothy Lightbourne - Attorney General and Minister of Justice, who made it clear in no uncertain terms that she signed the extradition request for Dudus with a heavy heart, because there were issues with both the evidence and the manner in which the request was made.

Then there was Mr. Karl Samuda – Minister of Industry, Investment and Commerce, who stated in no uncertain terms that he knew who Dudus was and had met him on numerous occasions, but was also quick to make it clear that he did not know him in the capacity that he was accused of. AND TO CAP IT OFF - The very Prime Minister of Jamaica, the Hon. Bruce Golding, testified under oath [March 18th 2011] at the above mentioned enquiry - that he also knew Dudus, and in his own words - QUOTE: "He (Dudus) was typical of what is called dons in various communities," - END OF QUOTE.

Developments and revelations like those have left more questions than answers, questions mainly pertaining to the integrity of the Country's leadership. In a very literal sense, almost every Jamaican has heard of Dudus and what it's *said* he was about, so should Jamaicans believe that Minsters of Government likewise are not aware of who he was, or who he was *said* to be, and shouldn't the very suggestion that he was who he was, be enough for association with an individual of that nature to be off limits for Government officials?

The 'Dudus', Manatt Commission of Enquiry, aired daily on national television, [*for transparency purposes*] became somewhat of a *Political Soap Oprah*, and according to many Jamaicans, served only one good purpose – the purpose of showcasing the type of leadership that is really in charge of the country – like one man puts it, *"dem can hide from man but Jah not sleeping, fi him courtroom run offa a different order, so mek dem gwaan, time longer than rope."* **TRANSLATED**: *"They can hide from man, but God is not sleeping, His courtroom runs off a different order, so let them continue, time has a funny way of making all things right."*

But as usual, it didn't stop there, because as revealing and as dramatic as it was to watch public officials grapple to find words that wouldn't implicate them while on the stand, there was also the very real and heart wrenching issue of mothers still in search of their sons, who were said to have been taken away from their homes by members of the security forces, during the incursion, but have not been accounted for since.

AN EXCERPT FROM AN ARTICLE ON THE SUBJECT [Jamaica Observer – Tuesday, November 9, 2010] **READS**: *Every day since May 25 when soldiers and police took 16-year-old schoolboy Dale Anthony Davis from his home in Tivoli Gardens, his mother stood at the gate of her house hopefully, anxiously awaiting his return. The day after the security forces mounted a bloody assault on the community against Christopher "Dudus" Coke's militia who manned barricades to prevent his capture and extradition to the United States to face drugs and two gun charges, Dale was seen being taken away by policemen and soldiers. There has been no sign of him and two other boys missing since the Tivoli Gardens incursion.*

Reports are that many law-abiding residents killed by the security forces were not at the barricade fighting, but apparently the security forces did a complete job and there were a lot of extra-judicial killings in the community. All told, more than 74 people were killed in Tivoli Gardens and elsewhere in West Kingston. The last time Dale's family saw him was on May 25 when the soldiers and police were taking him away. When his sick grand-aunt, whom Dale helped to take care of, often cooking her meals, asked where they were taking him "because 'im no do nothing", a policeman in the party replied that he was going to the detention centre at the National Arena to be checked out. But residents told investigators that they heard shots in a neighbouring house and shortly afterwards they saw a body wrapped in a sheet being taken out by police and soldiers. "They seemed to have checked him down," said an angry resident. The investigators have not been able to establish the identity of the police and soldiers who carried out the body.

Despite the best effort by the investigators from the Bureau of Special Investigations to find Dale, interviewing and showing photographs of him to juveniles who were held at the National Arena, visiting several places where he could have been, there was no sign of him. His was not among the bodies videotaped and photographed by the BSI. There was no structured or organised attempt by the security forces to identify those killed during the operation. This aspect was clumsily handled by the security forces. A truck moved through the community and picked up the bodies one by one and carried them to the Kingston Public Hospital morgue where they were stacked high to the ceiling.

The hope of Dale's mother finding her son alive has dimmed, but at least she would like to get hold of his body to give him a decent funeral. She told me that Dale "was not a bad boy; he was not a robber or a murderer, and as young as he was he cared for the family".

NOTE: One of the missing boys was eventually indentified by DNA – February 2011.

GROTESQUE INCIDENTS OF SUCH MAGNITUDE CITED ABOVE should never be a part of the circle of a developing nation with hopes of first world status by *2030*, but as great and admirable as that may all sound, and as fast paced as Jamaica is moving, on the flip side of the coin, the reality that incidents of this nature are still a very relevant part of this growing Nation is simply SAD – with an even more devastating after effect for those like the mother of *Dale Anthony Davis* – a reality that again leaves one question and one question alone to be answered, *what was it all for*?

ADDITIONAL TESTIMONIES OF ATROCITIES: Helana Pinnes, an elderly resident of Tivoli Gardens, said she saw soldiers shot two young men at a house across the street from her. **QUOTE**: *"They take them out of that house. They take them out and kill them,"* she was heard telling a reporter from the Guardian of London. *"There wasn't a shootout with anybody."*

Another witness, Timothy McIntosh, said soldiers fired at unarmed residents. *"Most of these people that died weren't involved in any fighting."*

IF JAMAICAN AND THE WORLD IS TO BELIEVE PUBLISHED REPORTS AND PUBLIC ADDRESSES, THE POLICE ARE NOW IN CHARGE, the big bad wolf is gone, but – STOP – although one thing is being said, the day to day reality of Jamaica tells a totally different story, because the bodies are still piling, and the guns are still blazing – so again, the question remains, what was all that for, if indeed the problem remains? Or better yet, is the problem even way bigger than it was initially assumed to be?

IN SHORT: Dudus is in New York, awaiting his day in court, Sandy Coke, his sister was told to stay away from Tivoli Gardens, placed on restricted activity by law enforcement. Livity is in police custody, awaiting trial on a variety of charges, which include firearms charges and impersonating of military personnel. Tivoli Gardens as most people once knew it is no more. The Presidential Click is dismantled, or at least gone underground. There isn't even *Passa Passa* anymore [a weekly street dance, which was said to

Aerial shot of Passa Passa

be famous the world over and so crime free that tourists were known to leave five star hotels to be a part of the ghetto festivity, with no fear of being robbed or taken advantage of in any way. This was the

order]. **SPECIAL NOTE:** This event – *Passa Passa* – held on Spanish Town Road, at one of the many entrances into Tivoli Gardens, was the only event that had one hundred percent free reign, going until 7:00 a.m. [regular cut off time for outdoor parties or events is set at 2:00 a.m.], disrupting the morning traffic of commuters heading to work and children heading to school, as well as vendors from the rural areas heading to downtown markets. An issue that according to many was never *once* addressed by law enforcement until the extradition of Dudus to The United States.

According to many interviewed for this volume, **A LOT HAS CHANGED,** some for the better, and some for the worse. With Dudus gone, so is the *subsidy* that many in Tivoli Gardens and Western Kingston at large have become accustomed to, and literally depended on for their survival. No longer is there a West Kingston Jamboree aimed at giving the children the type of festive season that had now become commonplace in the community. **NOTE:** In December of 2010, members of law enforcement made an effort of staging a Christmas treat for the children of West Kingston - an effort which *paled* in comparison to Dudus' weakest effort, and to many residents of West Kingston, was an effort simply aimed at showing them that there was a new *don* in town – the *Dudus* era was over!

No longer is there a *Champions in Action*, which was said to have assisted many with the funds needed for back to school supplies at the start of every new school year. The avenue of job creation paved by Dudus is now blocked with debris of uncertainty in the aftermath of his exit, which has left many without the opportunity to earn.

The order that once existed in the downtown section of the city is seemingly gone – *the inmates are running the asylum* – and many feared that the days of trepidation are on their way back – the days when downtown, Kingston was a place that many avoided at all cost.

A LOT HAS CHANGED: Dudus may be gone, but he didn't take crime with him, crime is still a very dominant reality on the Island of Jamaica – and from all observations, it's also clear that the influence he once had, still remains what it has always been; a fact made extremely clear according to one news report entitled - *WAR FOR TIVOLI DONSHIP - Battle lines drawn over who should be next strongman* – printed in local Jamaican tabloid, The Star, on January 24, 2011 - see excerpts from the article below.

Exhibit Y

- War is looming in sections of West Kingston as a group of young thugs are said to be working hard at ensuring that nobody, unless appointed, rises as don of the area.

THE STAR *has learnt that the young men are the sons of a number of high-ranking men from Tivoli Gardens, and they have reportedly made it known across west Kingston that only men related to them can be considered to take up leadership of the community.*

In a recent interview, Deputy Superintendent Arthur Brown, head of the Kingston West Division, said the police were urging anybody who has intentions of filling the shoes of Christopher 'Dudus' Coke to think twice.

Since his extradition, a number of men expressed interest in becoming west Kingston strongman. These intentions have, however, been met with resistance by both the police and thugs from the area.

Last November (2010), the police asked Andy Miller, also called Andy Fowl, to turn himself in after getting information that he was one such person interested in taking over west Kingston.

Two Fridays ago, Winston 'Black John' Pennington, was found with a single gunshot wound to the head in a section of Tivoli Gardens known as 'Top Ten'.

While the police say they are yet to identify any suspects in the murder, checks with persons from the community found that fingers are being pointed at a man said to be the son of a very influential resident of west Kingston.

*"Yo, a some young yute a run di place now, when mi seh run di place mi nuh mean as in dem a di don, but a dem a mek sure seh only man weh inna fi dem link can run west Kingston and nobody else dem seh. Di likkle man dem hot and dem naw tek no talk," one thug said when **THE STAR** visited the community on the weekend.*

Pennington's murder is said to be a clear message to those like him, and those who supported his dreams of donship.

"Right now di people kinda a fret because di man dem weh did a support 'Black John' a seh a eediat ting gwaan because him was a good person and him did a look out fi everybody, not just Tivoli people but all people from Denham Town and Hannan Town," another man explained. As a result, there is said to be tension among men from various sections of west Kingston as some persons side with the sons, while others say they do not appreciate their views and actions.

***THE STAR** spoke with one of the young thugs who chose his words carefully before saying, "some man feel seh cause dem an' certain big man was fren dem can just jump up and talk bout dem waa run place. A nuh suh it go, orders affi send before anything like dat can gwaan and di two man dem weh can give dem orders deh nuh deh yah now suh until one a dem come back a we a hol' it off fi dem."*

_____End of Excerpt

A LOT REMAINS THE SAME, BUT STILL, A LOT HAS CHANGED: Another interesting development is that residents of Tivoli Gardens have even complained about being disrespected by their very own Councillor, and Mayor of Kingston and St. Andrew, Desmond McKenzie; who gave them jobs to *bush* the heavily vegetated May Pen Cemetery, off Spanish Town Road, adjacent to the Tivoli community, but when it was time to pay up, they were treated as if they were beggars, which resulted in one irate Tivoli resident and worker making her grouse known with the stinging: **And I quote**: *"if ah did Dudus (former West Kingston strongman Christopher Coke) did give we work we woulda did get we money long time without no problem and see dem send him way gone ah America under all kind a treatment and Desmond McKenzie ah come feisty wid we, say him nah buy nobody vote."* - **End of quote**...

IN THE AFTERMATH these are just some of the realities being faced by those left to pick up the pieces now that the Dudus saga has subsided. A scenario in which it seems literally everyone has been affected in one way or the other, from politicians to the common man or woman in the streets – and sadly, this is a saga which may continue to produce fruits with a bitter aftertaste, for years to come.

PRESI: All that has occurred because of or due to Dudus is without doubt tragic, but as some would say, he made his bed hard, and now he has to lay in it, it's just that simple, if those who subscribe to that stance have a say in the matter. No doubt he was a creation of a system way bigger than he ever was, or could ever dream to become, but even within all that, Michael Christopher *Dudus* Coke was an individual, an individual who had the privilege of *choice*, and he chose what has eventually brought him to his *waterloo*.

What must not be overlooked in the overall final analysis of Michael Christopher *Dudus* Coke; is that he was not average by a long shot, and neither were his opportunities. Unlike most children, who were born or grew up around the time he did, from the same or similar communities; Dudus was provided for in ways they only dreamed of, and in the *context* of this conversation, it makes no difference by which source those means came - ill gotten or otherwise – the fact that he was privileged is what matters here.

His high school transcripts tell a story of a young man with a bright future. He was intelligent, sharp and witty, and he used all he had in a way that didn't amount to much after all was said and done, because regardless what he has done, or owned, there is little doubt that he would rather be a free man in Jamaica, than being in the confines of a US jail cell, facing the possibility of a life sentence, with new evidence steadily mounting against him with each court appearance.

No doubt the choice was his, and he could've easily utilized what he had in a way that would have kept him above reproach, but he didn't – and like it is said and universally accepted, *for every action, there is a reaction* - and Dudus is presently awaiting the by-product of his actions.

CHILDREN LIVE WHAT THEY LEARN: – There's no denying that, so, maybe Dudus did have an excuse after all, but stop, what about *choice*? – That one syllable verb that changes the entire dynamics of perception and reality. Like all of us, he always had that, but he chose or allowed the influence of his reality to become the dictator of his destiny.

There was no rule that said he had to become what he eventually became, and it made no difference who his father was either – that was what it was, but it can also be viewed as an outright excuse if we fail to see Dudus for what he *himself* truly became; regardless of DNA make up. **LET'S FACE THE FACTS**: If what our parents were dictated what we *all* became, a lot of us would be in totally different places, and doing totally different things, SO REGARDLESS WHO HIS FATHER WAS, in the bigger scheme of things, it really made no difference. It didn't even make a difference what he saw growing up or where he lived while growing up. Yes, all those contributions did have an impact on his future, but they were not excuses, and should never be treated as such.

Michael Christopher Coke, may not have been the typical don, but he was who he was – a don of the highest order, according to the very community he was from and the streets in general. Sure there is the twist to the story that what is said about Dudus may not even be 100% true, and that some of it may have even been *edited* for reasons of sensationalism, but regardless of what is true and what isn't, it is clear that if he wasn't who he was, in even the *least* possible of ways, then he would not be implicated in the ways he had always been, and eventually fell victim to. So it stands to reason that there is indeed some truth to the stories that he was who he was; operating in the background without all the flash or bling, while forging loyalties, eliminating competitors and raking in millions. The issue of who Dudus was and who he wasn't, isn't even a matter of opinion anymore; the evidence *shouts* for itself, so regardless of what is said, it's clear, Dudus was who he was - a *don* – according to the understanding of dons in Jamaica and criminality at large.

- Agree ( ) or Disagree ( )

To some Dudus wasn't a don, but was merely the devoted father and community patriarch – a man who was respected in the majority of garrisons across Kingston, where he was a literal folk hero. Residents were known to revere him for providing handouts to the poorest of the poor. He was also credited for orchestrating neighbourhood security, helping to maintain law and order by using his clout to punish crooks in an area where law enforcement had little presence. He was also known for providing jobs through his legitimate businesses, which included the construction company; *Incomparable Enterprise* – and so on and so forth the stories go – but on the flip side of all that, according to others, as kind hearted as he was to those around him, the tenacity was the same at which he was known to address his rivals and those who violated - with deadly precision - AND ACCORDING TO THE UNITED STATES OF AMERICA, he is also one of the world's most deadly drug dealers.

The opinions differ in some ways and correspond in others, but regardless what one thinks or how this may or may not all play out, one thing is sure – Dudus is in the custody of the US authorities – the same people/system who wanted, but never got his father. The prosecution against him is claiming to have star witnesses, and some are said to be prominent Jamaicans. Dudus was connected, there was no doubt about that, but as it presently stands, time will tell how this will all play out, because regardless how connected he was, all that means nothing at this stage, because not only is this no longer a Jamaican issue, but above all that, the game has changed, so much the league is now of an *international* nature.

Michael Christopher Coke aka *Dudus*, may've been all that he was said to be, and may've perpetrated all he was accused of, but like so many infamous notables before him; his fate is no longer in his hands, and he's now faced with a system that is literally foreign to him. No witnesses will be intimidated here. The documents won't get lost in the shuffle. The evidence won't just one day mysteriously disappear, and it makes no difference if witnesses show up to court or not – the game has changed, and in the American justice system, circumstantial evidence is just as good as any other evidence. And there is plenty of that according to speculation.

BUT ABOVE ALL THAT, what needs to be realized here even more than anything else, is the *deadly* end result of politics and corruption. *Duduses* are a dime a dozen, hundreds have been born since he was extradited. He was not the first and he won't be the last to face such a fate, and therein again is the problem - because if Jamaica is to move forward as a nation, and this type of behaviour is to be confined to the pages of history, then the line between gangsterism and politics *must* become an electronic fence. Without this achieved, all we will see is a repeat of the same; just new and improved. So let your imagination run wild if you may , and just imagine for a second what type of *Dudus* can and will be produced in let's say - 2017, if indeed practices of this nature aren't eradicated from the reality of Jamaican politics.

Just look at the not so distant past, [Claudius Massop, Copper, Jim Brown, Jah T, Curly Locks and General Starkey, just to name a few of Jamaica's most notorious politically affiliated thugs] and we will undoubtedly get a vivid idea of how we are to gauge the future, if indeed there is no real and lasting change in the system of governance and political practices that have long been entrenched in the Island of Jamaica.

O—➤ *The solutions of any tomorrow - rest on the decisions of today.*

Selah…

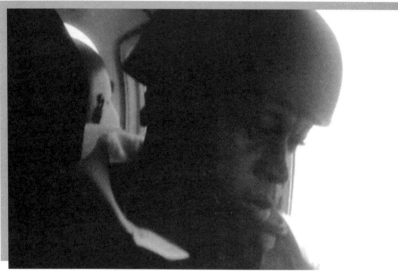

"All through history, there have been tyrants and murderers, and for a time they seem invincible, but in the end they always fall, always!"

Mahatma Gandhi

K.C. Samuels

COMING SOON